LIBRARY CLASSIFICATION

LIBRARY CLASSIFICATION

By

Bhagwatiben Govindbhai Prajapati

M.A., B.Lib., M.Lib., B.Ed.

Librarian

Special Education College

Palanpur

(India)

DISCOVERY PUBLISHING HOUSE PVT. LTD.

NEW DELHI-110 002

Published by:
Namit Wasan
DISCOVERY PUBLISHING HOUSE PVT. LTD.
4383/4B, Ansari Road, Darya Ganj
New Delhi-110 002 (India)
Phone : +91-11-23279245; 23253475; 43596065
E-mail : discoverybooksindia@gmail.com
discoverypublishinghouse@gmail.com
namitwasan9@gmail.com
web : www.discoverypublishinggroup.com

***First Published:* 2013**

***Reprinted:* 2021**

ISBN: 978-93-5056-388-5

Library Classification

Printed at:
Infinity Imaging Systems
Delhi

Contents

Preface

Library classification of a piece of work consists of two steps. First, the "aboutness" of the material is ascertained. Next, a call number based on the classification system in use at the particular library will be assigned to the work using the notation of the system.

A library classification is a structure of coding and organizing documents or library materials according to their subject and allocating a call number to that information resource. Bibliographic classification systems group entities together that are relevant to the same subject, typically arranged in a hierarchical tree structure. A different kind of classification system, called a faceted classification system, is also widely used which allows the assignment of multiple classifications to an object, enabling the classifications to be ordered in multiple ways.

Library classification form part of the field of library and information science. It is a form of bibliographic classification. It goes hand in hand with library cataloging under the rubric of cataloging and classification, sometimes grouped together as technical services. The library professional who engages in the process of cataloging and classifying library materials is called a cataloguer or catalog librarian. Library classification systems are one of the two tools used to facilitate subject access. The other consists of alphabetical indexing languages such as Thesauri and Subject Headings systems.

—Author

1

Knowledge Organization

AN OVERVIEW

The term *'knowledge organization systems' (KOS)* is intended to encompass all types of schemes for organizing information and promoting knowledge management. Knowledge organization systems include classification schemes that organize materials at a general level, subject headings that provide more detailed access, and authority files that control variant versions of key information. They also include less-traditional schemes, such as semantic networks and ontologies. Because knowledge organization systems are mechanisms for organizing information, they are at the heart of every library, museum, and archive. Knowledge organization systems are used to organize materials for the purpose of retrieval and to manage a collection.

A KOS serves as a bridge between the user's information need and the material in the collection. With it, the user should be able to identify an object of interest without prior knowledge of its existence. Whether through browsing or direct searching, whether through themes on a Web page or a site search engine, the KOS guides the user through a discovery process. In addition, KOSs allow the organizers to answer questions regarding the scope of a collection and what is needed to round it out. All digital libraries use one or more KOS.

Just as in a physical library, the KOS in a digital library provides an overview of the content of the collection and supports retrieval. The scheme may be a traditional KOS relevant to the scope of the material and the expected audience for the digital library, a commercially developed scheme such as the Yahoo or Excite categories, or a locally developed scheme for a corporate intranet. The decision of what knowledge organization system to use is central to the development of any digital library. The KOS must be applicable, either automatically or by human catalogers, to the resources included in the digital library. Once the material is included in the collection, the KOS must be meaningful to its users. This part outlines the characteristics of KOSs, describes the common types, and discusses their origins and traditional uses.

Common Characteristics of Knowledge Organization Systems

It is often said that humans are inherent organizers. From an early age, children play sorting and matching games. We cope with our ever-changing world by comparing new objects or experiences with those with which we are familiar, identifying patterns and categorizing what is new into our existing frame of reference.

The emphasis on developing comprehensive KOSs can be seen in the writings of our earliest philosophers, many of whom continue to influence our view of the world. For example, Aristotle's effort to categorize knowledge into groups is reflected in our language, our education, and our science. The original classification scheme of the Library of Congress, used between 1800 and 1814, was based on the philosophical works of Sir Francis Bacon and inherited from the English tradition. Beginning in 1814, the influence of Thomas Jefferson can be seen on the Library of Congress collection. Jefferson, who reclassified the library, reflected a more humanist philosophy. There is no single knowledge classification scheme on which everyone agrees. Michael Lesk speculates that while a single KOS would be advantageous, it is unlikely that such a system will ever be developed. Culture may constrain the knowledge classification scheme so that what is meaningful to one culture is not necessarily meaningful to another. Therefore, we live in a world of multiple, variant ways to organize knowledge.

Despite their diversity, KOSs have the following common characteristics that are critical to their use in organizing digital libraries:

* The KOS imposes a particular view of the world on a collection and the items in it.
* The same entity can be characterized in different ways, depending on the KOS that is used.
* There must be sufficient commonality between the concept expressed in a KOS and the real-world object to which that concept refers that a knowledgeable person could apply the system with reasonable reliability. Likewise, a person seeking relevant material by using a KOS must be able to connect his or her concept with its representation in the system.

Types of Knowledge Organization Systems

A review of some typical knowledge organization systems shows their scope and applicability to a variety of digital library settings. While there are specific definitions for many of these KOSs in the computer science and information science literature, and even in standards documents, there is debate over these definitions. Terms are often used, particularly in the popular press and in the book trade, in nonstandard ways. Reflecting the scope of this practice, a recent *National Information Standards Organization* (NISO) work shop on electronic thesauri emphasized the need to improve the definitions of "terminology relating to terminology".

The descriptions given here provide an overview of possible systems for organizing digital libraries. The descriptions are based on characteristics such as structure and complexity, relationships among terms, and historical function. The list is not comprehensive; nor are the definitions of these terms contained in specific standards documents. They are grouped into three general categories: term lists, which emphasize lists of terms often with definitions; classifications and categories, which emphasize the creation of subject sets; and relationship lists, which emphasize the connections between terms and concepts.

Term Lists

Authority Files

Authority files are lists of terms that are used to control the variant names for an entity or the domain value for a particular field. Examples include names for countries, individuals, and organizations. Nonpreferred terms may be linked to the preferred versions. This type of KOS generally does not include a deep organization or complex structure. The presentation may be alphabetical or organized by a shallow classification scheme. A limited hierarchy may be applied to allow for simple navigation, particularly when the authority file is being accessed manually or is extremely large. Examples of authority files include the Library of Congress Name Authority File and the Getty Geographic Authority File.

Glossaries

A glossary is a list of terms, usually with definitions. The terms may be from a specific subject field or from a particular work. The terms are defined within a specific environment and rarely include variant meanings. Examples include the *Environmental Protection Agency* (EPA) Terms of the Environment.

Dictionaries

Dictionaries are alphabetical lists of words and their definitions. Variant senses are provided where applicable. Dictionaries are more general in scope than are glossaries. They may also provide information about the origin of a word, variants and multiple meanings across disciplines. While a dictionary may also provide synonyms and through the definitions, related words, there is no explicit hierarchical structure or attempt to group them by concept.

Gazetteers

A gazetteer is a list of place names. Traditional gazetteers have been published as books or have appeared as indexes to atlases. Each entry may also be identified by feature type, such as river, city, or school. An example is the U.S. Code of Geographic Names. Geospatially referenced gazetteers provide coordinates for locating the place on the earth's surface. The term *gazetteer* has several other meanings, including an announcement publication such as a patent or legal gazetteer. These gazetteers are often organized using classification schemes or subject categories.

Classifications and Categories

Subject Headings

This scheme type provides a set of controlled terms to represent the subjects of items in a collection. Subject heading lists can be extensive and cover a broad range of subjects; however, the subject heading list's structure is generally very shallow, with a limited hierarchical structure. In use, subject headings tend to be coordinated, with rules for how they can be joined to provide concepts that are more specific. Examples include the *Medical Subject Headings* (MeSH) and the *Library of Congress Subject Headings* (LCSH).

Classification Schemes, Taxonomies and Categorization Schemes

These terms are often used interchangeably. Although there may be subtle differences from example to example, these types of KOSs all provide ways to separate entities into "buckets" or broad topic levels. Some examples provide a hierarchical arrangement of numeric or alphabetic notation to represent broad topics.

These types of KOSs may not follow the rules for hierarchy required in the ANSI NISO Thesaurus Standard, and they lack the explicit relationships presented in a thesaurus. Examples of classification schemes include the Library of Congress Classification Schedules, the Dewey Decimal Classification and the Universal Decimal Classification. Subject categories are often used to group thesaurus terms in broad topic sets that lie outside the hierarchical scheme of the thesaurus. Taxonomies are increasingly being used in object-oriented design and knowledge management systems to indicate any grouping of objects based on a particular characteristic.

Relationship Lists

Thesauri

Thesauri are based on concepts and they show relationships among terms. Relationships commonly expressed in a thesaurus include hierarchy, equivalence and association or relatedness.

These relationships are generally represented by the notation:

* BT (broader term),
* NT (narrower term),
* SY (synonym), and
* RT (associative or related term).

Associative relationships may be more detailed in some schemes. For example, the *Unified Medical Language System* (UMLS) from the National Library of Medicine has defined more than 40 relationships, many of which are associative. Preferred terms for indexing and retrieval are identified. Entry terms point to the preferred terms to be used for each concept. There are standards for the development of monolingual thesauri and multilingual thesauri. In these standards, the definition of a thesaurus is fairly narrow. Standard relationships are assumed, as is the identification of preferred terms, and there are rules for creating relationships among terms. The definition of a thesaurus in these standards is often at variance with schemes that are traditionally called thesauri. Many thesauri do not follow all the rules of the standard but are still generally thought of as thesauri. Another type of thesaurus, such as the *Roget's Thesaurus*, represents only equivalence. Many thesauri are large; they may include more than 50,000 terms. Most were developed for a specific discipline or a specific product or family of products. Examples include the Food and Agricultural Organization's *Aquatic Sciences and Fisheries Thesaurus* and the *National Aeronautic and Space Administration (NASA) Thesaurus* for aeronautics and aerospace-related topics.

Semantic Networks

With the advent of natural language processing, there have been significant developments in semantic networks. These KOSs structure concepts and terms not as hierarchies but as a network or a web. Concepts are thought of as nodes, and relationships branch out from them. The relationships generally go beyond the standard BT, NT, and RT. They may include specific whole-part, cause-effect, or parent-child relationships. The most noted semantic network is Princeton University's WordNet, which is now used in a variety of search engines.

Ontologies

Ontology is the newest label to be attached to some knowledge organization systems. The knowledge-management community is developing ontologies as specific concept models. They can represent complex relationships among objects, and include the rules and axioms missing from semantic networks. Ontologies that describe knowledge in a specific area are often connected with systems for data mining and knowledge management. All of these examples of knowledge organization systems, which vary in complexity, structure, and function, can provide organization and increased access to digital libraries.

The Origin and Use of Knowledge Organization Systems

In the physical library, classification schemes such as *Library of Congress* (LC), Dewey Decimal System, and the Universal Decimal Classification reflect, among other things, the need to store a single item at a single location on a shelf. To provide multiple access points beyond the limits of a single physical location, subject headings are applied. Libraries use subject heading schemes such as LCSH, Sears, or other specialized schemes developed for specific content or specific collections. At the level of specific content, libraries have used authority files to control variant forms of personal, organizational, and geographic names. However, KOSs can be found in settings other than libraries. An awareness of the KOSs available from alternative sources is valuable when considering the development of digital libraries for a specific audience.

Abstracting and Indexing Services

Abstracting and indexing (A&I) services developed as an outgrowth of traditional bibliographies and the explosion of journal literature. In the sciences, the development of A&I services was spurred by the post-World War I concerns about inadequate access to scientific information. In the 1950s, investment in A&I services was fueled by the Cold War and Sputnik. Abstracting and indexing services in the humanities, such as the Bibliography of the History of Art or the *Modern Languages Association* (MLA) Bibliography, generally took a different growth path than did their scientific and technical counterparts, but they also quickly became important resources for scholarship in the online environment.

The scope of A&I services varies from broad discipline-oriented services to narrowly defined aspects of the literature and subdisciplines. Special KOSs, such as thesauri and subject categories, were developed to support A&I services and their specific products and audiences. These organizations applied increasingly complex schemes to provide subject access to the literature in a variety of subjects. By the 1960s, A&I services were moving from the provision of printonly products to print and online services through large online vendors such as Dialog. Later, the products were distributed on CDROM and now, increasingly, on the Web.

In many cases, the KOSs migrated from print to electronic media following the products they supported. While increased computing power, more sophisticated search engines, and more independent end-user searching have led to changes in some KOSs, most have retained their importance, even in the Web environment. For many years, the KOSs related to A&I services were applied only by catalogers and indexers trained in using the KOS indexing for a particular product or products. The primary users of KOSs were librarians and other professional searchers. However, the proliferation of electronic data, the explosion of electronic publishing, and increasing concerns about the difficulty of locating information have led to a renewed interest in these KOSs for use not only by professionals but also by end users.

Publishers

As publishers have migrated to electronic composition systems, they have become increasingly involved in the production of A&I products. Large journal publishers such as Academic Press and Elsevier have developed their own systems to provide bibliographic records linked to the full text of documents. As the content of online journals has grown, it has become necessary to move from systems that provide browsing by table of contents and journal issue to systems that support searching by both free text and by KOS. Electronic journals have resulted in additional KOSs, particularly classification and categorization schemes. For example, Elsevier's Web site has a subject categorization scheme to provide access to individual Web sites of its more than 2,000 titles.

Trade, Professional, and Governmental Organizations

A variety of authority files and classification schemes are used to support business and commerce. They range from the *Standard Industrial Classification* (SIC) code and the *North American Industrial Classification System* (NAICS), used in procurement and government statistics, to disease codes used to communicate patient illnesses and treatments among physicians, hospitals, and insurance companies. As more organizations develop Web sites, additional KOSs are being developed to support them.

Internal Projects

Organizations are among the most prolific creators and users of KOSs. Developers of corporate intranets and knowledge management systems have discovered hundreds of specific classification schemes, glossaries, categorization schemes, and other vocabularies in use within organizations. Many of these are geared towards specific tasks and are, therefore, very narrow both in subject scope and target audience. However, for these audiences, they can also be rich sources of information. For example, the *Department of Energy* (DOE) *Environmental Management Science Programme* (EMSP) and the Office of Scientific and Technical Information are developing a digital library to support EMSP programme managers.

Programme managers and researchers have developed "needs categories" and "science categories" to organize the *Environmental Science Network* (ESN). The categories are used primarily to support the process of grant submission and award; however, the ESN also uses them to provide access to related material from within DOE and from other distributed databases from the EPA, the Department of Defence, and NASA. Vocabulary is currently being organized around these categories for use with a Web mining tool that will provide highly relevant Web resources for project managers in specific areas.

LINKING DIGITAL LIBRARY RESOURCES TO RELATED RESOURCES

This part emphasizes the ability of knowledge organization systems to link digital library resources to other related resources. The basis for this linking is the identification of information within a digital resource that can be extracted and used to search and locate information within a KOS. The KOS may then be used to expand codes to more explanatory full text, to provide more descriptive records, or to link entity names to resources of physical specimens.

EXPANDING CODES TO FULL TEXT

Practitioners of a discipline use coding schemes to facilitate communication within that discipline. It is often helpful to connect these coding schemes to the full names for which the code stands. The examples provided here include links between databank registration codes and the biological sequence data, and between industrial codes and the full name that the code represents.

Linking Sequence Numbers to Biosequence Databanks

The lengthy biochemical and genetic sequences that molecular biologists, biotechnologists, and geneticists identify each day are kept in databanks. Several databanks have been developed, for example, to cover protein sequences, nucleotides, and cell lines. One of the largest databanks contains information on the mapping of the human genome. As molecular biologists began to discover these sequences, they reported them in scientific journals. Difficulties in composing, proofreading, and printing the text soon arose. Through an ad hoc standards process, major biomedical publishers agreed to require the inclusion of codes or databank numbers for these sequences in objects when they are published. In addition, the sequence itself must be registered in a databank before the paper can be published. Some of the most frequently referenced databanks are listed on the Web site of the National Center for Biotechnology Information. They include GenBank and the Research Collaboratory for Structural Bioinformatics Protein Data Bank. Each sequence number is different, but all begin with a persistent code identifying the databank.

How can the link be made between the literature and the databank? Through a search profile, a text analysis programme, or keyword indexing, the text can be analysed and the sequence databank numbers identified. An active link can be embedded. The active link consists of a search strategy to locate that sequence number in the databank where the actual sequence is stored. When the user clicks on the active link, the script is generated and launched from the user's browser. The Web-enabled database is searched, and the sequence record is returned to the user. Depending on the services provided by the databank site, the user can analyse the sequence using a number of tools provided by the databank or download the sequence for local manipulation. This type of connection exists between the *National Library of Medicine's* (NLM) search service, PubMed, and GenBank at the National Center for Biotechnology Information. If a search in PubMed yields records that have GenBank numbers, the user can automatically search and display the sequence records from GenBank.

Linking Individual Industrial Codes to the Full Scheme

In business, classification schemes serve to communicate important facts about a company or product. These codes are generally controlled by a government, professional, trade, or international standards organization. They often serve as shorthand for users interested in material in a particular area of industry or a specific business sector. Perhaps the most familiar scheme is the SIC code, which was last updated in 1987. The SIC codes have been used by the U.S. government, economists, financial markets, regulators, and procurement offices to identify manufacturing, agriculture, and service sectors of the economy. In 1997, a new scheme was approved for use within the United States. The North American Industrial Classification System was developed with Canada and Mexico as a means of providing an agreed-upon scheme for the collection, reporting, and analysis of information about the economy by sector, both within and across borders. Information about NAICS is available from the Web-site of the U.S. Census Bureau.

The digital library can provide related information by using the authority files for the coding schemes as a linked authority file. If a company or economic sector mentioned in the digital library's collection can be linked to an SIC or NAICS code, the code can be searched against the official tables of definitions maintained by the U.S. Census Bureau. These files provide definitions of the codes and place each code in the classification scheme with other economic sectors. The digital library's content can be further enhanced by making a link between the SIC and NAICS codes. If the digital library resource has the SIC code, it can be extracted and searched against the Census Bureau's *1997 NAICS and 1987 SIC Correspondence Tables.* The table returns the corresponding code from the alternate scheme.

LINKING TO DESCRIPTIVE RECORDS

Linking the name of an entity, such as a personal name, organization, or location, to additional information about that entity was one of the first uses of hyperlinking. Knowledge organization systems such as dictionaries, glossaries, and classification schemes can be used to link the entities in one resource to richer descriptions of that entity in another resource. This is particularly helpful for users who are new to a topic and in cases where the additional information can make the user's task more efficient. The examples that follow are from three disciplines. The first example links organism names to records that not only describe the species more fully but also put it in the context of the overall classification scheme for living organisms. The second example links chemical names to descriptive records and molecular structures. In the third example, proper names are linked to the biographies for the person.

Linking Organism Names to Taxonomic Records

Genus-species names are the Latin names for organisms, *e.g.*, plants, animals, and microorganisms. Taxonomists, who study and classify living organisms, create records for each of these organisms. Generally, these records are linked relationally to the other organisms in a hierarchy. Beyond the organism name and the information that it and its placement in the hierarchy convey, taxonomic records use other elements to describe the organism. These may include distribution patterns, the authority for naming and classification, and the date the organism was identified. Scientists base the information on specimens that are retained because they serve as the physical evidence of the description. Natural history museums, private collections, and individual scientists number, or code, the specimens in their collections. Sometimes specimens are supported by photographs or line drawings, which may be digitized.

By using a taxonomic authority file as an intermediate authority file, one can link a text or an image file containing a name or picture of an organism to additional related information. By automatically processing the text or embedding a link from the organism name in the text or from the image to the taxonomic authority record, one can extend the knowledge conveyed by the text. The text can include the descriptive and historical information in the taxonomic record and, ultimately, link to a photograph, a drawing, or appropriate video or audio segments. Because of the ambiguity in organism names, many examples of this type are now created manually.

However, depending on the extent of the files involved, the ambiguity of the Latin and common names for organisms can be overcome. An example of a taxonomic intermediate file is the *Integrated Taxonomic Information System* (ITIS). ITIS is a partnership of U.S., Canadian, and Mexican government agencies, private organizations, and taxonomic specialists cooperating to develop an online, scientifically credible list of biological names of North American plants and animals. It is used by many U.S. government agencies for consistent naming of plants and animals for regulatory and monitoring purposes. To link textual material in a digital library to the ITIS record, the organism name can be identified manually or automatically in the text and submitted as a query to the ITIS database. When a match is found, ITIS presents the ITIS record, which provides essential information about the organism. The information includes synonymous names, including some common names, and an indication of the placement of the organism in the larger taxonomic classification scheme.

Linking Chemical Names to Molecular Structures

The unique identification for a chemical substance is not its name but its molecular structure. However, chemical names are commonly used in research documents, project plans, catalogs, and directories, all of which may be resources in a digital library. There are competing systems of nomenclature as well as common and commercial synonyms. The ambiguity is resolved by providing links between the chemical names in the text and the molecular structure. This is done through a chemical registry number or code that is connected to a particular chemical name and an authority record that provides additional information about the chemical. This information includes the chemical's synonyms and some of its chemical and physical properties.

Most important in today's research environment is the link from this authority file to a chemical structure file. Structure files, used with the appropriate software, graphically depict the molecular structure. This sophisticated software allows for three-dimensional visualization, rotation, and substitution of the chemical bonds. An example of the use of the chemical registry number to link chemical names with molecular structures can be seen in the work of BIOSIS, the world's largest not-for-profit producer of biological and biomedical databases. In 1993, BIOSIS began processing its bibliographic citations to automatically identify chemical names. BIOSIS assigns CAS Registry Numbers (RNs) to the chemical names identified in this process. In the STN International online system, hosted in the United States by CAS, a user of BIOSIS can select one or more of the records resulting from a search and extract the RN.

The extracted RN can be applied against the CAS Registry File, which contains more than 21 million substances, including organics, inorganics, biosequences, metals, and alloys. The registry file record for the chemical name, including the link to the synonyms for the chemical name and the structure file itself, can then be accessed. With special tools developed by CAS, the structure can be viewed and manipulated. It can be imported into modeling tools that allow the chemist to manipulate the structure and thereby envision new chemicals. Alternatively, the user can start with any database that contains CAS RNs and extract the resulting RNs to perform a search for complementary bibliographic records in the BIOSIS database. Linking chemical names to structures using RNs on a large scale is neither inexpensive nor easy.

There are two approaches to identifying chemical names in text. Some journal objects include the CAS RN for the major chemicals discussed. In this case, an analysis of the text for the terms "RN", "CAS RN", and variations preceding numerics can identify RNs that can be used as a link. Alternatively, a programme to identify chemical names in text, similar to that developed by BIOSIS, could be devised. Developing the identification programme, as well as searching chemical databases, is costly; however, if the digital library has license agreements for chemistry databases, this type of linkage may be possible. In addition, many organizations have small chemical files of their own that may include RNs and other information of particular relevance to the organization's research. It may be possible to link to these local databases using methods that are more direct.

Linking Personal Names to Biographical Information

A common type of authority file is the personal name authority, which controls variants of personal names. For example, the *Library of Congress Name Authority File* (LCNAF) is used to control variant personal names for authors, editors, artists, and others. The *Union List of Artist Names* (ULAN), developed by the Getty Vocabulary Programme, is another example. Name authorities serve as tools for catalogers and indexers. They ensure that the proper form of the name, rather than an unapproved variant, is used and bring together all works by or about the person. A name authority file can also be used to link a bibliographic record or document containing the person's name to a variety of other related materials. If the digital library's resource has a standardized form of the name, it can be identified and searched against the authority file to locate variants. The standardized and variant forms can be joined in a search against a variety of other resources that can provide related information. For example, in the case of a digital library of images of artists' works or biographical or critical text, a name authority file such as the ULAN or the LCNAF can act as an intermediate file to provide additional information.

The file, which contains integrated variant names, can be searched by the name appearing in the digital library collection. When the record is found, the information about the artist can be displayed, providing a wide range of contextual material for the user. Citations to significant biographical or critical works about the artist, some of which may also be available on the Web, may also be provided in the name authority file. The variant names from a name authority can also be used to locate and provide automatic links from the personal name in the text to a biography, without requiring that the name be presented in the same fashion in the two resources. One such resource that could be linked to for biographical information is Gale's Biography Resource, which contains more than 142,000 biographies and related citations from more than 1000 periodicals.

However, to produce this kind of link, there must be a mechanism for locating personal names in text. Several programmes can do this type of text analysis; among those that have been developed commercially are NameFinder from the Carnegie Group and the Intelligent Agent from IBM. In addition, variant names can be extracted from the name authority itself, grouped, and run as a search against the text to locate name occurrences.

LINKING ENTITY NAMES TO PHYSICAL SPECIMENS

In some cases, it is possible to go another step and connect entity names in the digital library resources to physical specimens. The curation of physical specimens or artifacts is critical to the advancement of many disciplines. Exhibition catalogs describe the art objects in a particular exhibition. Museum catalogs provide inventories of the art, natural history, or cultural objects held by a particular museum. These catalogs, increasingly available as computerized databases, are knowledge organization systems that not only provide descriptive records but also point to the location of the object in a museum, an archive, or another collection. For example, in biology, a physical specimen is particularly important when it is the result of the discovery and description of a new organism or of the reclassification of a known organism. A type specimen is the example collected from the field by a taxonomist to serve as the prime example for the description of the organism and the validation of its taxonomic classification and naming.

These specimens are held by natural history collections, and their deposit is required by the rules of various taxonomic societies. As part of the curatorial activity, the collections assign identification codes. While the primary use of identification codes has been to organize the physical collections, numerous projects are under way in the natural history community to digitize photographs of specimens and create database records for the specimens, including their identifiers, and thereby make them more readily accessible. The degree of digitization varies from specialty to specialty.

For example, in botany, virtually all significant research herbaria are digitally cataloging their type collections instead of maintaining paper records. Many are also making digital photographs of the type specimens available over the Web. The publication of identification codes in the journal literature is also changing. Historically, identification codes have been presented in the "Materials Used" parts of journal objects. The level of specificity of the identification code has varied, depending on the biological discipline. For example, botanical journals tend to list only the institution and the catalog, while vertebrate journals provide the code to the specimen level.

The current trend is to require lists of specimens that are more detailed. As the lists become longer and the printing costs increase, journal publishers are beginning to request links to independent Web sites maintained by the researchers or their organizations that carry all the specimens used in the study and provide some level of identification. If the digital library collection contains resources that include the identification codes, these codes can be extracted and matched against the Web-based catalogs or databases. This link can provide users with location and contact information to allow them to access the physical object mentioned in the digital library resource. Curators or registrars of artistic, archaeological, and cultural history collections also assign inventory or accession numbers to items in their collections. Identification numbers may also be found in scholarly catalogues raisonnés. Links similar to those described for natural history can be made between text related to works of art and the physical work in a particular collection

An object about a work of art can be linked to additional information about the physical specimen by linking the identification number in the text with an online catalog containing the number and additional information about the work. As museums digitize their collections to establish a presence on the Web or to reduce the handling of the physical objects, KOSs that can link the digital library resources to the physical object are being developed. If there is a museum with a collection that complements that of the digital library, it is worthwhile to discuss ways in which the digital library and digital museum collections may "co-evolve."

MAKING RESOURCES ACCESSIBLE TO OTHER COMMUNITIES

Someone recently compared the Web with a large room filled with books that were scattered all over the floor. The Web is the world's largest mass of bits and bytes. It is a meeting place that brings together disparate communities. The "Internet Commons," as this meeting place has been called, requires connections between and among disparate communities in order for an "economy" to develop. This economy will provide the framework within which both commercial and noncommercial transactions can occur.

KOSs are one means of connecting these disparate communities. Knowledge organization systems can be used to:

* Psrovide alternate subject access,
* Add modes of understanding to digital library resources,
* Support multilingual access, and
* Supply terms for expansion of free-text searches in domains that are relatively unknown to the user.

PROVIDING ALTERNATE SUBJECT ACCESS

Alternate subject access refers to the provision of one or more additional subject orientations that make the resources of the digital library accessible to different audiences. This approach is particularly valuable when the digital library resources appeal to groups that do not share a common terminology. It can be a system of subject headings, a classification scheme, or any other subject-oriented system.

Alternate subject access can be provided by:

* Indexing or classifying the resources using multiple schemes,
* Retaining original schemes from organizations that contribute to the digital library, or
* Mapping between the primary scheme and an alternate scheme.

Indexing the Material with Multiple Schemes

The most direct method for providing alternate subject access to a collection is by classifying or indexing the resources with multiple schemes, but it may also be the most costly. This approach requires redundant cataloging or catalogers who are knowledgeable in both schemes. It may also require modifications to the cataloging tools and procedures. However, if the cataloging is at a high level or if the schemes are not difficult or detailed, it may be a reasonable approach.

Retaining Alternate Indexing from Contributors

If the digital library is being built through contributions from a variety of sources, the originating organization may have applied an alternate scheme that could be used. For example, the NASA database on aeronautics and astronautics receives relevant bibliographic records from other U.S. agencies, such as the Department of Defence and the Department of Energy. The controlled vocabulary terms assigned by the contributing organization are processed through a machine- aided indexing process to create candidate indexing terms from the *NASA Thesaurus* for review by NASA's indexers. However, the final records contain both the *NASA Thesaurus* terms and the controlled vocabulary terms from the contributing organization, with the alternate indexing terms retained in a separate data element in the bibliographic record. The terms collected from other organizations can be viewed as an alternate access point, so that at least part of the collection is accessible through another discipline's terminology.

Mapping Multiple Schemes

The third method for providing alternate subject access is the most indirect, that of mapping one or more schemes. Several examples of this approach can be found among A&I services. Both BIOSIS, the world's largest private sector A&I service in the life sciences, and the NLM apply MeSH to BIOSIS documents. The records that BIOSIS contributes to NLM's TOXLINE database are processed automatically to have appropriate MeSH terms added. This is based on a mapping of the natural language terms that occur in the toxicology literature and BIOSIS' normalized natural language keyword indexing with the MeSH terminology. In the new BIOSIS relational indexing structure, BIOSIS builds and maintains authority files that connect natural language disease names to the MeSH-controlled disease terms. When the BIOSIS indexer assigns the free text keyword for the disease name, the appropriate MeSH term is also added to the record as an alternate access point.

The assignment is based on the development over time of a mapping between the terminology used by BIOSIS and the MeSH-controlled terms. In addition to providing alternate access points to BIOSIS products, the inclusion of the MeSH terms makes it possible to perform cross database searching on the indexing field with MEDLINE and other databases that include MeSH terms. From 1999 forward, users can search BIOSIS databases using MeSH disease terms. The disease terms can be extracted from the MeSH authority file or from a MEDLINE record and then used in a search against the BIOSIS files, or vice versa. This helps users find relevant records that are unique to either BIOSIS or MEDLINE. The inclusion of terms from an alternate KOS, such as MeSH, therefore supports the use of BIOSIS by medical librarians and practitioners who are familiar with MeSH terminology. A more extensive example of mapping variant schemes is the metathesaurus developed by the NLM's *Unified Medical Language System* (UMLS). This system has linked more than 40 separate KOSs from various medical specialties. They range from MeSH to coding and classification schemes used by insurance companies and physicians to describe treatments and diseases on patient records.

The UMLS is licensed by many other organizations for inclusion in applications that can bridge various health care communities. How can digital libraries use alternate indexing? While many digital libraries do not have the A&I resources of large database producers such as NLM and BIOSIS, the concept of applying alternate indexing can be scaled to fit. While the systems described deal with item-level bibliographic records, alternate indexing can be applied at several levels. Alternate subject access can be applied only at the resource level, for the database, electronic book, electronic journal, or image collection, so that other communities can identify resources of interest that must then by searched or browsed individually. This concept is conducive to use with portals that provide access to the same resources with different views for different audiences. Alternatively, if the digital library has bibliographic records or metadata records at a very detailed level, it may be possible to develop switching programmes that will translate concepts from the original organization of the digital library or resource to that of the alternate scheme.

ADDING NEW MODES OF UNDERSTANDING TO THE DIGITAL LIBRARY

People perceive the world through many modes, including textual and graphical. Some people comprehend information more easily in one mode than another. Most people benefit from a variety of modes that reinforce one another or that can be used when appropriate to the context. Many digital library projects remain text-based; however, this text-only dimension is changing as digital libraries become oriented more to multimedia and as other modes of information presentation become viable on the Internet. KOSs can be used to bring new dimensions to an information resource or a collection in a digital library. In the digital library environment, these dimensions can be viewed as layers that can be added on top of one or more objects.

Various tools and services can be developed that are geared to a particular mode. For example, the results of a text search can be presented in graphical or visual form, based on the number of occurrences of a term or concept or on the occurrences of documents from a particular country, journal title, or author. A more complex dimension that can be added is the geospatial dimension, which emphasizes access by place. A "geolibrary" is defined as a digital library consisting of "geoinformation," or material that can be accessed by place. This so-called georeferencing can be either direct or indirect. Georeferencing of textual objects is facilitated by a gazetteer, which brings together the place name and the spatial footprint for its location. Many gazetteers also include feature types for each footprint. The vocabulary used for the feature types varies among gazetteers, but may include terms such as "airport," "harbour," and "railroad station."

Although many organizations, including federal and state agencies, are currently required to provide geospatial referencing as part of the National Spatial Data Infrastructure Programme, the geospatial referencing is not readily available for older works. How can the data sets of today be integrated with the textual information of yesterday? The answer is by adding geospatial referencing to the text resource. Geospatial referencing requires that the text name for a place have an associated spatial footprint. This can be achieved by using a georeferenced, digital gazetteer that provides geospatial footprints for place names. Through this type of knowledge organization system, place names in a library catalog or bibliographic database can have footprints assigned.

If one or more of the library's resources have latitude or longitude coordinates in the catalog record or in the full text but no place name, the coordinates can be extracted and submitted to the gazetteer service. The service will return the place name for the footprint. Alternatively, the resource may have a textual place name. This place name can be extracted and searched against the gazetteer, and the footprint can be provided to a mapping application. The latter search may result in more than one footprint, since place names may be ambiguous. Therefore, it is important that the user interface be designed to allow the user to distinguish the locations. Once the footprint has been determined, a user can access the text resource through a geographic mapping tool. Alternatively, a user of the text resource can find a set of results and have the place names displayed as footprints on a map. In disciplines such as ecology, environmental science, and even public health and epidemiology, it would be beneficial to build a digital library with access to such a digital gazetteer service. Users could then access the system through the text mode or the geographic mode, depending on their comfort level and the type of information needed. Presenting the results on a map allows users to make new associations and analyse the results more easily. Through a geospatial KOS, they can see connections between disparate data, because the data are presented in an alternate mode.

PROVIDING MULTI-LINGUAL ACCESS

A third way that KOSs can support the use of digital libraries by disparate communities is to provide multi-lingual access. A variety of sources, including multi-lingual dictiona-ries and multi-lingual thesauri, can support this type of access. One of the most extensive multi-lingual thesaurus efforts is the *Generalized Multi-lingual Environmental Thesaurus* (GEMET) from the *European Environment Agency* (EEA), produced by Italy's research council, the *Consiglio Nazionale delle Ricerche* (CNR). The GEMET is available in 12 languages, and plans for a global environmental thesaurus in many more languages were recently announced. GEMET is available by agreement with the EEA.

The European Topic Centre on Catalogue of Data Sources in Germany is developing a system that will link data sources and metadata information in a virtual library. GEMET will be used to convert a search in one language into searches for the same concepts in other languages. Users will retrieve documents not only in their native language but also in other languages. This will allow data systems from throughout the EEA and beyond to be accessed as a virtual library collection with both controlled vocabulary and free-text term searching in multiple languages.

EXPANDING FREE-TEXT SEARCH TERMS

Free-text searching is the main method of searching on the

Web. Only a small percentage of Web resources have metadata, and an even smaller percentage have controlled vocabulary assigned. However, variations in natural language make free-text searching problematic. Even a knowledgeable user may not know all the terminology that can be used in the literature to express a concept. The problem is exacerbated when the user is unfamiliar with the topic or is interested in an interdisciplinary area. How can the user expand his or her search to overcome these terminology differences? One possibility is to use KOSs as aids to the selection of free-text keywords.

The Getty Vocabulary Project emphasizes support for searching as a significant application of its vocabularies. Harpring reports that the vocabularies are increasingly being used in search engines to look for different terms that refer to the same concept. The Getty vocabularies are particularly rich in equivalence relationships. "When these equivalence relationships are exploited in search engines, there are typically two possible scenarios: the user may be allowed to first query the vocabulary database, locating appropriate terms, and then applying those chosen terms in a query across target databases; or there may be little or no user interaction with the vocabulary, when the vocabularies are used behind the scenes [to expand the search]...". Getty developed a prototype called *a.k.a.* to experiment with the use of equivalence terms to broaden or narrow searches across databases on the Web.

In addition to expanding routine search queries, KOSs can be used in Web mining tools. Northern Light has developed a Web mining tool that reportedly returns a high degree of relevant hits. The KOS that supports the Northern Light site was built by ingesting large existing vocabularies and thesauri. The result was then organized under an extensive classification scheme developed by Northern Light. The terms can be used to extend a user's search or to distinguish between multiple meanings of the terms supplied by the user. The results of a search are organized into "folders" based on the classification scheme. These high-level categories, represented by the folders, help distinguish multiple meanings of the same term. For example, an ambiguous word such as "pitcher" might result in two folders being presented to the user. One folder would be titled "Sports", the second "Decorative Arts". The user who chooses only the Sports folder will be presented with only those Web resources that use "pitcher" in the baseball sense. The user who selects the folder called "Decorative Arts" will be presented only with those resources that are related to water pitchers. KOSs can be very powerful in supporting free-text searching within digital libraries and in integrating Web resources into existing digital libraries. However, these systems must be used with caution. KOSs have generally been developed for a specific discipline, task, or function, or for the indexing of a specific collection or database. Therefore, depending on the domain in which the KOS is being used and the complexity of the system, it may or may not suggest relevant free-text terms. Expanding a search with related terms, rather than pure synonyms, may return hits that are only peripherally relevant to the user.

PLANNING AND IMPLEMENTING KNOWLEDGE ORGANIZATION SYSTEMS IN DIGITAL LIBRARIES

This part provides general guidelines that may be useful for an organization that wants to use knowledge organization systems to organize a digital library. The framework described is applicable for KOSs of any type or subject.

PLANNING KNOWLEDGE ORGANIZATION SYSTEMS

Analysing User Needs

Of primary importance to any digital library project is an analysis of its users' needs, in terms of content and functionality. Many volumes have already been written about needs assessment, and providing detailed guidance on this subject is beyond the scope of this paper. However, when analysing how a KOS might be used with a particular digital library, it is essential to thoroughly understand the environment of the user. One must look not only at the needs for organizing the digital library materials but also at possible links between content within and outside the digital library walls. This is particularly important for KOSs that are acting as intermediate authority files, because in such cases the links may not be readily apparent. It is important to consider other views that might be valuable for users and peripheral communities that might benefit from the digital library's content were it accessible to them through a KOS.

Locating Knowledge Organization Systems

Once the user's needs have been analysed, it is necessary to locate KOSs to meet the need. While an alternate system can be built locally, it is preferable to find an existing KOS for several reasons. First, it is costly and time-consuming to build a KOS. Second, KOSs often benefit by having been built over time. Many of the systems described in this report have been built over decades. The value of a KOS comes from its acceptance by the user community; sources built by noted authorities such as learned societies, trade associations, or standards groups will be viewed as more trustworthy than those built internally. Finally, the networked environment has resulted in both an explosion of primary materials, including documents, electronic journals, and Web-based databases, and in an equivalent explosion of KOSs on the Web. There are several ways to identify KOSs that may be of interest. Many users are already aware of KOSs on the Web within their discipline. Developers may also turn to directories, librarians in the field, and reference sources, or they may perform a general search of the Internet.

Planning the Infrastructure

It is necessary to make decisions about the architecture of the KOS in the context of the digital library setting. The physical location of the KOS is important. Will the system be held externally or internally? There are pros and cons to either approach. If the system is available on the Web, it is possible to consider linking to the KOS as an external system. This architecture requires a script or some search query to locate the resource. One must then launch a query against the resource to obtain the piece of information that will serve as the key between the two files. This key could be a *universal resource locator* (URL) or input to another search query. A query may be necessary if the KOS is stored in a database.

The script may transfer log-on information from the digital library system to the external KOS, in order to provide access to the Web-enabled database. In the case of a more direct link, the access may be by URL. However, the use of a URL as the link has the same problem with persistence as does direct access via a URL from a browser. The organization may move the KOS, thereby changing the URL that is being used as the key. It is important to determine how often the URLs in the KOS change, whether there is a means of notification of these changes, and whether it is possible to consider an alternative that would be more persistent. Schemes such as the Digital Object Identifier and the Persistent URL have been devised to enable resources to be physically moved among servers without having their names changed.

Another alternative is the use of other *Uniform Resource Identification* (URI) schemes and the *Uniform Resource Name* (URN), which can be sent from the newer Web browsers. The benefit of linking to a remote resource is that the resource will always be upto- date. The maintenance of the KOS is in the hands of the owner, not the digital librarian. It may also be more apparent to users that the KOS is not owned by the digital library. Linking to a remote KOS also has disadvantages. Persistence and unexpected changes in the organization and content of the system may cause problems. The software or telecommunications route between the digital library server and the KOS may be unreliable. In systems requiring fast response time or large amounts of data transfer, and, therefore, high bandwidth, the fact that a connection must be made between the digital library and the external KOS may make the system unacceptable to the user.

Alternatively, the KOS may be obtained from the owner and loaded locally. In many cases, this requires licensing that may not be required when the KOS is accessed remotely, because a copy of the whole resource is being provided to the digital library. Loading a KOS locally also requires that one consider issues such as maintenance, local system administration, and disk storage. If the KOS uses special software, such as a database management system, loading the KOS locally will require a copy of that software, which may require additional purchase or licensing. Other considerations are the need for firewalls and interface design. On the positive side, the KOS is under more local control.

Therefore, it may be possible to improve the response time by not accessing the KOS over the Internet.

If the KOS is to be used behind the scenes, concerns of speed and integration become more important. If additional modifications need to be made to the KOS to integrate it with the digital library, it will also be necessary to load the KOS locally. If the digital library intends to incorporate numerous secondary KOSs, it is important to consider the degree to which the architecture is scaleable. The National Library of Medicine's UMLS incorporates more than 40 different sources. While its main purpose has been to develop a metathesaurus for moving among these vocabularies, the management of the systems, regardless of the mapping issues, has been a major consideration. Ingest has been a major concern, with the need to develop a system that can handle a variety of input formats-from ASCII text files to highly structured database output.

The architecture must also accommodate the character sets of the incoming sources. This is particularly important if a mark-up language has been used to represent special characters and diacritical marks. Systems that have been developed in Unicode, which extends ASCII to accommodate diacritical marks and non-Roman character sets, cannot be handled by systems that deal only with ASCII or extended ASCII sets. Since many digital library systems are being built as extensions or applications of existing *integrated library systems* (ILS), it is important to consider how the KOSs will integrate with the library system. Unfortunately, many ILS vendors have not considered links to external files or databases in their system designs. In some cases, the vendor may require that the information be stored in the proprietary format of the ILS.

The system may require that the files be on the same directory or server as the accessing ILS. The fields that can be linked to the Web or searched may be limited. Outside communications may require Z39.50 client-server connections. With relatively closed systems, ILSs may be a difficult environment in which to implement alternative and nontraditional KOSs. Digital libraries that are interested in using KOSs should consider this integration when developing requirements for the procurement of a system to support them.

Vendors should be encouraged to support relatively open architectures and to consider the extension of traditional library systems to support broader digital library functionality. In addition to these immediate concerns, it is important to consider the incorporation of future KOSs. Initial success may spur the desire for integration of additional KOSs or enhanced functionality for the existing KOS. Success may breed additional requirements and increase the strain on hardware, software, and network architectures.

Maintaining the Knowledge Organization System

For a digital library, an outdated KOS can be more of a hindrance than a benefit. Maintenance, both of content and of the system, should be considered when planning a KOS. This is particularly important if the digital library is to be self-supporting or revenue generating. Version control of the KOS is extremely important. Reloading a new version from the system provider is one way to accommodate changes; however, this may not be acceptable if the locally held version differs substantially from that held by the system's provider. If there has been significant transformation or processing of the original KOS, it may be difficult, or impossible, to reload the original and recreate the changes that have been made.

A transaction-based approach, whereby only changes are transferred between the KOS provider and the library, is also possible; however, this requires that the system provider have the infrastructure, both machine and human, to produce these transactions. It also requires that the changes to the original KOS be identifiable in order to create change transactions. For example, Stuart Nelson of the NLM's UMLS Project recently reported that many systems can create annual transaction records to inform the UMLS about the changes that have occurred to the original system. However, the changes are often not indicated with enough detail to support automatic change transactions in the UMLS. If a change date, for example, is recorded only at the level of the concept record, it is impossible to tell whether the term has changed or if the relationship between this concept and another concept has changed. Since the UMLS splits the incoming terminology and its relationships into a variety of files, it is often difficult to tell how the UMLS files must be change based on the changes made during the maintenance of the original KOS.

Presenting the Knowledge Organization System to the User

In addition to deciding which KOS should be used and what functions it should serve, the digital library will need to determine how to present the KOS to its users. A KOS may be exposed to the user or made relatively transparent. The KOS can be exposed to the user in different ways. Material can be grouped into KOS-related themes or categories on the digital library's Web site. The KOS may be used at a higher level to identify specific portals for different uses or users. If the content of the digital library includes metadata records, the KOS may be displayed as index terms on the records or in its entirety as a navigation aid to searching. In other cases, the KOS may be transparent. For example, a thesaurus can be used behind the scenes to extend the user's search to include synonyms, to connect the digital library's resources to other information and resources, or to filter or rank the information obtained.

IMPLEMENTING KNOWLEDGE ORGANIZATION SYSTEMS

Acquisition and Intellectual Property Issues

It is critical to properly handle the acquisition of knowledge organization systems. The first question is whether the KOS is under copyright. If so, the copyright holder should be contacted concerning the KOS. It is important to ensure that the apparent contact is the official one. Many references have been reprinted or put on the Web without proper acknowledgment of the real owner.

Once the contact has been made, there are several points for discussion:

* If the provider maintains the KOS, how will the digital library find out about any changes that may be made in it? Is there a notification mechanism in place? How frequently must the information be updated to be of benefit to the digital library's users? Will the maintenance be self-evident, or must the agreement

include notification requirements? What will the owner do if the maintenance can no longer be performed?

* What will happen if the provider discontinues the product or sells or transfers it to someone else?
* What uses can the digital library make of the KOS under the proposed agreement? As with other licensing, it is advisable to aim for the broadest permissions and the longest term possible. At a minimum, the library should be able to renegotiate the terms of the agreement relatively easily.
* In a networked environment, it is beneficial to develop mechanisms for linking to online versions rather than to maintain a local copy of the resource. This ensures that what is presented is up-todate, and acknowledges more clearly the ownership of the KOS. However, there are numerous factors to consider. Will the KOS be used on an intranet or behind a firewall, where access to the outside or information coming into the organization might be prohibited? Does the KOS service use "cookies" or require knowledge of the user's Internet provider address? Does it require a user ID and password?
* If the KOS is to be accessed remotely, are there service issues? Is it likely to be accessed with bandwidth, model, and computer speeds that are adequate for outside connections of this type? Is the use of such a critical nature that unreliable service on the part of the KOS or the Internet connection will cause the digital library itself to be viewed as less useful? Does the KOS require a specialized search engine or search query formulation? Can the digital library system properly display the results, or would the results be better displayed through the KOS system? Will the resulting information be used in its native form or must it be extracted or transformed? If the KOS is to be loaded locally, in what formats can the content be received?
* If the KOS is not available electronically, can it be digitized? Is the owner interested in a cooperative

venture, and are the human and financial resources for such an effort available?

Making the Link

There are two parts to establishing the link between the digital library and the KOS. The first is locating the key anchor information in the digital library's resource. The second involves the look up against the target file. The creation of this link may be more or less automatic, depending on the particular situation. The characterization of this activity is meant to be general and to allow both "on-thefly" links and embedded links. Regardless of what function the KOS is going to serve in the digital library, the essential information contained in the digital library resource from which the link is to be made must be identified.

The mechanism for doing this depends on the type of object from which the link is being made and on the information that is expected to be identified in the digital library's resource. The first step is to review any metadata related to the digital library resource. Do the metadata carry the term that is needed to make the link? If this information is included, the level at which the metadata are assigned should be reviewed. If the metadata indicate the subject matter of the specific resource in which the user will be interested, the metadata can be used to make the links. However, in some cases, the terms that appear in the title or description at the resource level may not be indicative of the subject at the individual item level.

Automatically making a link on the basis of the content description for an entire book may misrepresent the content of a chapter. Whether or not the metadata can be used will depend on the amount and type of information given in the metadata and the level at which the metadata are assigned. If a text resource in the digital library provides no appropriate metadata, the procedure for identifying the key information may involve text analysis. A programme to perform simple string searching or a search engine that can preserve hit locations can be used if the text string has distinguishing characteristics, such as a database acronym, or a specific structure, such as a latitude and longitude coordinate. If the text string has no such cues, text mining or more complex textanalysis tools may be necessary.

These tools use a variety of semantic and syntactic algorithms to locate key information. There have been significant advances in commercially available text-mining tools, such as IBM's Intelligent Agent, which includes specific algorithms for identification of names of places and persons. The second step of the linking activity is to make the connection to the KOS. The methods for doing this vary, depending on whether the system is being loaded locally or is referenced remotely. If the system is loaded locally, it is possible to perform a significant amount of processing to match the two files, assuming that computer resources of this type are available to the digital library organization.

If the system is only available remotely over the Web, the interaction will require knowledge of scripting and various Web-based access techniques. Scripting should be considered in both local and remote approaches, since the more integrated the linking is with the resource, the more maintenance may be required if there are changes in either the resource or the KOS. Regardless of the approach that is taken, making the link requires an analysis of both the information in the original digital library material and the corresponding information in the KOS. If the KOS is being used as an intermediate file to bridge between the digital library's resource and another resource, it is also important to understand the data and the process whereby the search is performed and information returned from the target resource.

If the KOS must return a value to the original digital library resource, the data and process must be evaluated in a bidirectional sense. Choosing the linking mechanism is equally important. The link may be fixed or "on-the-fly." In the case of a fixed link, a specific URL is embedded at the link point in the digital library material. However, as stated before, problems of persistence are inherent in this approach. Alternatively, a URN can be used. The URN requires the creation of a namespace on the point of the target file, and the search is to this namespace rather than to a specific URL. Persistent locators (PURLs) and digital object identifiers (DOIs) can also solve this problem. These schemes are sufficient if the material is an HTML document. Content in databases is more difficult to retrieve. The National Library of Medicine now supports the searching of a variety of its databases through its Internet Grateful Med (IGM) URL function. IGM users can create URLs that will actually perform searches against the databases.

Information on the syntax for creating such a URL is provided on the NLM Web site. While the intent is that the search URL will be bookmarked by an individual user, the same concept can be used for creating an active link at the anchor point for the link. With additional scripting, the creation of the term *pneumonia* can be automatically replaced with an active link that picks up the term where the link has been made.

THE FUTURE OF KNOWLEDGE ORGANIZATION SYSTEMS ON THE WEB

As online databases moved to the Web, they began to provide their products, including vocabulary aids, in this environment. Portable document format (PDF) versions of printed vocabulary aids are common, since PDF can be easily produced from a Postscript file and it retains the look of the printed product. With Adobe's tools for indexing and searching, the PDF file can provide some level of support for linking. Many of these aids, however, remain in the form of HTML files only—there is no database structure to easily support the linking and searching. In some cases, the full structure of the KOS is not made available on the Web; the only format for a Web-based thesaurus may be an alphabetical list of terms that does not enable the user to navigate easily the hierarchical structure.

As unique ways of using these resources are developed, it is hoped that more KOS providers will be encouraged to provide their systems in formats that are conducive to such networked uses. Some of the requirements for such electronic KOSs were identified at a workshop entitled "Electronic Thesauri: Planning for a Standard" and sponsored by NISO. While the focus of this meeting was digital thesauri, consideration was also given to other KOSs in digital form. The identified requirements include persistent identification at the concept level, the need for a simple protocol for the distributed querying and response from a KOS, and the development of a standard set of metadata attributes for describing a remote KOS. To facilitate the search and display of information from a previously unknown KOS, the system must have unique and persistent identifiers for each of the concepts in the system.

For example, the California Environmental Resources Evaluation System and the U.S. Geological Survey have developed a system for remote querying and response. It requires that each concept in the thesaurus have a unique identifier. In the case of the ITIS, which is accessed remotely by the CERES system, the ITIS record number is used as the identifier. Other unique identifiers could include the DOI, or a classification notation that has been made unique by appending the scheme name or the URL to the notation. The second requirement is a protocol for the distributed querying and response of KOSs. This is particularly critical for highly structured systems such as thesauri, semantic networks, and ontologies. Work has been done in this area within the Z39.50 community.

A profile has been proposed by the Zthes Working Group to tailor the Z39.50 protocol to operate on thesauri that follow the Z39.19 standard. A similar effort is under way at the CERES Project. Instead of a Z39.50-based protocol, CERES has developed a structure that is based on the Resource Description Framework (RDF) and the HTTP protocol of standard browsers. The RDF's concept of containers is a natural for managing the hierarchical structure of complex systems such as thesauri.

The structure proposed by CERES is likely to be encoded using XML, a mark-up format that lends itself to structured information. This protocol for linking distributed vocabularies will support both searching and cataloging. The user will be presented with remote vocabularies that can be displayed and navigated by a local client. The third major finding from the NISO workshop was the need for a metadata content standard for the description of KOSs.

Such a standard is key to provision of knowledge organization services over the Internet. The metadata identify the Web resource as a KOS and provide important information to allow an application to use it remotely without prior knowledge of its content or structure. A draft set of attributes for describing KOSs available in a networked environment has been developed by a task group of the Network Knowledge Organization Systems (NKOS) Working Group, an ad hoc group of terminology experts from organizations that are interested in issues related to the use and interoperability of KOSs over the Internet.

The draft attributes are based on work originally done by Linda Hill and Michael Raugh. The attributes describe the KOS so that content from the system can be transferred over the Internet and handled by a remote browser or client application. The attributes include the depth of hierarchy, the types of relationships included, the subject, storage format, copyright and rights management, and contact information. To facilitate the transfer of information, the attribute set also includes information on character set and file size. To facilitate the acquisition and licensing of the KOSs, the draft content description includes point of contact information.

During discussions about the metadata content standard, workshop attendees identified three methods for storing the metadata for a KOS. First, the metadata could be stored with the KOS, as metadata elements for that resource. Second, the metadata could be stored in a physically separate knowledge organization registry. The third possibility is a hybrid approach, where a minimal set of metadata elements is contained in a central registry. There is significant interest in the use of KOSs to organize and search material on the Internet. It is hoped that this interest will result in knowledge organization services that will make these sources more readily accessible to a variety of software applications and to a variety of users. As services and enabled software proliferate, it will be easier to integrate these KOSs into digital libraries.

CONCLUSION: ENHANCING DIGITAL LIBRARIES WITH KNOWLEDGE ORGANIZATION SYSTEMS

Given that the digital library field is still quite new, it seems strange to be talking already about enhancing digital libraries. However, in this fast-moving environment, the initial digital libraries resulting from digitization projects, or even virtual collections, are being enhanced as user expectations and technology capabilities allow. In the midst of this furious activity, it is valuable to analyse users' needs and interests and then to identify KOSs that can be used to enhance the digital library. Knowledge organization systems refer to a range of traditional and nontraditional systems for the organization of knowledge. The systems have been developed in numerous environments outside the traditional library environment, including those of A&I services, publishers and professional organizations, and corporations.

Examples exist in many disciplines and for many target audiences. Knowledge organization systems can enhance the digital library in a number of ways. They can be used to connect a digital library resource to a related resource. The related information may reside within the KOS itself or the KOS may be used as an intermediary file to retrieve the key needed to access it in another resource. A KOS can make digital library materials accessible to disparate communities. This may be done by providing alternate subject access, by adding access by different modes, by providing multilingual access, and by using the KOS to support free text searching. A well-planned infrastructure for KOSs is required.

This includes the resources, processes, and policies for analysing user needs; locating KOSs to answer these needs; and acquiring, implementing, and maintaining the KOS. Traditional and nontraditional KOSs provide an opportunity to extend the boundaries of the digital library. By going beyond the initial organization of the digital library, digital librarians can use the network environment to provide additional value to its users.

2

Understanding the Library Classification

NEED AND PURPOSE OF LIBRARY CLASSIFICATION

As a participant in this course you are either a library worker or wish to be one. You are aware that libraries keep various types of documents. At the outset, it is necessary to know that libraries hold several types of collections like printed books, journals, manuscripts, maps, charts, micro-documents, CD-ROMs, video and audio cassettes. etc. All these collections should necessarily be arranged systematically.

There are three possible ways in which a reader may demand library material. He may ask by the name of the author whose works he wishes to read, or by the title of the book. The third situation is that he may need book(s) on a particular subject. This last one is known as subject approach. In short, subject approach is the means of securing unknown items from the collection, and classification is the means of facilitating it. Library classification yields subject-wise arrangement of library materials in which documents are arranged by subject and each subject is followed by another subject related to it, *e.g.*, physics following mathematics. This is known as systematic arrangement.

The other important activities in a library such as book selection, circulation and reference services are somewhat indirectly dependent upon library classification. It is thus no wonder that classification is widely regarded as the foundation of librarianship. Classification can ensure full exploitation of library material and strengthen other services in a library. The need for classification is all the greater in modern libraries, as they store different types of documents requiring diverse storage media. In other words, documents on the same subject(s) get scattered throughout the collection because of their diverse physical forms. Classification, however, is the means of bringing books on the shelves and their entries in a catalogue or index at one place. Let us, therefore, acquaint ourselves with these different types of documents that modern libraries acquire and store.

DOCUMENTS

We find in libraries various types of documents, *viz.*, manuscripts, printed books, periodicals, pamphlets, reports, photo reproductions, sound records, films, musical scores, microfilms, maps, atlases, charts, illustrations and electronic media items, such as CD-ROMs, through which human thought is communicated and preserved. Proper collection, storage and maximum use of these documents is the prime concern of present day libraries.

Nature of Documents

The problem of collection, storage and retrieval of documents has been complicated by the following factors:

* The steady growth in the output of various types of documents popularly known as the "knowledge explosion" or "information explosion" or "information flood" or "information boom or bloom".
* The publication of documents in various languages of the world. The production of documents in diverse physical forms. '
* The nature and complexity of the thought content of the subject matter presented in various forms of documents.
* The complexity of readers' approach to documents and libraries.

Each document, like an individual, is not only unique but also exhibits relations of considerable complexity with other documents. Extrinsic features like size, colour, volume, binding, year of publication and intrinsic features like thought content and their arrangement inside the document, or the nature of information, *i.e.*, textual, numeric, bibliographic or graphic, also add to the complexity of the problem of libraries for achieving the objective of maximum utilisation of their collections.

The complexity of thought content and the nature of relationships between various types of documents must be known and clearly established for their maximum use.

The maximum use of documents can be ensured by:

* Personal assistance to readers,
* Systematic arrangement, and
* Proper display of materials in the library.

If the collection of a library is arranged in a systematic way documents can be located and retrieved easily. A classification scheme is the map or device for the arrangement of books in the library.

Collection and Storage of Documents

From the dawn of civilization man has recognised the need for collecting and preserving the records of human thought. Books and other graphic material are the records of human thoughts, action and achievement and can serve as the basis for future achievement. Their value to society, thus, cannot be exaggerated. These records are collected and preserved in libraries for the benefit of present and future generations. These records, diverse in form and content, are referred to by the generic term documents.

Factors Determining Arrangement of Documents

Documents can be arranged in various ways in a library, *e.g.*, by author, or by title, or by, subject or by basis such as size, language, colour of binding or any other such criterion. The needs of the readers may be the criterion one can consider for arrangement of documents in a library. Mills, in his book Modern Outline of Library Classification, lists the following possible characteristics determining the arrangements of documents:

* *Age of reader*: Children's books are distinguished from adult's books.
* *Conditions attached to the use of the material*: Books for lending are distinguished from those to be consulted

within the library. Generally "Reference Books" come under this category.

* *Documents of unusual size*: Documents of an abnormal size, oversize or undersize, are shelved separately. This is done to conserve space in the stack area.
* *Documents of unusual gross body*: Micro cards, gramophone records, tapes, slides and other audio-visual material and electronic documents are shelved separately.
* *Thought content of the document (subject matter)*: Factual literature is arranged by subject, imaginative literature by language or author.
* *Language of the document*: Documents in foreign languages are separately arranged in their original languages.
* *Value of the document*: Manuscripts and rare and costly documents are shelved separately.
* *Peculiarities of form of presentation*: Files of bound periodicals are separately shelved.
* *Date of printing*: Incunabula - early printed books - are shelved separately.
* *Local history collection*: Documents dealing with various aspects of a place, locality or region are shelved separately.
* *Gift collection*: A large number of hooks may be gifted with the condition to shelve them separately.

The factors influence the arrangement of documents in libraries. But thought content or subject arrangement (fifth in Mill's list) is still the dominant and important facto- for deciding the sequence of documents. All other factors in the list are functional. Though a collection can be diviued into several parts on the basis of any of the functional factors, it would still be helpful to arrange documents in each part on the basis of subject matter. This leads to parallel sequences in the various collections in libraries.

In any library, the total collection gets divided into some separate collections of general books and reference books, textbooks, journals, etc. There are, thus, many sequences of books on one and the same subject in the library. These sequences are known as "parallel sequences".

Arrangement of Documents in Libraries

Until the end of the 19th century library collections were small in size. Not as many subject fields had developed as one notice now, and publishing was not as wide spread. The readership was not as large as we notice in the present times. Libraries of yesteryear attempted to arrange their collections on the basis of fixed locations. This method was employed to allocate each and every document a particular and permanent place on a particular shelf of the library. Each new document, irrespective of its thought content, was assigned to the place immediately next to the one previously added to the collection.

The fixed location failed to bring together documents embodying the same subject. Fixed location implied chronological order of accession under broad subject categories.

In some of the older libraries, attempts where made to arrange the collection on the basis of extrinsic characteristics such as colour, size, year of publication and type of binding of documents. All these arrangements or sequences are not as helpful as the subject arrangement.

Approach of Readers for Documents

As state l earlier, documents can be arranged in libraries on the basis of the colour of the binding, the size, the language, the year of publication, the accession number and so on. But these methods are outdated and unhelpful, as they cannot bring to the notice of the reader the author, the title or the subject matter of a document. There is little or no chance of your finding today a library, which arranges its collection on the basis of colour, size, year of publication or even the name of the publisher. It was possible to use these characteris-tics for arranging books when the collections were very small in size.

There are a few libraries where the collections are arranged on the basis of accession number or serial number. The other methods by which documents are usually arranged are by title, author or subject. This is because in present-day libraries, the reader's approach for a specific document is by title or author or subject. It is common practice that fiction is arranged by author, periodicals by title and scientific factual literature by subject. In some libraries, you can find that even imaginative literature (belles letters) is arranged first by language, and within each language by form followed by author and, if necessary, by work number.

It has already been explained, that a reader may demand a document by a particular author or of a particular title or on a particular subject. There are, thus, mainly three approaches to a collection, *viz.*, author, title and subject.

Author Approach

Generally readers go to a library to find:

* A particular document whose author is known or
* What documents by a particular author are in the library.

But the arrangement of documents on the basis of the author is not always helpful. If you want a particular document, or documents on a particular subject, the author arrangement fails to bring documents having the same specific subject and related subjects at one place. Here is an example:

*	Marsten, R.B.	:	Communication Technology
*	Marston, A.N.	:	Encyclopaedia of Angling
*	Marston, E.H.	:	Dynamic Environment
*	Marston, Elizabeth	:	Rain Forest
*	Marston, John	:	Dutch Courtesan
*	Marston, J.E.	:	Nature of Public Relations
*	Marston, Phillip	:	Breeder of Democracy
*	Marston, P.B.	:	Collected Poems
*	Marst, R.M.	:	Electronic Projects
*	Martell, P.	:	World Military Leaders

Title Approach

Sometimes you may go to a library to get a document whose title you know. If the books in the library are arranged by title, it will meet your requirement. But the method of arranging documents on the basis of title is also not very helpful. There is always a chance of a title being misquoted. Titles sometimes change from one edition to another. The title of the same document would differ when translated from one language to another. Sometimes the same document is published in different countries under different titles, though the language may remain the same. Title arrangement, like author arrangement, fails to bring together documents having the same specific subject at one place. Because of these limitations; the arrangement of documents on the basis of title is not very helpful.

Here is an example:

* Instant Astrology by Jack London
* Instant Beauty Tricks by P. Brooks
* Instant Book Keeping by D.C. Conaway
* Instant Chicago by J. Graham
* Instant College by R.W. Graham Classification
* Instant Divorce by S. Rosen
* Instant English Handbook by M. Semmelmeyer
* Instant Medical Advisor by J. Smith
* Instant Paintings by N. Koni
* Instant Quotation Dictionary by B.O. Bolander

Subject Approach

In academic, special, technical and research libraries, and to a large extent even in public libraries, you will find that the majority of readers approach documents on the basis of the subject. This subject approach by readers has increased due to the growth in science and technology and also to a large extent in social sciences where the author and the title of a document are important but not adequate. Due to the enormous output of documents in these fields, it is often difficult to recall a specific title or author correctly except in the case of classics.

Therefore, one finds that in well organised libraries documents are arranged on the basis of subject matter. This arrangement helps to bring documents embodying the same specific subject together and those on related subjects in their close proximity on the shelves. This would result, as Ranganathan puts it, into an APUPA arrangement that will give reader the greatest satisfaction at the moment in full conformity to all the Five Laws of Library Science. In this arrangement, the focal point of one's main interest is the UMBRAL REGION. This is followed on, either side by the PENUMBRAL REGION represented by subjects on either side of the UMBRAL region having successfully a decreasing bearing on the umbral region. The penumbral region will ultimately thin into ALIEN REGIONS. This is helpful and convenient especially on open access libraries. Readers can directly go to the shelves and browse through the library collection. Generally, the objective of libraries is to have an APUPA ARRANGEMENT EVERYWHERE.

Subject arrangement, hence, helps bring together on the shelves documents on one and the same subject followed by those of related subjects. Suppose you are looking for a specific document on say, physics, you can find, where subject arrangement exists, documents not only on physics, but also those related to it in close proximity, *i.e.*, chemistry. It may so happen that if a specific title wanted by you is not available, you can find another title on the subject that may very well meet your requirement. Some scholars may need everything available on their topic. You will notice that near the books on chemistry you will also find books on related subjects like mathematics and astronomy on one side and chemistry and biology on the other.

Subject arrangement of documents enables you to know:

* What documents the library has on a specific subject; and
* What is the quality of collection on that subject, and what are the gaps in the collection?

This kind of arrangement is known as 'filiatory sequence'.

In large and special libraries, having several parts such as:

* Text books
* Reference books
* Theses and dissertations
* Pamphlets
* Bound volumes of periodicals

You will find that all these different collections are arranged by subject using a scheme of library classification:

It has been the considered opinion of experts that the arrangement of documents on a basis other than subject may not meet the requirements of the majority of readers in modem libraries. Nowadays the subject approach to books is predominant. Eminent classificationists like Melvil Dewey, J.D. Brown, C.A. Cutter, W.C.B. Sayers, S.R. Ranganathan, H. E. Bliss and others advocate the subject arrangement of documents. Subject arrangement, however, does not mean that there is no scope for the author and title approaches. These approaches are taken care of through the author and title catalogues. Subject arrangement, then, is paramount and the basis for it is the subject content of documents. Library classification is the technique used in libraries for mechanising of this subject content documents: It is a technique for making libraries more helpful.

CLASSIFICATION

Meaning of Classification

Systematic grouping of entities (both abstract and concrete) to meet one's requirement is known as classification. Classification lies at the root of all human activities. Our daily life is very much dependent on the process of classification, however, elementary this process may appear. You can surely recall a number of activities around you where classification plays its part. Take, for example, the arrangement of contents in a railway time table, the display of goods in a grocery shop, the arrangement of modules in a departmental store to facilitate the selection of goods by customers, the seating arrangement in a theatre or stadium, the assignment of registration numbers to various motor vehicles by a state transport authority, or the sorting of letters by postmen first by the city, then by the street and lastly by the house numbers for quick delivery of post. These are simple examples of how we use classification in our activities.

The word 'classification' was derived from the Latin word classes which meant order or rank of mobility in Roman society based upon birth and wealth. Classification is a mental process by which we group or separate things on the basis of common characteristics. For example, things grouped together on the basis of a common characteristic like writing material. In other words, classification is an attempt to identify a class for like things. We succeed in our attempt by applying a characteristic and isolating all like things on that basis from unlike things. Classification in essence means dividing into groups, grouping, sorting, arranging, ordering, ranking and relating one entity to the others.

Dr. S.R. Ranganathan, in his *Prolegomena to Library Classification (1967)*, elaborately discusses the meaning of classification. In the case of physical objects, division and assortment are the two results of classification, According to Ranganathan, while division implies sorting objects into two or more groups, assortment additionally denotes arrangement of these groups in a predetermined sequence. Further, in library classification, the sequence of objects, *i.e.*, documents, is so mechanised by the use of notation that it is reflected in the notation when a document is withdrawn or added.

Thus, one can see that the term 'classification' is a homonym.

Ranganathan, therefore, tried to resolve the homonym by examining the various ways in which the term has been used:

* Classification in Sense 1 is DIVISION.
* Classification in Sense 2 is ASSORTMENT.
* Classification in Sense 3 is CLASSIFICATION IN SENSE 2 plus representing each entity by an ordinal number taken out of a system of ordinal numbers, designed to mechanise the maintenance of the sequence,
* Classification in Sense 4 is CLASSIFICATION IN SENSE 3 when complete assortment is made of an amplified universe· - that is when the entities and the pseudo-entities arising in the process of successive assortment stand arranged in one filiatory sequence.
* Classification in Sense 5 is CLASSIFICATION IN SENSE 4 with all the entities removed but only the pseudo-entities or classes retained.

It is classification in Sense 5 that is used:

* Either when the universe classified is infinite,
* When some of the entities are unknown and unknowable at any moment, even though the universe classified is finite.

It is classification in Sense 5 that is practised by the library profession. The primary,concern of libraries is to establish the most helpful arrangement of documents. Library classification, therefore, presupposes the use of notation, *i.e.*, a brief symbol for the names of subjects. It is in this sense that the word classification is used in this and other units.

Definition of Library Classification

Having understood the meaning of classification in library science, let us now go through a few well-known definitions of library classification.

Library classification has been defined by both the classificationists and the critics, all necessarily underlying its utilitarian aspect. According to Margaret Mann, classification is "the arranging of things according to likeness and unlikeness. It is the sorting and grouping of things, but in addition, classification of books is a knowledge classification with adjustments made necessary by the physical form of books". W.C. Berwick Sayers defines it as the arrangement of books on shelves or description of them in the manner which is most helpful to those who read". Arthur Maltby revises Sayers definition as "the systematic arrangement of books and other material on shelves or of catalogue and index entries in the manner which is most useful to those who read or who seek a definite piece of information". Ranganathan is more elaborate in his definition.

According to Ranganathan:

* "it is the translation of the name of the subject of a book into the preferred artificial language of ordinal numbers, and the individualisation of several books dealing with the same specific subject by means of a further set of ordinal numbers which represent some features of the book other than their thought content".

In this definition, we find three important phrases, viz.,

* Artificial language,
* Ordinal numbers, and
* Specific subject.

These three phrases need some explanation.

Artificial Language

In library classification we use symbols to denote subjects. The names of subjects are in ordinary language understandable to an ordinary person. Therefore, we call it the natural language which comes naturally to the human being living in a society. On the other hand, the symbols that we may use to denote a subject, say B, or 510, or QA for mathematics, are artificial in the sense that the common man will not ordinarily understand the meaning of these symbols. Hence these are artificial and intelligible to a specifically trained class of professionals. Their value is only ordinal, which means that these symbols have no quantitative or qualitative value; they only determine the sequence/order of documents on the shelves. These symbols also maintain/preserve the chosen sequence as the books will be replaced at their proper place after taking them out for reading or lending. These symbols do not indicate anything except the order/sequence of these documents on the shelves.

Ordinal Numbers

These are used not for the purpose of counting but ordering and mechanising the arrangement of things. For example, participants in a conference can be listed in a desired sequence on the basis of some suitable principle and then this sequence can be mechanised with the help of ordinal numbers.

Melvil Dewey (1851-1931), the father of modern library classification, was the first classificationist to use simple Indo-Arabic numerals (0-9) as ordinal numbers for the systematic listing of subjects both broader and narrower, in his Decimal Classification first published in 1876. Since then the system of ordinal numbers-notation as it is called in library classification-has been the principal element in the design and use of library classification schemes.

Specific Subject

The contents of a document may deal with some field of knowledge. It is a prerequisite for a classifier to know what subject matter the document exactly contains. After ascertaining the exact subject, or specific subject, the classifier translates that specific subject into the artificial language or ordinal numbers of the classification scheme used. In order to know the specific subject of the document the classifier has to examine its title, contents page, preface and introduction, and to scan through some chapters, and, if necessary to go through the entire book. There may be certain occasions where a classifier has to consult an expert to ascertain the specific subject of a document.

Ranganathan defines the specific subject of a document as "that division of knowledge whose extension and intension are equal to those of its thought content". Extension means the scope (if the subject treatment and intension means the depth of the subject treatment in a given document.

Palmer and Wells define it as "that division of knowledge which exactly comprehends all the major factors that go in its making". Let us take an example and perform an analysis to ascertain the specific subject.

It is possible to interpret the contents of this book as '*Mstory*' or '*History of India*' or 'History of India during the Mughal Period'. All these possible subjects are not specific enough and are too broad to convey the actual thought content of the book. It is, therefore, necessary to add one more phrase to the analysis to make it complete, and that phrase is 'Reign of Akbar'. All these aspects should now be brought into the class number. If you omit any of these aspects, the extension and intension will not be equal to the thought content of the book.

The specific subject of the book can be arrived at as follows History:

* Indian History
* Mughal Period
* Akbar
* Reign

When you analyse the thought content of the document on the lines, the extension (scope) decreases and the intension (depth) increases with every successive division. This sort of subject ordering is called "general to specific".

Ranganathan's definition of classification refers to two objectives: Translation of the subject into an ordinal number and individualisation of a given document in the total order of documents in a library. The subject of the document is translated into a class number with the help of a notation. But, several documents are likely to bear the same class number and the problem of individualisation arises. The class number is, therefore, not enough. It has to be supplemented by one, or if necessary, by two, additional elements.

These additional elements are:

* Book number and
* Collection number.

Class number, book number and collection number constitute the call number of a document. It is only the call number that individualises a given document in a library.

Call Number

The call numbers' for a document consists of three elements, *viz.*, class number, book number and collection number. The following example will show the presence of these three elements in a call number.

Jawaharlal Nehru: An Autobiography with Musings on Recent Events in India, Bombay, Allied. 1962.

The call number for this book by Dewey Decimal classification is:

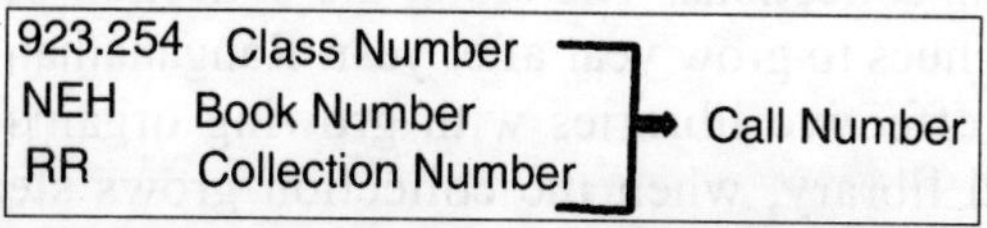

The explanation of the above call number is:

* *923254*: Biography of an Indian statesman (that is the subject of the book, *i.e.*, Class number
* *NEH*: Nerhu (the first three letters from surname of the author, Book number)
* *RR*: Reading Room Collection (the nature of the collection in the library *i.e.*, collection number

Thus, with the help of book number and collection number a document is fully individualised. It means that the call number of a document is unique. Different methods are in use to devise book number and collection number. It is left to individual 'libraries to follow one of these methods, or, if possible, devise their own method or practice.

Purpose and Function

We have so far studied the meaning of classification. We also have studied the importance of a call number. We would now do well to see what exactly is achieved by classifying documents and arranging them in a systematic way in a library.

In the era of the information revolution, the role of libraries in acquiring and organising various types of documents hardly needs any emphasis - Libraries as service institutions acquire documents for use. These acquisitions should systematically be arranged so as to meet the ever growing needs of readers precisely, exhaustively and expeditiously.

If documents are arranged in library on the basis of factors other than subject matter, the arrangement will not be helpful in meeting the requirements of the majority of readers who usually approach a library for subject material. In other words, documents should be classified and arranged on the basis of their subject content.

We are witness to the information revolution. Documents are published in various languages in various disciplines in diverse forms. Libraries have always been acquiring books and adding them to their collections. Therefore, the collection of an active library continues to grow year after year. Ranganathan compares active and effective libraries with growing organisms, In an unclassified library, when the collection grows steadily into thousands and lakhs of volumes, it t would be difficult for the library staff to lay hands on a particular document required by a reader. To meet the subject approach of readers the collection must necessarily be classified by subject.

In libraries where the collection is arranged by accession number, or author or title, and not by subject, books on the same subject will be scattered throughout the collection. Even if the books are arranged alphabetically by subject, the resultant sequence will not be helpful, as unrelated material will come together.

For example:

* Adult education
* Agriculture
* Algebra
* Alloys
* American history
* Anthropology

* Applied mechanics
* Arithmetic
* Astronomy
* Atomic energy
* Australian history.

This type of sequence of subjects surely is far less useful and will fail to meet the requirements of readers. Alphabetical sequence leads to alphabetical scattering of logically related subjects; as shown in the example. It is through systematic arrangement that a filiatory sequence or collection of closely related subjects can be achieved. For this we require a scheme of library classification. Here is an example of arranging documents on the basis of Dewey Decimal Classification which brings documents dealing with different aspects of economics systematically one after another at one place in a collection.

*	330	Economics explained	by R.L. Heibroner
*	331	The economics of work and pay	by Albert Reas
*	332	Essentials of finance	by R.G. Jones
*	333	The economics of natural resources	by R. Leconber
*	334	Cooperative housing	by M. Digby
*	335	Socialism without the state	by E.Lurd
*	336	The fiscal system of HongKong	by H.C.Y. Ho
*	337	Building Europe: Britain's parterns in EEC	by K.J. Twitchett
*	338	Production economics	by M. Fuss
*	339	Macroeconomics	by J.B. Beare

Within each class the arrangement is carried out finally and minutely, *e.g.*,

*	300	Social sciences
*	330	Economics
*	332	Financial economics
*	332.1	Banks and banking
*	332.11	Central banks
*	331.110 954	Reserve Bank of India

Libraries stock various types of documents for different purposes. Classification helps achieve a 'systematic arrangement of different types of documents'.

In big libraries, the collection is segregated in different parts or departments. This is done for the efficient and effective use of library collections and for the convenience of different types of readers. In each department, the collection requires a classified arrangement. An Classification unclassified collection, even though equipped with necessary guides, would be of no use as the readers feel lost in the ocean of books wasting their valuable time to find documents. It has rightly been said that to locate a book in an unclassified library is as difficult as to locate a needle in a hystack. On the other hand, a systematic arrangement helps readers to get documents without loss of time. Thus the time saved by the library staff can be utilised for rendering personalized reference service for the benefit of readers. A systematic arrangement of documents creates order out of chaos. It provides a panoramic view of documents available in a library on a given subject along with those on closely related subjects. This filiatory sequence of subjects facilitates readers not only in getting his/her documents, but also helps them know the strength and weakness of the collection.

The second, third and fourth Laws of Library Science, *viz.*, Every reader his/her document, Every document its reader and Save the time of the reader, as expounded by Ranganathan, can be practised by libraries through the systematic arrangement of documents. The First and Fifth Laws, *i.e.*, Books are for use and A library is a growing organism also advocate a systematic classification of books in libraries.

The arrangement of documents on the shelves is in a progressive order of complexity, *i.e.*, from the general to the specific. Colon Classification is able to arrange documents in an APUPA pattern. Such an arrangement is in pedagogical order, *i.e.*, it is self-educative and reflects the progress of that subject in an evolutionary order.

In the light of the discussion in this subsection, the functions of library classification can be summarised as follows:

* Library classification helps to arrange documents in a systematic order, which is most convenient to the reader and the library staff. It brings related subjects in close proximity, called collocation by Henry Bliss.

* It helps the identification and location of a document on a given subject wanted by a reader whatever may be the size of the library collection. Documents can be quickly retrieved from and replaced to their original positions. The location, lending and replacement of documents are completed mechanically in libraries.
* It helps to arrange documents into organised groups, like pigeonholes; and when a new document is added to the collection, classification finds an appropriate place for the newly added documents among the other documents on the same subject.
* The universe of knowledge is dynamic, continuous, infinite and ever growing. New areas or subjects are being continuously added to the sum total of human knowledge, When the first document on a new subject is added to the library collection, it finds itself at the appropriate place among the already existing related subjects, *i.e.*, among its kith and kin and according to the level of its relationship to them. The functions stated in (ii), (iii), and (iv) are also known as mechanisation of the arrangement.
* It helps to organise book displays and exhibitions. It facilitates withdrawal of certain documents from the main collection for special purposes and occasions such as book talks, seminars, symposia, conferences and special exhibitions, on a given topic.
* It helps in recording the daily issue and return of documents on various subjects at the circulation counter of a library. This facilitates the compilation of statistics on issues, which reflect the pattern of use and demand of documents on different subjects. The feedback helps in the allocation of funds to various subjects and guides the book selection policy of the library. The statistics so collected can be included in the annual report of the library.
* Stock verification is a very important aspect of library administration. Library classification, through the medium of shelflists, facilitates an efficient and thorough stock verification of the library's holdings.

* It helps in the compilation of reading lists. This facilitates facet analysis of the reference queries on various aspects and 'indirectly helps in an efficient reference service.
* It helps in the compilation of subject union catalogues and bibliographies of books and other reading material. The union catalogues are very important tools for resource 'sharing and cooperation among libraries.
* Classified catalogues are only possible with a classification scheme. In a research library classified catalogues are preferred over dictionary catalogues.
* It assists in systematically deriving subject entries. It also aids the cataloguer to use the alphabetical list of subject headings for deriving specific subject headings through class numbers, *i.e.*, by the chain procedure.
* Classificatory principles are used in subject headings and thesaurus construction.
* It helps the library staff, especially the classifiers, to be aware of and comprehend the complexities in the development of the universe of knowledge, which is the basis for a systematic arrangement of documents in libraries.
* Nowadays classification finds immense uses in OPACs (*i.e.*, online public access catalogues). In a computerised catalogue, the class number field can be used in combination with other fields such as language, date or even subject heading and can be used with logical operators such as AND/OR/NOT or the Boolean logical operators. Class numbers can be used to broaden or narrow the searches. Class number searches in combination with other fields increase the efficiency (recall and precision ratios) of the information retrieval system, of which classification is a tool.
* It is the basis for the organisation of knowledge emb6died in documents for maximum use. It is the basis for efficient bibliographic control and retrieval of

documents. It is a great time saving device for the reader and the library staff. As Hulme puts it, "it is a mechanical time saving device for the discovery of knowledge in books".

MODES OF FORMATION OF SUBJECTS

UNIVERSE OF SUBJECTS

Library service is, in essence, the retrieval and dissemination of embodied knowledge to individual members and groups in a community.

Hence, the two essential parameters which affect the value of library services are:

* Universe of Readers; and
* Universe of Subjects.

In order to achieve efficiency of services to readers, it has become imperative to adopt and develop such tools and techniques which would facilitate the classification of subjects embodied in documents and thus help in retrieval and service to the satisfaction of the laws of library science.

But, for this to happen, it is essential that the discipline of library science must keep developing itself to meet changes in the value of each of the parameters. In the succeeding parts, we shall consider the concern of library science with one of the parameters, namely, the Universe of Subjects (UoS).

Laws of Library Science vis-$\overline{\alpha}$-vis Universe of Subjects

The study of the structure and development of the UoS by the information professional can be shown to be a necessary implication of the five laws of library science.

Law 1 and Its Implications

The first law is "Books are for use". Here, the term "book" is a generic term to denote all kinds of documents, including books themselves, periodicals, technical reports, patents, specifications, non-conventional and meta-documents.

The document, in its turn, is a trinity of:

* Soul - embodied knowledge;

* Subtle body - language and expression of the knowledge; and
* Gross body - physical body of the document.

The term "use", on the other hand, implies essentially the use of organised, expressed and embodied knowledge - that is, the subject dealt with in documents - by the readers, although the subtle body is indispensable for the acquisition of knowledge and as a vehicle `for its communication, and the physical body is a convenient means of transport of the embodied knowledge across space and through time. A document retrieval system is, therefore, essentially concerned with the classification, search, retrieval, and service of the "subject".

A subject, in. its turn, is an organised or systematised body of ideas, whose extension and intension are likely to fall coherently within the field of interest and comfortably within the intellectual competence of and the field of inevitable specialisation of a normal person.

Implication

To satisfy law 1, the arrangement of documents and the main entries should primarily be based on the characteristics of the subjects embodied in the documents. The study of these characteristics is, therefore, essential for the efficient classification, search, and retrieval of subjects and service to readers.

Further, the criterion for "use" assumes significance. Therefore, it may be helpful to examine the differences, if any in the respective purposes of the reader. Certain affinities and dissimilarities among the subjects will then be recognised.

Law 2 and Its Implication

The second law "Every reader his book" implies that the classification and arrangement of documents and/or the main entries for them should bring together at every point of approach just those documents relevant to the interest of the reader at the moment, and also arrange them on either side in the decreasing degree of affinity. In other words, an APUPA (Alien, Penumbral, Umbral, Penumbral, Alien) pattern everywhere of documents and/ or main entries is desirable.

Law 3 and Its Implication

The third law "Every book its reader" implies that at the time of retrieval no document relevant to the interest of the reader at the moment should be missed, irrespective of his approach. Again, a study of the structure and development of the UoS indicates that no single tool of library science can fully satisfy this law. Several of its tools and methods have to be used concurrently or in succession according to need to meet the interest of the majority as well as the minority.

Law 4 and Its Implication

The fourth law "Save the time of the reader and of the staff" implies that:

* The intellectual and mental potential of the reader should be conserved by pinpointed and expeditious retrieval; and
* The retrieval and service should be done in the most economic manner.

To Satisfy Law 4 One Requires

An analysis of the UoS to recognise each of its constituents and their relevant characteristics; and formulation of a methodology for the design and development of a document retrieval system which can implement, the findings. The work done and to be done in this context pertains to the constituents/ characteristics of the Uos.

Lawn 5 and Its Implication

The fifth law "Library is a growing organism" implies that the UoS is ever growing and, therefore, library science is ever growing. Hence, a historical study of the pattern of development and the structure at different stages of growth will help to recognise the modes of formation of subjects and thereby it would be possible to develop and refine techniques tools for efficient information retrieval and dissemination. From the foregoing account, it becomes clear that the study of the structure and development of the UoS by the librarian is a necessary implication of the five laws of library science.

Modes of Formation of Subjects

In order to give unique co-extensive representation to each subject in the UoS, the classificationist has to ascertain the various attributes - infinite, turbulently dynamic, continuum, manifold multidimensional quality, different modes of formation of subjects, etc., in the UoS that affect library classification. While many of the attributes are self-explanatory, the attribute "modes of formation of subjects" is complex.

The modes of formation of subjects that have been recognised are.

* Lamination
* Loose Assemblage
* Fission
* Fusion
* Distillation
* Clustering
* Agglomeration.

Lamination

Lamination is construction by an over layering facet, just as one makes a sandwich by layering a vegetable over a layer of bread. According. to Ranganathan "when the basic layer is a basic subject and the other layers are isolate ideas, a compound subject is formed". Lamination is of two types:

Lamination 1

In this mode, one or more isolate facets are laminated over a basic facet. This results in compound subjects.

Example:	1) Anatomy of the human body				
	Basic facet		Medicine		
	Isolate facets	=	Human body (P)		Anatomy (MP)
	2) Treatment of diseases of plant				
	Basic facets	=	Botany		
	Isolate facets	=	Plants, *(P)*	Diseases, *(MP)*	Treatment *(E)*

Lamination 2

In this mode two or more sub-facets of a compound facet are

laminated over one another. Such subjects were called earlier as non-main basic subjects, the components of which were host main subject. The latter had the canonical/special/ environment/system component.

For example, the ayurvedic system of medicine is a non-main basic subjects. In this example medicine is the host-main subject and the ayurvedic system is the system component.

The following table gives the revised terminology:

Original Terminology	Revised Terminology
Non-Main Basic Subjects or Basic Subjects (BS)	Non-Primary Basic Subjects (BS)
Canonical BS	Secondary BS
Compound BS	Compound BS

Other Examples:

* Medicine = Host-main subject
* Child = Special component
* Mathematics = Host-main subject
* Geometry = Canonical component

The sequence among the non-main components is System Environment - Special

Loose Assemblage

Loose assemblage is assembling together of two or more of:

* Subjects (basic or compound)
* Isolate ideas (in one and the same facet, or isolate ideas in one and the same array)

Assembling is done to express one or the other of possible relations, between the components of the assembly. The result is a complex subject, or a complex isolate idea, or a complex array isolate idea, as the case may be. Loose assemblage may be of three kinds. They are: Loose Assemblage of Kind-1, Kind-2 and Kind-3.

Loose Assemblage of Kind-1

Two or more subjects - simple or compound - are studied in their mutual relationship. It is called "inter subject phase relation" and can be one of the following five types:

* General;

* Bias;
* Comparison;
* Difference and
* Influencing.

Loose assemblage results in complex subjects.

Here are examples of complex subjects:

* General relation between political science and economics
* Statistics for librarians
* Influence of geography on history

Loose Assemblage of Kind-2

Two or more isolates taken from one and the same schedule are brought into a mutual relationship. This is called an "intro facet phase relation" and results in a complex isolate.

Examples:

* Influence of Buddhism on Christianity
* Difference between Lemuroidea and Anthropoidea

Loose Assemblage of Kind-3

Two or more isolates taken from one and the same array of an order higher than I in one and the same schedule are brought into mutual relation. This is called an "intra array phase relation" and results in a complex array isolate.

Canonical Basic Subject

This denotes a traditional division of a main subject. The traditional division is denoted by the term "canonical constituent".

Examples:

* C3 : Sound
* C4 : Heat
* C5 : Radiation

Special Basic Subject

This denotes a division of a main subject (MS), in which the subject of the study is restricted in some special manner, not amounting to any of the anteriorising common isolates or any other isolate ideas. This special division is denoted by the term "special constituent" of the MS. Generally, the class number for a special BS is got by the enumeration device.

Examples:

*	L-9C	:	Child medicine
*	L-917	:	Geriatrics
*	L-9H	:	Female medicine

Environmental Basic Subject

This denotes a division of a MS, in which the entity of the study of the MS is within an extra normal environment, such as those enumerated in the schedule of environment divisions.

Examples:

*	D-9Uk2	:	Desert engineering
*	D-9Um7	:	Mountain engineering
*	D-9V4	:	War engineering

System Basic Subject

This denotes a division of a MS or a non-main BS expounded according to a specific system, or School of Thought, other than what is currently popular.

Examples:

*	B2-N	:	Boolean algebra
*	L-B	:	Ayurvedic system of medicine
*	S-N	:	Gestalt psychology

When all non-main constituents occur in a compound basic subject, the sequence among them should be system constituent, environment constituent, special constituent, and canonical constituent.

Example:

* Medicine ayurvedic system—tropical environment — child

Fission

The initial set of primary basic subjects (PBS) included in a scheme for library classification results from a division/fission of the UoS in a manner similar to the division of the UoS by scholars among themselves as convenient fields of specialisation. It may not be possible to discern a specific characteristic used in this initial division.

Fission is the process of division or splitting or breaking up into parts. This process has, until recently, been denoted by the term "dissection". However, dissection usually implies the splitting, breaking up, etc., of an entity into parts by an outside agency. On the other hand, fission is an internal process of division without the involvement of an outside agency.

Example:

In CC, the initial schedule of traditional Primary Basic Subject (PBS) was derived by a direct' fission of the UoS and the following broad groups may be noted:

* Primary BS covering natural sciences
* Primary BS covering useful arts
* Primary BS covering humanities
* Primary BS covering social sciences

The term "dissection" is used to denote fission when we consider an array of divisions of an isolate or of a basic subject, resulting from fission.

On the other hand, the term 'denudation' is used to denote fission when we consider one and only one of the subdivisions of an isolate or of a BS, resulting from fission. Prolegomena defines as "Denudation is the progressive decrease of the extension and the increase of the intension (or the depth) of a BS or an isolate idea, even as we scoop out the flesh of a soft-fruit from deeper and deeper layers or as we excavate the well". In the words of J.H. Shera, denudation is "the exposure of a new area of knowledge by erosion or divestment through research or enquiry"..

Example:

Philosophy

Logic

Deductive Logic

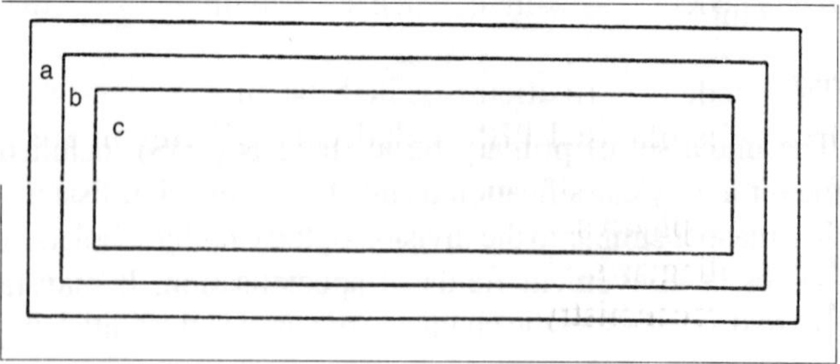

Fusion

One result of interdisciplinary research, which is characteristic of present day organisation and conduct of research programmes, is the emergence of new ideas and new subjects of an interdisciplinary character. Often, an interdisciplinary subject may be deemed to go with more than one of the existing primary basic subjects (PBS). The subjects going with this PBS will usually contain the core entity whose attributes are examined by the research team. Let us call.this host PBS 1. The subjects going with another PBS - that is, host PBS 2 may be related to the subjects going with the host PBS1 in a variety of ways, *e.g.*, phase relation (*i.e.*, application of statistics to biology).

In due course, as the field develops, there may be a number of new ideas arising out of the interdisciplinary research, such that:

* The classificationist may find that they cannot be conveniently and helpfully deemed to go with the host PBSI selected earlier;
* These new ideas attract for themselves a group of specialists; and
* A new field of specialisation concretises with normative principles/ theory of its own, in addition to using the normative principles/ theory of the subjects going with the host PBS 1 and 2.

At this stage, the classificationist may find it helpful to deem the new field of specialisation to go' with a new PBS - which is not already enumerated in the schedule of PBS in the scheme of classification concerned. Subjects going with this new PBS may contain isolate ideas drawn from the schedules of the host PBS 1 and 2 as well as ideas special to the new discipline. The new PBS may be considered, for convenience, as a combination of the host PB S 1 and 2.

This mode of formation is called fusion.

Examples of fused PBS included in CC edition are given below:

* Astrophysics
* Biolinguists
* Astrochemistry

* Sociolinguists
* Bio-physics
* Educametry
* Medical Jurisprudence
* Socio-cybernetics, etc.

In other words, in this mode, two or more PBS are fused together in such a way that each of them loses its individuality with respect to the schedule of isolates needed to form the compound subjects going with it. This mode may be taken to be equivalent to what Boulding describes as "hybrid discipline".

Distillation

In this mode, a pure discipline is evolved as a PBS from its appearance-in-action in diverse compound subjects going with either different BS or one and the same BS. It gives rise to PBS by distillation. This mode may be taken to be equivalent to what Boulding describes as "Multi-hybrid with common methodology". Thus, distillation may be of 2 kinds (Kind 1 and Kind 2. In Kind 1, the new PBS essentially accommodates the theory of discipline emerging 'or distilled out of an idea(s) occurring as a practice - in-action in subjects going with diverse BS. However, it should be remembered that, even after the formulation of a new pure discipline, the appearance of the idea as a practice-in-action will continue and should be treated as such - that is, it should be placed as an isolate idea in the subject concerned.

On the other hand, in distillation of Kind-2, the idea occurs in subjects going with a particular BS only and there may be a trend towards the formulation of a new discipline with recognisable literary warrant, and, perhaps, some principles and postulates for guiding its development.

Examples: Statistical calculus, Microbiology, Anesthesiology, International relations, Ergonomics, Forestry.

Clustering

In the past, in the Universe of Documents, the general trend has been to narrow the extension of a subject embodied in a document taken as a whole. Therefore, there has been a general tendency not to bring into one and the same document, compound subjects going with the different basic subjects, except in the case of complex subjects involving phase relation and the subjects involving the use of subject device in forming or sharpening isolate facets. In recent years, however, interdisciplinary team research has often, for practical convenience, necessitated bringing together in one and the same document two or more compound subjects going with different BS.

For example, for the convenience of organising research, the preliminary results and data obtained in work falling in different subject fields involved in the study of one phenomenon or entity may be brought together in one and the same document and treated disjunctively that is, without any substantial integral treatment. Subsequent elaboration of the work falling in different subject fields may be by specialists in the respective subjects and the results may be published separately. The document in which the preliminary results are brought together just as in a collection, taken as a whole, presents a subject field in which there is a core entity of study with inputs or viewpoints or work on it coming from specialists in subjects going with diverse BS. This feature is something like clustering around a nodal idea - that is, forming a group of similar entities, because of their relationship with each other, or their simultaneity of occurrence or for convenience in treatment or discussion.

Examples:

* Area study, in which geographical area forms the focus of the cluster, like Sinology (Chinese studies), Nippinology (Japanese studies).
* Generalia person study, in which a multi-faceted personality forms the focus of a cluster Gandhiana.
* Study of entity or phenomena forming the focus of a cluster Soil science, Surface science.

Agglomeration

Agglomeration (earlier called partial comprehension) is the process of collecting together of entities into larger masses without cohesion among the components. An agglomerate can be a BS, or it can also be an isolate idea. Agglomeration may be made up of consecutive constituents or even non-consecutive constituents with respect to a classification scheme.

Examples in CC:

* Natural sciences,

* Humanities,
* Social sciences

METHODOLOGY FOR THE STUDY OF SUBJECTS

Until recently, information consolidation products (ICP) were prepared by subject specialists themselves on the basis of the documents furnished by libraries and information centers. But with advances made in the held of library and information science, especially in the techniques of organising and displaying information, the library and information science (LIS) personnel have started playing a dominant role in the preparation of ICPs.

But, for them to play an useful role, the following prerequisites become necessary:

* Familiarity with the different aspects of the subject;
* Familiarity with reader's requirements on the subject of his pursuit; and
* Knowledge of the helpful methods of presentation of ideas in an ICP.

Understanding the Highways and Byways of Subjects

The majority of the queries/questions that LIS personnel will have to deal with are about subjects. An answer to such a query, in whatever form it may finally be presented to suit the requirements of the reader, will be derived from the subjects embodied in documents. Therefore, the LIS personnel should become familiar with the subjects they have to deal with predominantly. The more intensive the knowledge they have of the subjects, the more helpful it will be in making the information services productive.

Obviously, such a knowledge of all the subjects cannot be acquired by one person. A person with a basic background in a subject - say, at the graduate or post-graduate level - can build upon it through experience, - such as doing research and/or teaching the subject, But the LIS personnel's work does not admit of doing research simultaneously (other than in library and information science). Further, it is not the intensive specialisation in a narrow region of a subject that will be useful in the work of the LIS personnel. What they require is a broad perspective that is, the highways and byways of the different subjects with which their clientele are concerned.

Specific Implication

In general, the kind of knowledge that the LIS personnel should gain about the subjects may be specified as follows:

* Scope of the subject as a whole;
* Its main branches and subdivisions within each branch and the scope of each of them;
* The ideas generally falling in relation to the subject and their grouping in relation to the branches and subdivisions within each branch of the subject;
* The interrelation between the component ideas and the relevant characteristics on the basis of which they can be grouped;
* The landmarks in the evolution of the subject: the important contributors and their respective contributions;
* The state-of-the art and trend in each of the different branches of the subject;
* The interrelation of a subject with other subjects; and
* The technical terminology of each of the different subjects.

Systematic Study of Subjects through Documents

Reading about Major Subject Fields

LIS personnel should recognize the major subject fields related to the work of the institution concerned. Further, it would be helpful to group the subjects as of umbral and penumbral interest. This implies that the person should develop the ability to read through the documents in such a way that the ideas relevant to his purpose are picked up without his plodding through each and every sentence in the document.

Kinds of Documents for Study

The following varieties of documents may be helpful in the systematic study of a subject to acquire the kind of knowledge mentioned under the heading Specific Implication.

* Standard general dictionaries and technical glossaries for definitions and synonyms of terms,
* Articles in general encyclopaedia for getting an overview of the scope and major divisions of the subject.
* Specialised encyclopaedias, if any, mainly" devoted to the subject for getting a deeper knowledge of the subject than that from the general encyclopaedias.
* An orientation book, specially written with a flair and/ or with a bias to the requirements of the LIS personnel.
* Books on the history of the subjects for sensing the landmarks in the evolution of the subject.
* Treatises for getting a deeper knowledge of the ideas falling in the different divisions 'of the subject, their interrelations, and also to get a proper perspective of the subject as a whole.
* Good review articles and trend reports for sensing the current developments and trends in the subject.

Proforma for Collection and Organisation of Information

In the course of reading about a subject, it is helpful to make a record of the information selected in a systematic way.

A systematic proforma may be used for this purpose.

* *Introduction*: Statement of the purpose and the plan of the project on "Study of Subjects", indicating also the need and method of keeping the results of study up-to-date.
* *Definition*: The definition of a term denotes the subject concerned given in different authoritative sources. A comparative study of the collected definitions showing their similarity and differences is called for.
* *Terminological Development*: Terminological development of the term used to denote the subject, if any; the current synonyms, and different views on them. This generally applies to a subject which has been denoted by different terms at different points of time. For example, this applies to the term "library science". It started as "library economy"; passed through' librarianship' and, now it is denoted by the term' library science'.
* *Scope*: General scope of the subject as a whole. The

general scope of the subject is to be taken note of under the following subheadings:

* *Divisions and Subdivisions*: This includes all topics studied under the subject concerned - that is, primarily its divisions and subdivisions. For the purpose of this part, the terms (including synonyms) denoting the different broad divisions and their respective immediate subdivisions along with the definition and scope of each are to be given. It would be convenient to take note of the divisions and subdivisions from a selection of representative textbooks and advanced treatises on the subject concerned by analysing their contents. This would amount to taking note of the classificatory treatment of the subject concerned by specialists for the purpose of study, teaching, learning, etc. Definitions are to be collected from different authoritative sources.
* *Application*: Topics to which the subject concerned may be applied for their development. For example, when physics is the subject of study, engineering sciences, chemical sciences and biological sciences are the areas of its application.
* *Tool-Subjects*: These are subjects applicable to the subject concerned for its development. For example, when chemistry is the subject of study,mathematics, statistics, physics, etc., are applicable to it as tool-subjects, for its development.,
* *Classification*: This part, is intended to take note of how the subject concerned, and its divisions and subdivisions, are treated by the different schemes for classification - general and special. The first point of interest would be to find out the rank of the subject concerned in the whole Universe of Subjects, as recognized by different classificationists. *For example, the rank of the subject "chemistry" in the Universe of Subjects is commonly recognized as follows*:

– Universe of Subjects
– Sciences
– Natural Sciences

– Physical Sciences
  – Chemistry

The use of the indention in the example is to show the superordinate-subordinate relationships.

Treatment of the subject concerned in different schemes for classification is to be noted under the following subheadings:

* *Special Classification*: This subsection is intended to take note if there is any special subject classification designed by specialists for the purpose of a deeper understanding of the entities falling within the purview of the subject as a whole, or of any division or subdivision of it; for example, the taxonomical classification in geology, botany, and zoology, and the periodic table in chemistry. For the purpose of this subsection, generally a summary table of comparatively broader classes, with introductory remarks and a short description of the scheme, is to be given.
* *Document Classification*: This subsection is to take note of the treatment of the subject in classification systems, including thesauri and lists of subject headings. Such a scheme may be general in scope; for example, the Dewey Decimal Classification, Colon Classification, Thesaurus of Engineering and Scientific Terms, Thesaurofacet, etc. Such a scheme may be special in scope; for example, the Classification Schedule and Alphabetical Index for Packaging Documentation, the London Education Classification, the INIS: Thesaurus, the Thesaurus of Federal Aviation Agency Descriptors (USA), the Medical Subject Headings (MeSH), Subject Headings for Engineering (SHE), etc. Besides, if there is an indexing or abstracting periodical on the subject concerned, it would normally be expected to follow a special document classification scheme. Taking note of the treatment would consist of extracting a summary table from each of such schemes. When the scheme consists of a systematic part and an alphabetical part,it would be necessary to look for the subject concerned

in both the parts to extract relevant portions from them.

* *Development of the Subject*: The development of the subject concerned is to be noted down under the following subheadings:
* *Landmarks*: The landmarks in the development of the subject - that is, the contributions - are to be noted down, as far as applicable, under its broad divisions and subdivisions. Under each divisions or subdivisions as the case may be, the part will consist of entries arranged chronologically. *Each entry, as far as ascertainable, will consist of the following items of information*:
  - The year or period of contribution as far as determinable;
  - The name of the contributor;
  - A short biographical note of the contributor;
  - Each of his significant contributions;
  - The title and the year of publication of the original document, giving wherever applicable, its host and locus
* *Trend of Research*: The trend of research in the subject concerned., This can be collected from review documents, indexing and abstracting periodicals, etc. The idea is to mark out the broad areas in the subject concerned in which research is in progress. Additionally, attempts are to be made to ascertain in general the growth of literature (documents) on the subject concerned; and the degree of documentary seepage, and the scatter of information on research results in the subject concerned.
* *Trend of Education*: The trend of education in the subject concerned. This part is intended to take note of the development of education in the subject concerned and of its different levels - such as, undergraduate, graduate, postgraduate, research, etc.
* *Sources of Information*: This includes the information on the subject concerned. Three varieties of sources of

information are readily recognisable. They are:

- Documentary sources;
- Institutional sources; and
- Human sources.

This part is intended to take note of the various sources of information on the subject concerned. As such, information about the various sources is to be collected under the subheadings. For this purpose, different standard proforma are to be used. The specification of these proforma will be provided separately. Each entry pertaining to the sources of information is to be classified according to a standard scheme for classification. The entries under each subsection are to be arranged systematically according to the scheme used. The sources may not always be directly turned on the specific subject concerned. For the purpose of the subsections of this part, it would be required to take note of the sources on the:

- Specific subject;
- The subjects of extension greater than that of the specific subject; and
- The subjects of extension smaller than that of the specific subject.

For example, when the specific subject of study is "chemistry", the subjects "science", "physical sciences", "chemical sciences", etc., are subjects of greater extension; while the subjects "inorganic chemistry", organic chemistry", "physical chemistry", etc., are subjects of smaller extension.

* *Documentary Sources*: This subsection is intended to take note of the various documentary sources of information on the subject concerned. *Such sources fall in two distinct categories*:

- Primary, and
- Secondary.

The sources in each of these two categories are many. To start with, it would be necessary to take note of a selection of the outstanding documentary sources - both primary and secondary. In the primary category will fall:

- Outstanding textbooks;
- Advanced treatises; and
- Primary periodical 'publications.

In' the secondary category will fall:

- Conventional refe-rence books - that is, encyclopaedias, handbooks, directories, dictionaries, glossaries, etc.;
- Adhoc bibliographies;'
- Indexing and abstracting periodi-cals; and
- Review documents (annual reviews, advances in, year's work, etc).

As a part of this subsection, it would be helpful to add a list, of the organisations (with addresses) specialising in› the publication of documents in the subject concerned.

* *Institutional Sources*: This subsection is intended to take note of the various institutional sources of information on the subject concerned. For the purpose of 'this part, the conferences and projects turned on the subject concerned are to be taken note of. The idea is to identify the institutions, including conferences and projects, specialising in the subject by way of research, education, or organisation. As such, they are in a position to provide information on many aspects of the subject which is not readily available from other sources. Selection should include, as far as practicable, the institutions in the following three categories:

- International;
- National; and
- local.

* *Human Resources*: This subsection is intended to take note of the human sources of information on the subject concerned. The idea is to identify the living persons recognized as specialists in the subject concerned because of their educational achievements and experience. Such a specialist, when consulted, may be

in a position to provide specific information on the subject concerned which is not readily available from any other source. The selection should include, as far as practicable, living persons of repute at the international, national and local levels.

* *Information Transfer Processes*: This part is intended to take note of:
  - The information transfer process among the users of information on the subject;
  - The information seeking Behaviour of persons specialising in the subject; and
  - Typical informa-tion queries on the subject. Information about these aspects of the subject is to be collected primarily from documents dealing with these aspects as a whole, or some portion of it, or some broader subject comprehending-the subject concerned.

  When no such specific treatment is available, general information on information transfer processes and information seeking behaviours is to be taken note of. Typical information queries on the subject may have to be formulated on the analogy of such queries in other subjects; for, in the majority of cases, they may not be readily available.
* *Conclusion*: The conclusion may focus attention on any one of the following aspects relating to the subjects concerned;
  - The impact of research on the growth of the primary documents;
  - Adequacy or otherwise of the secondary documentary sources of information;
  - Problems of physical access to the sources of information;
  - Problems of organising information; and
  - Remarks and suggestions relating to any aspect of the subject falling within the purview of the study.
* *References*: This part is intended to list the documents actually used to compile the handbook. For the purpose of this part, a short entry is to be prepared for each

document. The entry is to be prepared according to the prescription of a standard code for cataloguing practice. In the majority of cases, an entry for a macro document is to be prepared in the following style:

* ATKINS (Kenneth R). Physics – once over – lightly 1972. If a particular portion of a macrodocument is referred to, its exact location is to be incorporated as the last item in the following style; Part 2; or Chap 3; or Sec. 52; or Page 20-28; etc., depending upon what the document admits as appropriate. Normally an entry for a microdocument is to be prepared in the following style:
* ROBERTSON (Andrew). Behaviour pattern of scientists and engineers in information seeking for problem-solving.
* *Entries prepared in the styles are to be arranged alphabetically and serially numbered*: The serial number of the document is to be used in the appropriate part of the text to indicate the sources from which the information has been collected. On the other side, the part number is to be used as a part of the appropriate entry. As a result, an entry in the Reference Part will appear in the style analogous to the following:
* 5 Sec 32 ATKINS (Kenneth R). Physics - once over - lightly. 1972. Chap 9.

Contents and Index

Evidently, for the purpose of the project on the "Study of Subjects", necessary information is to be collected from the existing documentary sources of information - both primary and secondary. The techniques to be employed for this purpose in the majority of cases will be the technique of "abstracting" - that is, briefly, summarising the essential contents. When the collected information is systematised according to the prescriptions of the proforma, it will result in a handbook of information on some facets of the subject concerned, considered to be essential for professional information work and service.

In order to turn this handbook into an effective externalised memory, it has to be equipped with:

* A detailed list of contents; and
* A good alphabetical subject index

The preparation of the list of contents will be largely governed by the headings in the proforma. For the purpose of indexing, a suitable procedure of indexing is to be adopted. The.Indian Standard on this maybe used with advantage.

Use of Scheme for Classification

Among the tools and techniques used in a library, classification is concerned with the analysis' and structuring of subjects. embodied in documents. Here, classification essentially denotes the process of recognising the component ideas of a subject, determining the degree of interrelationship among these ideas and arranging the ideas in a sequence preferred by the majority of the specialists in that subject.

Such an analysis and arrangement of components should preferably be guided by explicitly stated postulates and principles, such that a consistent pattern of structuring of subjects is secured. Thus, a study and use of a scheme for classification, based on a set of helpful postulates and principles, and examining the way in which it throws the components of each subject into a sequence preferred by specialists and also arranges the different subjects in a helpful pattern, would naturally aid the LIS personnel in understanding a subject in such a way that he can make use of the knowledge so gained in designing an information consolidation service to meet the specific needs of users. Of course, incidentally, he also becomes increasingly more familiar with the terminology of the subjects concerned.

Design and Development of a Scheme for Classification

In recent times, the dynamic development and rapid. pace of growth in the Universe of Subjects have made it necessary for the, classifier to play the role of classificationist-in-little, from time to time for no scheme can anticipate and make provision for accommodating all the future developments in the Universe of Subjects. Therefore, even as.a classifier, he will find it necessary to extend and develop the capacity of the preferred scheme for classification for co-extensively structuring the newly emerging subjects and providing them with class or code numbers. Hence, classifying present day documents requires not merely a knowledge to use a ready made scheme for classification but also a knowledge of the foundation and the methodology of the design and development of schemes for classification.

Steps in Designing

The major steps include a study of the appropriate documents on the subjects in a. graded sequence so as to recognise the component ideas, their interrelations, the modes of combination of the components and the sequence of the components preferred by the majority of specialists in the subject. Irrespective of the model on which the designing of the classification is based.

Inference

It is obvious that the design and development of a classification scheme provides an excellent opportunity to the LIS personnel to learn about subjects, keeping up with the development in each of them, and to some extent, envisage the likely development in the near future.

Other Methods

The following are the other varieties of opportunities and methods by which LIS personnel may learn about the highways and byways of subjects.

* Attending and participating in lectures and discussions by subject specialists oriented to the needs of LIS personnel;
* Consultation with subject specialists while designing a scheme for classification;
* Attending other lectures by and discussions among subject specialists; and
* Attending new-entrant-training schemes, which are in the form of a series of lectures by senior personnel in the organisation - and sometimes from outside the organisation - spread over a period of three to six months.

LITERARY WARRANT

The Library of Congress collections serve as the literary

warrant (*i.e.*, the literature on which the controlled vocabulary is based) for the Library of Congress subject headings system. The number and specificity of subject headings included in the Subject Authority File (the machine-readable database containing the master file of Library of Congress subject headings from which the printed list, the microform list, the CDMARC SUBJECTS, etc. are generated), are determined by the nature and scope of the Library of Congress collections. Subject headings are established as they are needed to catalog the materials being added to the collection or to establish links among existing headings. In recent years, headings contributed by libraries engaged in cooperative activities with the Library of Congress based on the needs of their collections have also been included.

3

General Principles and Theory

GENERAL THEORY

In this chapter, an attempt has been made to present in brief the general theory of library classification. A theory refers to an organised set of principles, which provide the basis for further investigation into, and the development of a subject. It explains existing phenomena. A theory goes through the process of development from time to time and is constantly changing and improving. This is equally true with the development of the theory of library classification.

There are two distinct stages in the development of the general theory of library classification. In stage-1, we notice the emergence of the descriptive theory distilled out of the past practices in designing schemes of library classification and their use. In stage-2, on the other hand, we find.the development of a dynamic theory for guidance in designing schemes with a greater degree of detail.

In stage-l, stalwarts like J.D. Brown, E.C. Richardson, Edward Hulme, W.C.B. Sayers, H.E. Bliss and S.R. Ranganathan through their writings, and some of them through their classification schemes, contributed to the development of the descriptive theory of classification. The descriptive theory formed the basis for the development of the dynamic theory in stage-2. In other words, these stalwarts laid the foundation for the general theory of library classification.

In stage-2, we notice the development of the dynamic theory. It was called dynamic because it was capable of carving out a methodology for library classification. Ranganathan was the chief architect of this dynamic theory. He formulated basic laws, postulates, canons and principles which gave a completely new direction to the development of the theory of library classification. This new theory helps in designing schemes of classification, which can withstand the challenges posed by the growth and development of knowledge and their evaluation. Ranganathan, thus, turned classification from an intuitional flair to a science based on objective methods.

THEORY OF LIBRARY CLASSIFICATION

Before we attempt to study the Theory of Library Classification, it is necessary for us to know the importance of developing a theory. It is equally necessary for us to recognise the need for such a theory.

IMPORTANCE OF A THEORY

At the outset, one must know what constitutes a theory and how it is important for development of a subject. A theory refers to an organised set of principles, which provides the basis for further investigations into and the development of a subject. It explains the what and why of the existing phenomena. It qualifies the subject to be accepted as a discipline. It provides a scientific basis far' a subject and brings respectability and status to it. Its importance for the growth and development of a subject hardly needs emphasis.

NEED OF A THEORY

If we look into the history of library' classification, we find that during the early stages of its development it handled a small number of subjects constituting the whole of knowledge, and a broad classification met the requirements of that time. The schemes were prepared largely in response to the exigency of the time. These schemes seem to have been guided by the purpose on hand rather than a theory that would stand the test of time. These schemes solved the immediate and short-term problems. However, with the passage of time the number of subjects into which knowledge could be divided steadily increased, proving the existing schemes inadequate. With the growing complexity of subjects enshrined in documents it became necessary to classify knowledge minutely. This complexity called for a theory of library classification which could meet the -challenges posed by the turbulent growth in knowledge.

DEVELOPMENT OF A THEORY

In any sphere of life, practice precedes theory. Life force stimulates man to improvise, design, and develop various aids - both at the physical and mental levels. After a long experience is gained with an improvised aid, a theory is developed in order to understand the, aid deeply and to systematise, improve, refine and develop it. So also it has been with classification. Within fifty years: after the design of Decimal Classification, Richardson add Sayers made comparative studies of the then known schemes for classification; and they also evolved a Theory of Classification. It was largely a "descriptive1rmulation" and "interpretative explanation". It was static and not dynamic. The emphasis at this stage, according to Parkhi in his book *Library Classification, Evolution of a Dynamic Theory*, was on the description of the practices followed by the classificationists in designing their schemes and were considered as norms for designing schemes.

On the other hand, after 1949, Ranganathan and his associates slowly evolved a *Dynamic Theory of Classification*. The first consolidated account of this *Dynamic Theory* was published in 1957 in the Prolegomena to Library Classifica-tion, by Ranganathan. This 'was further refined after the establishment of DRTC at Bangalore in 1962, which provided facilities for deepening the Theory of Classification and making it more dynamic and applicable both to book classification and article classification. Consequentially, active work in the design of depth classification schedules for the classification of articles progressed. The need for such a dynamic theory is obvious as it only.could provide guidelines-for the development of subject classification in the future.

DESCRIPTIVE THEORY LIBRARY CLASSIFICATION

In the beginning there was no theory; only practice was

followed. Practice gave rise to descriptive theory. Thus, the descriptive theory was the first stage in the development of library classification. This theory was able.to meet the requirements of the universe of subjects, as it existed at that time. The descriptive theory was based on the practices in vogue based on different schemes of classification then available. The descriptive theory, distilled out of the contemporary schemes, held its sway until the early 1950s. The schemes designed before the 1950s were based on 'the flair or natural gift of the designers and not on any objectively worked out theory of library classification.

Their methods were empirical. The development of the descriptive theory is attributed to several stalwarts like Brown, Richardson, Hulme, Sayers, Bliss and Ranganathan. The period between 1898 and 1937 witnessed the genesis and development of this theory. These stalwarts, through their schemes and writings, enunciated certain principles of library classification which greatly contributed to the development of a General Theory of Library Classification.

J.D. BROWN (1862-1914)

J.D. Brown was an English librarian, whose contribution to the General Theory_ of Library Classification was small but significant. He brought out three different schemes of classification. The first of these three was developed in 1894 jointly with J.H. Quinn and was known as Guinn-Brown Scheme. This scheme did not make much impact. Three years later, in 1897, Brown independently brought out another scheme and called it Adjustable Classification. This scheme also proved inadequate even in those days. In the year 1906, Brown published the first edition of his Subject Classification, the scheme for which he is mostly known. Its second edition was brought out in 1914 and the third; edited by J.D. Stewart; in 1939.

Brown's Subject Classification was founded on the principle that every science and art spring from. Some.definite source. In the order of things, there were first two factors, *viz.*, matter and force. These, in turn, gave place to life. Life, in course of time, led to the mind, which in turn gave birth to records.

In addition to the shove principle, Brown also advocated - two other principles. The first of these two was his one place theory. According to this principle, each subject has only one place in the scheme inrespective of its' aspects and numerous manifestations. For example, the subject of rose may be viewed from the viewpoints of botany, horticulture, history, geography, decoration, -bibliography, etc. The subject of rose, according to Brown, is concrete, while the various viewpoints represent its aspects. He was of the opinion that the interest of the scholar in 'rose' is constant, unlike that of the bibliographer whose interest is only occasional. He, therefore, preferred to place rose under one concrete or specific heading. It means that his arrangement of books was not ht, discipline (as in the Dewey Decimal Classification (DDC) or Library of Congress, (LC); but by topic. It was an experiment, which failed.

The other principle advocated by Brown was the science and its applications theory. According to this principle, he places each subject as nearer as possible to the science from which it has sprung. Thus, rose is placed under botany, libraries under library economy, coal under mineralogy, and persons under biography. Theory and practice are collocated. As a result of this principle, Brown dispensed with "conven-tions, distinctions and groupings, which are arbitrary rather than scientific". for example, the distinction between Pure and Applied Sciences, between Fine Arts and Useful Arts, between Currency and Numismatics, between Architecture and Building and between Costume and Press was not made.

He faithfully followed these principles in his Subject Classification.

E.C RICHARDSON (1860-9939)

E.C. Richardson was the first librarian of Hartford Theological Seminary, USA, and later took over as librarian of the Princeton University Library. Richardson is regarded as the first classificationists to have ma4e a systematic attempt to set down a theory of library classification. In 1910, he published his book Classification, Theoretical and Practical. It was the first textbook on classification, which later influenced W.C.B. Sayers. In the introduction to this work, he enumerated basic laws and principles meant to guide the work of designing a scheme of classification.

These principles, called as Criteria of Classification, are as follows:

* Classification should follow the order of things; classes should be arranged in historical sequence.
* Division of classes should be minute.
* Arrange things according to likeness and unlikeness.
* Books are collected for use; they are administered for use, and hence, it is the use, which is the motive behind classification.
* A scheme of classification should be provided with a notation. The notation should be amenable to indefinite subdivisions preferably using a mixed symbol with decimal base and with mnemonic features.

Richardson asserted that "things: nature aye already classified and roan has to trace only the order -of the classification and record if."

E.W HULME (9659-1954)

Hulme was the librarian of the Patent Office Library, London. In 1911-1912, he published his book Principles of Book Classification in the library Association Record. Has principles influenced the later theories of book-classification. In the words of W.C.B. Sayers, the contribution of Hulme was " A valuable leadup to the more complete and satisfactory theories today".

According to Hulme, all classifications could be arranged into two groups (categories), viz.,

* Mechanical and-
* Philosophical

According to this categorisation, book classification is mechanical Hulme's principles of book classification are as follows:

* Book classification is the plotting of areas pre-existing in literature, and coincidence with a philosophical order is no guarantee of accuracy.
* Book classification-is mechanical assembly of material into classes.
* The division and coordination-of classes in literature

is determined mainly upon formal and non-philosophical lines.

* Classification should be based literary warrant.

Hulme states that mechanical classifications are left uncoordinated. But in book classification, systematic coordination of classes is introduced. His theory of literary warrant immensely attracted the attention of later classificationists. E.A. Savage (1877-1966) revived the term. Hulme ragards books as "concrete aggregates of facts selected from the common stock of knowledge". What Hulme meant by concrete aggregates is that if there are books on the subject of electricity and magnetism there is literary warrant for providing a number for such a class named "electricity and magnetism". Literary warrant simply means that a subject cannot be listed in the scheme unless some literature has already appeared on it. Cr, the existing literature on a subject only justifies the inclusion of that subject in the scheme.

Hulme's principle of literary warrant greatly influenced the Library of Congress Classification (LC). Ranganathan also made use of this principle, but not exactly in the sense Hulme made, use of it. According to Ranganathan, when the literature on a particular subject grows in size, there may arise a need for providing a separate class for it in the scheme. Ranganathan's principle of literary warrant states that "the subjects in an array of subjects or the isolates in an array of isolates may be arranged in the sequence of decreasing quantity of the documents published or anticipated to be published on them, except when any other overwhelming consideration rules it out." Hence, it requires that the various aspects of such a new subject should be so listed as to bring those aspects first on which more literature have appeared.

W.C.B. SAYERS (1881-1960)

William Charles Berwick Sayers, an English librarian and teacher of S.R. Ranganathan made a remarkable contribution to the development of the theory of classification. He is referred to as the first grammarian of library classification. He is responsible for interpreting and systematising the ideas of other theoreticians. He never designed any classification scheme, though, through his theory he has shown the way for others in the designing of classification schemes. His theory of book classification first appeared in 1915 under the title "Canons of Classification". He expanded the outline of the theory contained in this book in three other books, *viz.*, Grammar of Classification, Introduction to Library Classification and Manual of Library Classification. It has now been revised by Rita Marcella and Robert Newton in 1994.

Sayers Canons of Classification

Sayers simplified his theory of classification by stating 29 principles. He called them canons, meaning rules, regulations, standard tests or criteria of classification. The 29-canons can be grouped under six categories as follows:

*	Canons of definition	... ...	6
*	Canons of divisions	... ...	7
*	Canons of terms	... ...	4
*	Canons of book classification	... ...	4
*	Canons of notation	... ...	4
*	Canons of book classification schemes	... ...	5

Definition

Classification is a mental process by which things or ideas are grouped according to their likeness. The likeness which exists in the universe of things and in ideas is called characteristic in classification. A characteristic is a basis of division or grouping of classes. In a scheme of classification, classes are to be arranged in a systematic order. The order is based on the theory of knowledge.

Division

Assembling things according to their degree of likeness and separating them according to their degree of unlikeness is the process of division. The chosen likeness or characteristic used to 'divide the given things may be natural or artificial. A natural characteristic is the inherent quality of a thing and hence, is responsible for its very existence. An artificial characteristic may be possessed by a group of things. For example, colour of clothes is an artificial characteristic. The division should proceed from greater extension and smaller intension to smaller extension and greater intension. The process of division should be gradual moving from general to specific. The characteristic used must be consistent at each stage of division.

Terms

A scheme of classification is a statement of knowledge using verbal terms. A term is the name for a class. It may be a word or a phrase. The terms should be unambiguous and unique with the same meaning whenever they are used in a scheme of classification. In a scheme of classification the terms used should always be non-critical.

Book Classification

A book classification is a device for the arrangement of books by subject or form in a logical order. It must be capable of admitting any new subject without dislocating the class of subjects already drawn.

Book classification schemes must be equipped with

* A generalia class;
* Form classes like poetry, fiction, drama, etc.;
* Forms in which subjects are presented like theory, history, dictionary, etc.; -
* A notation; and
* An index.

Notation

A notation consists of signs representing the class names in a scheme of classification. A notation should be brief, simple and flexible and have a mnemonic value.

Book Classification Schemes:

A scheme of classification should provide columnar schedules in the order of precedence of subjects. It is necessary to explain how to use the scheme. There should be a machinery for the revision of the scheme to keep it up-to-date accommodating new developments in the knowledge.

H.E. BLISS (1370-1955)

He Evelyn Bliss devoted his entire active life to the intensive study of the art and science of classification. In addition; which he contributed in library journals, his theories and principles of classification were expanded in his first work, titled Organisation of Knowledge and the System of Science (1929). In this work, he formulated scientific, philosophical and logical grounds for the study of bibliographic classification. This work is regarded as one of the basic texts on the theory of organisation of knowledge. He laid down the foundation for a relatively stable, scientifically acceptable and consistent scheme of classification. He also published another basic work on the theory of library classification titled Organisation of Knowledge in Libraries and the Subject Approach to Books. His work helped in establishing librarianship as a scholarly discipline. These two basic works convey to us the fundamental principles of classification which Bliss later tried to apply in his System of Bibliographic Classification (BC) whose outline was first published in 1935.

The basic concepts of classification as expounded by Bliss may broadly be categorised as:

* Consensus
* Subordination
* Collocation
* Alternative locations
* Notation.

Consensus

Bliss viewed book classification as basically knowledge classification. He felt that considerable agreement existed among the experts on the arrangement of various branches of human knowledge. He termed this as scientific and educational consensus. The growth, organisation and development of human knowledge are brought about through the process of science and education. The word consensus refers to a relative agreement on the major classes of knowledge, their scope, order of arrangement and the essential relation between them.

He believed that the natural order of main classes was close to this consensual order. Bliss felt that more closely a library classification reflected this consensus, the more stable, durable, flexible and efficient it would be. His order of main classes is based on this consensus.

Subordination

Bliss theorised that a classification scheme should observe two types of subordination, viz.,

* Subordination of the special to the general, and
* Gradation by speciality.

Subordination of the Special to the General

This is also referred to as the principle of decreasing extension. A scheme of classification should arrange subjects in the order of decreasing extension so that a general subject is followed by a special subject. The order of subjects in a scheme of classification should reflect the sequence from general to specific.

Gradation by Speciality

This concept is based on the philosophical notion of gradation by speciality. Gradation principle is employed for organising a series of topics of equal rank into a rational sequence. The principle is that some subject depend for their very existence on the works or findings of others, and those that so dependant should follow the disciplines upon which they rely. This is also known as the principle of dependency. For example, among the natural sciences, physics comes first because it deals with the fundamentals of natural phenomena. Chemical phenomena depend to some extent on the findings of the physicists and, therefore, chemistry follows physics. Bliss claims that "gradation by speciality is no mere arbitrary basis for classification but is a principle essential to the very process".

Thus, the order of classes will be:

* General treated generally.
* General treated specially.
* Special treated generally
* Special treated specially.

Collocation

It is a by product of the two principles. By collocation, Bliss means "bringing together in proximity subjects which are most closely related". Ranganathan termed this as filiatory sequence. The principles of subordination and gradation by speciality help to decide the sequence of broad subject fields or disciplines and, within each subject, the principle of decreasing extension and various orders in any array determine the sequence of the subject. It is also necessary for bringing together similar subjects, which are most closely related. Therefore, Bliss, in his Bibliographic Classification, collocated language with literature, because of their very close affinity with each other. Similarly, education is collocated with psychology, and chemical technology with chemistry. Collocation generally refers to coordinate classes. But, it may also refer to subordinate classes. Bliss subordinated sociology to anthropology and anthropology to biology.

Alternative Locations

A scheme of classification should meet the different needs and requirements of a special collection. Therefore, libraries may wish to- alter the order established by logical sequence. A scheme, if it is to be of maximum usefulness, should therefore provide for the adaptation of logical sequence to practical convenience in order to meet different views. Bliss did not believe in the rigid and unadaptable view of the order of knowledge. To meet this principle of practical convenience, provision has been made deliberately for alternative locations and treatments in his unique scheme, though it is somewhat contrary to the principle of consensus.

Provision has been made in notation for moving certain topics to other locations. For example, moving theology from the main class P religion to class AJ following philosophy; technologies like aeronautics or ship building from applied physics to useful arts and subordinating international law to political science or to law; and economic history to general history.

This principle provides flexibility needed to solve certain problems in classification faced by all classifiers of all systems. But it also proves that there is no absolute consensus on the order of subjects.

Notation

Bliss recognised three important qualities of a good notation. These are:

* It should be correlative and subsidiary.
* It should be simple and brief, *i.e.*, a notation should remain reasonably simple. He even suggested an economic limit of three to four digits in a class number.
* It should use synthetic features. This is to achieve economy in the printing and display of schedules resulting in the simplicity of structure and convenience in use.

Bliss achieved this by the provision of general and special systematic schedules for construction of coextensive class numbers.

S.R. RANGANATHAN (1892-1972)

Right from 1924, S.R. Ranganathan had been developing his theory of library classification. In the first edition of *Prolegomena to Library Classification (1937)*, he provided an integrated theory, mainly descriptive and comparative, of the practices in classification then in vogue.

Ranganathan went ahead of those classificationists, mentioned in the preceding sub-sections, by extending the principles put forward by them. He also provided the largest list of normative principles named by -him as Fundamental Laws, Postulates, Principles and Canons and evolved a special terminology, which is evident from the first edition of Prolegomena. These rightly belong to stage-2 in the development of the General Theory of Library Classification. His theory is now synonymous with the General Theory of Library Classification.

S.R. Ranganathan was instrumental in revolutionising the *Theory of Classification*. He propounded certain fundamental ideas and concepts, which are the basis for the development of the *Theory of Classification*. The consistently advocated that library classification should conform to the *Laws of Library Science*. He worked vigourously towards the most helpful sequence of classes in a scheme of classification based on the concept of Facet Analysis and Fundamental Categories. He totally rejected the earlier schemes, based purely on enumeration. His laws, canons and principles of library classification have been presented in his *Prolegomena to Library Classification*. This is regarded as one of the seminal works on the *Theory of Library Classification*.

Mapping of Universe of Knowledge

Ranganathan visualised the problem of transforming the multi-dimensional universe of knowledge into a uni-dimensional one. This was the fundamental and perennial problem faced by the classificationists in the design of schemes of classification. To meet this problem squarely, Ranganathan formulated the General Theory of Classification, which was guided by Basic Laws, Laws of Library Science, Canons, Principles and Postulates. With the help of these laws, canons and principles, the mapping of the universe of knowledge in a scheme of classification could be successfully represented.

CLASSIFICATION RESEARCH GROUP (LONDON)

After the Royal Society Scientific Information Conference in 1948 and on the suggestion of the eminent scientist J.D. Bernel, the Classification Research Group (CRG) London was established in 1952. It is an unattached society of volunteers pursuing classification as an additional off the job work. They meet regularly in London. Upto 1996, they have held 308 meetings. Its founder members D.J. Foskett, Bernard Palmer (1910-1979), B.C. Vickery and A.J. Wells (1911-1994) were greatly influenced by Ranganathan's work.

They mostly came from special, industrial and academic libraries. Their deep and thorough study led them to believe that none of the published schemes provided a satisfactory system either in arrangement or depth of details. CRG accepted Ranganathan's method of facet analysis though it did not accept his views on the restriction of the number of categories to be five. They named their categories as Entities, Properties and Activities. Nevertheless, in Ranganathan's Dynamic Theory, they found a sound base to be built up.

They published their manifesto in the periodical Library Association Record (1955) which emphasises on the-need for a faceted classification as the basis of all methods of information retrieval. B.C. Vickery wrote a small volume on the methods of constructing a faceted classification. Members of CRG designed many faceted classification schemes for specialised subjects ranging from diamond technology to soil science; music to education. Experience gained in designing such schemes led them to believe that the right approach should be to seek new principles for library classification.

Though they never produced any new general classification system, their contributions to the development of classification techniques' were many and innovating. A prominent member, Miss Barbara Kyle had a limited success in doing away with the necessity of main classes. Another member J.E.L. Farradane (1906-1989) incorporated the idea of relational analysis with operators into the construction of a faceted classification scheme. Later, a group member developed the Theory of Integrative Levels, which arranged entities in an evolving aggregation of complexities. Their work received publicity and wide discussion in their International Conference on Classification Research held at Dorking, England in 1957.

Another publication enshrining their work is Sayers Memorial Volume (1961) edited by D.J. Foskett and B.I. Palmer (London Library Association). At present, the CRG meetings are devoted to the discussion of the ensuing revised schedules of the Bibliographic Classification (BC2). Their major applied work remains in PRECIS formulated by Derek Austin, which had a classificatory approach. This Preserved Context Indexing System in 1971 replaced Ranganathan's Chain Procedure in the British National Bibliography - as required for the automated bibliography compilation work.

DYNAMIC THEORY OF LIBRARY CLASSIFICATION

The dynamic theory, according to R.S. Parkhi, is "a theory of library classification capable of carving out a methodology for the design of a scheme for library classification". It is regarded as stage-2 in the development of the General Theory of Library Classification. Such a theory enables us to organise emerging new subjects and the already known subjects in their proper places in a scheme of classification without disturbing the already established sequence. Its approach is futuristic.

The dynamic theory of library (classification, developed by Ranganathan between 1948 and 1955, was presented for-the first time in the second edition of has Prolegomena to Library Classification, published in 1957. A more advanced version of this theory appeared in 1967 in the shape of: the third edition of the Prolegomena. This dynamic theory has provided a sound and stable methodology for designing a scheme 9f library classification. This has also helped the classificationists to keep pace with the developments in the universe of knowledge to design more stable schemes of classification.

The formulation of a dynamic theory of library classification was marked by the recognition and separation of three planes of work: the Idea Phine, the Verbal Plane and the Notational Plane.

Before this was done, lack of capacity in the, Notational Plane inhibited free work in the Idea Plane. Nor was the Notational Plane cultivated. On the other hand, there was reluctance to cultivate it. There was even opposition to attention being paid to it.

The use of popular terms with all their homonyms and synonyms in the Verbal Plane caused confusion in the Idea Plane. Thus, the separation of work in the three planes laid bare the paramountancy of the work in the Idea Plane and the need to allow it to develop unhindered on its own: right.

By 1963, the dynamic theory was refined further and some of the new additions included the following:

* Identification of Property isolates as manifestations of Matter along with Matter-Material isolates with the result that some of the isolates forcedly included in the earlier years in the 'Problem Schedule', but later named forcedly as "Energy Schedules", were in reality Matter-Property isolates.,
* Prescription that life indicator digit, (,) 'comma' should be inserted before the first Personality isolate number/,
* Capacity of an array in the Notational Plane was increased by divesting Roman small letters of anteriorising quality and by restoring to digit (0)'zero', its natural ordinal value lying between the digits. 'z' and
* Postulation of digits T to Z as Emptying Digits which facilitates interpolation at any point P the Array.
* The theory in the Idea Plane formulated 18 principles

of helpful sequence and the powerful Wall-Picture Principle for helpful sequence of facets and of isolates.

These findings of the deeper and more dynamic 'theory of classification consciously developed have been incorporated in Colon Classification Version 3 making it a truly Freely Faceted Analytico-Synthetic Scheme for Classification. Thus, the basic laws, canons and principles enunciated by Ranganathan have greatly contributed to the evolution of the dynamic theory.

Basic Laws

Ranganathan formulated six basic laws, viz.,

* Law of Interpretation
* Law of Impartiality
* Law of Symmetry
* Law of Parsimony
* Law of Local Variation
* Law of Osmosis.

These basic laws govern the thinking process in general. These may be invoked when two or more Laws of Library Science or Canons for Classification lead to conflicting or equally valid different decisions.

Laws of Library Science

Ranganathan's Five Laws of Library Science are:

* Books are for use.
* Every reader his/her book.
* Every book its reader.
* Save the time of the reader.
* A library is a growing organism.

These were formulated in 1928 and were first published in the book The Five Laws of Library Science (1931). These laws have an impact on library functions and are invoked when two or more canons or principles of classification lead to conflicting or equally valid alternate decisions. These are useful in every branch of library and information science.

Postulates for Facets

The most significant contribution to the Theory of

Classification is the enunciation, of postulates dealing with the concept of facet analysis and fundamental categories.

Fundamental Categories

A subject may manifest itself in anyone or all of the fundamental categories. He postulated that "There are five and only five fundamental categories, namely Time, Space, Energy, Matter and Personality", PMEST; for short.

Facet Sequence

The five fundamental categories form the following sequence when they are arranged according to their decreasing concreteness PMEST.

Rounds of 'Energy'

Ranganathan also postulated that "the fundamental category Energy may manifest itself in one and die same subject more than once." These manifestations of energy are called rounds of manifestations. Similarly, the fundamental categories Personality and Matter may manifest themselves in Round 1,. Round 2 and so on.

Levels

He further postulated that the fundamental categories Personality and Matter may manifest themselves more than once in one and the same round within a subject. The first manifestation of a fundamental category within a round is said to be its level 1 facet in that round.

Space and Time manifest themselves in the last round. Principles of Facet Sequence: Ranganathan formulated four principles of Facet Sequence, namely,

* Wall-Picture Principle
* Whole-Organ Principle
* Cow-Calf Principle
* Actand Action-Actor-Tool Principle

These principles guide us in deciding the sequence of facets, which may appear in a compound subject.

Principles of Helpful Sequence

To achieve a helpful sequence of entities in an array,

Ranganathan formulated eight Principles of Helpful Sequence.

These are

* Principle of Later-in-Time
* Principle of Later-in-Evolution
* Principle of Spatial Contiguity
* Principles for Entities along a Vertical Line:
* Principle of Bottom Upwards
* Principle of Top Downwards
* Principles for Entities along a Horizontal Line:
* Principle of Left to Right
* Principle of Right to Left
* Principles of Entities along a Circular Line:
* Principle of Clockwise Direction
* Principle of Counter-Clockwise Direction
* Principles for Entities along long a Radial Line:
* Principle of Centre to Periphery
* Principle of Periphery to Centre
* Principle of Away-from-Position
* Principles for Quantitative Measure
* Principle of Increasing Quantity
* Principle of Decreasing Quantity
* Principle of Increasing Complexity
* Principle of Canonical Sequence
* Principle of Literary Warrant
* Principle of Alphabetical Sequence

Canons of Classification

Ranganathan provided a completely new direction to' the concept of classification originally formulated by Sayers.

Ranganathan formulated 43 canons and grouped them into three planes of work.

* Canons for Idea Plane (15).
* Canons for Verbal Plane (4).
* Canons for Notational Plane (24).

These are in total conformity with his Basic Laws and Laws of Library Science. These are normally invoked in the design of a scheme of library classification. Let us now discuss briefly these three groups of canons.

Canons for Idea Plane (15)

The four canons for characteristics deal with the process of division of knowledge. The characteristics selected for division should be easily differentiated, ascertainable, relevant and permanent. The three canons for succession of characteristics in the process of division of knowledge deal with the application of more than one characteristic and the sequence in which these characteristics are to be applied. The four canons for array (coordinate classes) state that the classes in an array should be collectively exhaustive and mutually exclusive, and the sequence among them should be helpful and gonsistent. The two canons for chain (subordinate classes) deal with the process of division of knowledge which should proceed from general to specific and it should be properly regulated. The two canons for filiatory sequence state that a scheme of library classification should clearly identify both coordinate and subordinate classes and they should be arranged among themselves according to their mutual affiliation.

The fifteen canons for Idea Plane are further grouped into

*	Canons for Characteristics	-	4
*	Canons for Succession of Characteristics	-	3
*	Canons for Array	-	4
*	Canons for Chain	-	2
*	Canons for Filiatory Sequence	-	2

Canons for Verbal Plane (4)

The four canons for Verbal Plane deal with the language and terminology aspects in a scheme of classification. The terminology used in the scheme should clearly indicate the context in which a particular term has been used and what aspects it comprehends. The terms used to denote concepts should be current and non-critical.

The four canons are:

* Canon of Context
* Canon of Enumeration
* Canon of Currency
* Canon of Reticence

Canons for Notational Plane (24)

These have been further grouped into:

* Basic Canons - 12
* Mnemonics - 5
* Growing Universe - 4
* Book Classification - 3

Notation means a system of ordinal symbols representing classes in a scheme of library classification. The basic canons, which are twelve in number, deal with the need for the removal of homonyms and synonyms in class numbers. The notation, according to these canons, should reflect hierarchy of classes. The base of the notation may be mixed or pure. However, the basic canons discuss the relative capacity of each of these two types. The notation may be faceted or non-faceted. The canons nevertheless deal with the relative advantages of both kinds. The class number should be co-extensive or non-co-extensive. The implications of these two varieties are also explained through these canons.

The five canons for mneanonics deal with the need for different types of mnemonic devices, namely

* Alphabetical,
* Scheduled,
* Systematic, and
* Seminal

The four canons for growing universe deal with the capacity of a notational system for admission of newly emerging classes into the fold of a scheme of classification.

Ranganathan called this capacity of a notational system by the terms hospitality in array and hospitality in chain. The 'notational system should be capable of admitting emerging new classes at the beginning, or at the end, or in the middle of an array or a chain. This is also known as extrapolation (at the beginning or end) and interpolation (in the middle) in an array.

The three canons for book classification dean with the provision of a system for construction of book numbers and collection numbers in a scheme of classification, and the sequence of these three elements - class number, book number and collection number – making up a Call Number.

Role of Postulates, Canons and Principles

The postulates lay down the process of work in the idea plane. The canons lay down the rhythm of classification. The principles deal with the details of the arrangement of the isolates in the schedules. The laws, postulates, canons and principles listed in the preceding paragraphs laid down a sound foundation for the Dynamic Theory of Library Classification. The application of the principles has amply been demonstrated in Colon Classification scheme. From the fourth edition, published in 1952, Colon Classification has been a freely faceted scheme of classification based on the laws, postulates, canons and principles. Prior to the fourth edition, Colon Classification was a rigidly faceted scheme.

The contribution of Ranganathan to the development of the General Theory of Classification is fundamental, unique and unparalleled. His concepts of facet analysis and fundamental categories have received wide acceptance. As a result, several special schemes of classification have been designed applying the concepts and principles formulated by Ranganathan in his Prolegomena to Library Classification (1967), and other books.

4

Types and Features of Classification Schemes

ENUMERATIVE: FACETED AND ANALYTICO-SYNTHETIC

Beginning

The world of information is today characterized by fluctuating borders that present challenges which impel continual, creative and proactive adaptations in strategies and solutions. Print-based and digital systems or structures that have been designed to organize or to provide access to information do not always provide optimal access to information and sometimes result in annoyance or impediment. Practitioners and researchers in the field of information science, whether in libraries or information centers, often find themselves engaged in the design, construction, and evaluation of promising tools and techniques, regardless of origin, as they search for strategies and solutions to organize and provide access to digital information. Any who venture into the digital flux of cyberspace are not free from these constraints on information seeking. The proposed research, concerned with one region of the information world, cyberspace, will investigate one promising tool to alleviate constraints on access to information.

Bowker and Star describe information organization and access as the bridge builder between the past and the future of *information science* (IS). The proposed research project postulates that information organization and access is best supported by mutable systems. Information organization and access devices in cyberspace serve, not as traditionally envisioned – as maps of all knowledge existent and potential in the universe but as reflections of the fluid associative and formal structured interrelationships among information packages that are best accessed through dynamic, responsive systems.

Clearly, a re-examination of the relationships and associations inherent in our systems of access and organization is important to provide a context for the proposed study. Although appreciation of the beauty of legacy systems of organization and access must be tempered by examination of their limitations and failures, such retrospection may result in the realization that there is no one best way, no one best access system, no single way to order knowledge. Preliminary phases of the proposed project included extensive original and archival research into the historical and theoretical underpinnings of classification theory in the late 19th and early 20th centuries. The goals of the past, to create a hierarchical ordering or mapping of all knowledge, today may seem audacious or inconceivable, but the need to order the universe of knowledge to facilitate retrieval has increased, rather than diminished, over the past century.

The proposed exploratory research is firmly grounded in the sociological and cultural milieu of the present even as it is anchored in the intellectual and theoretical foundations of information science. It seeks to unveil connections between the intellectual and theoretical foundations of information organization and access and the current practices of web design. People who are facile with theoretically-grounded systems of access and organization have the potential to create mutable, responsive systems instead of rigid unbending hierarchies. Such systems are versatile, as they can be well-suited to the needs of the task at hand while being applicable to the wider world of context and culture.

In 2001, a group of information architects and knowledge management specialists charged with designing websites and access to corporate knowledge bases seemingly re-discovered a legacy form of information organization and access: *faceted analytico-synthetic theory* (FAST). This group of has been instrumental in creating new and different ways for people to engage with the digital content of the Web. Some of these practitioners explicitly use the forms and language of FAST, while others seem to mimic the forms implicitly. Granted, simple use of forms and language characteristic of FAST is by no means incontrovertible evidence that the resultant organization and access systems have theoretical underpin-nings.

However, if web designers are not aware of underlying theory, then suggestions could be made to identify potential areas in which access and organizational structures may be improved or strengthened by the consistent application of existing theory. A review of the present situation may also reveal novel areas of practice with the potential to inform or to augment existing theory. This research proposes that a symbiotic relationship between theory and practice is possible. One potential contribution of the proposed study is the possibility to apply what is uncovered in the course of the study about web practices to enrich the current state of FAST theory, and in turn for FAST theory to enhance the design and construction of websites.

Research Questions

The proposed research seeks to answer the following questions:

* What types of access and organizational structures are used in websites?
* What is the evidence that there is use of faceted analytico-synthetic theory in website construction and design of website search tools?
* In what ways do the products of those Web designers who make explicit claims to utilize or be informed by faceted analytico-synthetic theory conform to or depart from the theory as described in LIS literature?

Research limitations

The proposed research will not deal directly with each of the many types of applications that may potentially be informed by FAST. It will not involve capture or analysis of metadata, even if a faceted scheme may be in use. It will not involve questions of thesaural development or the analysis of/or the creation of controlled vocabularies, even if faceted. Should content analysis of the sample of websites to be studied during phase one of the data collection or discussions during the interviewing of website designers during phase two of the research - reveal the use of such devices this will noted, and will be an appropriate area for future research. The proposed research will focus on capturing access and organizational structures are used in websites and whether or not there is evidence of the use of FAST in website construction and the design of website search tools.

Literature Review

Faceted Analytico-synthetic Theory (FAST): Early Development and Definitions

Faceted analytico-synthetic theory represents the dawn of a new era in information organization and access systems. Although earlier thinkers, including Paul Otlet and Henry Evelyn Bliss had explored the basic theoretical tenets, S. R. Ranganathan provided the essential descriptions of *facet analysis* (FA) and *faceted classification* (FC) in the 1937 and 1957 editions of the *Prolegomena to Library Science.* The 1967 edition provides a full exposition of the theory, postulates, and principles of (FAST) and the process of facet analytical approach (FAA). Both the process and principles of FAST and FAA captured the imaginations of a generation of practitioners and researchers in LIS.

Although the importance of the UDC and both editions of the Bliss Bibliographic Classification cannot be overstated, the fact that FAST retained its currency and continued to develop throughout the years is primarily due to the efforts of three groups who invested heavily in the intellectual/theoretical development of this new paradigm of information organization and access after WWII.

These three groups were:

* The Library Research Circle (LRC),
* The Classification Research Group (CRG) and
* The Classification Research Study Group (CRSG).

Members of the LRC, which formed in India in 1951, worked

closely with Ranganathan on the development and continuing revision of the Colon Classification and engaged in general discussion of the problems facing library science. This group met informally each Sunday on the veranda at Ranganthan's house. Questions and pragmatic problems encountered daily by the members were brought to each session for open discussion. The aim of the group was to "tidy up" definitions, axioms and postulates of classificatory technique and to promulgate classificatory principles.

Their approach was determinedly scientific and modeled after Russell and Whitehead's work in mathematics. The substance of these discussions was integrated into several books, such as *Depth classification* and the second edition of the *Prolegomena* Ranganathan's greatest contribution transcends the postulates and principles contained in these volumes and lies in his recognition of the provisional nature of systems of access and order. Ranganathan recognized the existence of a "two-fold infinity" in the universe of knowledge due to the multiplicity of individual worldviews and information seeking purposes, and the infinitely complex and dynamic nature of the universe of knowledge. This duality imposes the requisite features of flexibility and responsiveness as a measure of the success of any system. In 1962 the work of the LRC, which continues today and remains heavily influenced by Ranganthan's work, moved to a more formal setting, the *Documentation Research and Training Center* (DRTC) at the Indian Statistical Institute in Bangalore.

In England, instigated by J. C. Bernal, and formally organized in 1952 under the leadership of A. J. Wells and B. C. Vickery, the *Classification Research Group* (CRG) formed as a sister group to the LRC. This well-documented group is the best-known and most prolific of the three and still meets monthly in London. In 1955 the CRG issued a manifesto *The need for a faceted classification as the basis for all methods of information retrieval*, which rejected all "existing classification schemes as unsatisfactory, in one way or another, for the demands of modern documentation". The CRG, assisted by several other professional groups, also assembled an international group of practitioners and researchers in 1957 in Dorking, England. The proceedings of this conference, attended by Jesse Shera, Eugene Garfield, S.R. Ranganathan and N.T. Ball of the NSF, contain many papers which are still central to an understanding of FAST. Of perhaps greatest significance to the proposed study, members of the CRG created a number of special schemes for subject classifications at their places of employment, such as the Occupational Safety and Health Documents Classification Scheme, the English Electric Scheme, Coates' British Catalogue of Music and the Langridge's 1956 Classification of Enterprise Activities, thereby expanding the use and understanding of FAST while grounding it in fundamental and pragmatically practical concerns. Many of these schemes are still used today and may well serve as valuable manuals of practice.

The CRSG, formed in the United States and Canada in 1957, was modeled after the British CRG. Spearheaded by two women, Phyllis Richmond, then a librarian at Rochester University, and Pauline Atherton Cochrane, then assistant director of the Documentation Research Project at the American Institute of Physics. Throughout the mid-1960s the group held sessions in empty rooms at odd hours at the annual meetings of the professional societies - the American Library Association, the Special Libraries Association, and the American Documentation Institute.

The group "informally organized, with an open programme, with no visible means of support" was composed of members from academia, business and the government. The contributions of this group are difficult to measure, as few publications bear the CRSG imprimatur, but it is certain that CRSG programmes introduced FAST to many who were previously unaware of it and provided practical engagement with the theory for those who demonstrated interest. The 1965 volume, *Classification Research: Proceedings of the Second International Study Conference* edited by one of the co-founders of the CRSG remains a valuable companion to the proceedings of the Dorking Conference, organized by their British counterparts, the CRG.

This very brief overview provided a glimpse of the early practical and theoretical direction of FAST. Although descriptions of FAST began in the 1930's, it was not until the 1950s that it was codified by S. R. Ranganathan in the 1957 edition of the

Prolegomena to Library Science. The 1957 edition provided the theoretical test bed, for the postulates, and principles of FAST and the process of *facet analytical approach* (FAA). Three groups, one in India, one in England and the other in North America, found various ways to apply the theory to daily practice. The practical experiences of each of these three groups served to expose weaknesses, limitations and to further strengthen and augment FAST. Appreciation of the significance and impact of the growth and modern development of the theory requires some understanding of the language and concepts central to FAST.

The vocabulary of FAST can be confusing. Clarity of definition is important and consensus on terminology among various groups is desirable, if difficult to reach. The proposed research does not seek to impose new meanings upon traditional terms. The preferred meaning of each term, whenever possible, will be taken first from definitions provided by Ranganathan, and secondarily from the work of the CRG. The work of Ranganthan is considered the seminal work of FAST. The work of the CRG springs from that of Ranganan-than. While heavily influenced by it, it experiments with, strengthens and extends Ranganathan's work. Until his death in 1972, Ranganathan was supportive and encouraging of all efforts to extend FAST. Relying upon traditional or canonical definitions provides a return to terra firma, in stark contrast to the welter of often conflicting definitions available today.

Facet, the term most central to FA/FC is variously defined. Terms most often used as co-equivalents include: category, attribute, class, group, concept, and dimension. Ranganathan initially used the phrase "train of characteristics" while emphasizing that facets, "inhere in the subject themselves, whether we sense them or not." In describing a facet, he stated that "a classification of a particular universe is made on the basis of characteristics". In this sense, a characteristic is a parameter. Each parameter creates a dimension which usually falls into a small number of groups. Each group becomes a facet, and is itself multidimensional.

The central notion here is the ability to analyse an entity in a way that enables one to view it from every conceivable angle. Mills, an original member of the CRG and editor of the second version of the *Bliss Bibliographic Classification* (BC2), considers facets to be broad and of two general types: basic or relational. Relations between concepts lie at the heart of access and retrieval. In this view, concepts are represented by the words or terms which describe the entities or subject to be classified. The first step in identifying those relations is categorizing the concepts.

Faceted analytico-synthetic theory is a "deductive approach to concept organization" that observes the principles of logical division:

* One characteristic of division is applied at a time
* Division steps should be logical and proximate
* Division should be exhaustive.

Once identified, the facets are organized into mutually exclusive classes or arrays.

Facet Analysis (FA) and *Faceted Classification* (FC) are not synonymous, although these terms are often, at present, used in this manner. FA together with FC provide a framework, or "a simple and consistent method for analysis", "more than one way to view the world" and "may provide multi-dimensional and structured access points to collections".

There are many definitions for these two basic concepts, here Ranganathan and Vickery provide useful points of departure:

> Ranganathan describes FA as, "the mental process by which the possible trains of characteristics which can form the basis of classification of a subject are enumerated" and the exact measure in which the attributes concerned are incident in the subject are determined. Facets are inherent in the subject."

An FC, according to Vickery "is a schedule of standard terms to be used in document subject description" and assignment of notation. Broughton and Slavic in a modern statement of the CRG approach advise that, "Although *faceted classification* is regarded by many as a *structure* with specific characteristics, essentially *facet analysis* is a *technique*, and different models of the same universe of discourse can be derived to meet different local or subject-specific needs using different categories and variations on the syntax". It is best to heed Broughton's caution about the too "frequent use of the term faceted classification to mean any system of subject organization in which analytico-synthesis is used." This point cannot be overstated: the facet analytical approach is an iterative process but is one that stems from CRG extensions of Ranganathan's faceted analytico-synthetic theory.

These steps are generally followed:

FA ⇨ FC ⇨ FA

* Identification of a universe of entities to organize.
* Facet analysis of a representative sample of entities in terms of fundamental aspects and division of the entities into arrays.
* Once FA is complete, it is possible to create an FC which involves the formulation of filing and citation order, index and notation. It is not possible to create an FC without conducting FA.
* The process of FA then assists in the classification of entities by facilitating assignment of subject access points and notation.

The following four examples drawn from IS literature illustrate the diversity of definitions of FA:

* The essence of facet analysis is the sorting of terms in a given field of knowledge into homogeneous, mutually exclusive facets, each derived from the parent universe by a single characteristic of division. . . Facet analysis, by means of fundamental distinguishing characteristics or categories is the basic operation in constructing a faceted classification.
* Facet analysis is a mental process involving the analysis of a subject into its facets based on a set of postulates, canons and principles. It provides a framework to accommodate various types of terms along with rules for their combination.
* [F]acet analysis is interpreted in a much more restricted way. . . to mean that rigorous process of terminological analysis whereby the vocabulary of a given subject is organized into facets and arrays, resulting in a complex knowledge structure with both semantic and syntactic relationships clearly delineated.

* In analysing an entity one chooses descriptors from the appropriate facets. . . [T]he process is not one of division where the entities are subdivided into ever more specifically differentiated categories. It is not a process of decomposition, either in which the entities are broken… into component parts, each part different from the whole. Instead, the process of facet analysis is to view the object from all its angles – same object. . . different perspectives.

Central to the formulation of Ranganthan's FA/FC is the need to "uncover the thought-content of a written or expressed unit of thought" and to analyse both individual and aggregated groups of information entities, "in terms of entirety, rather than in terms of parts".

This necessitates a number of steps:

* All phases apprehended.
* All facets expressed.
* All foci uncovered.

It is important to note that the proposed research postulates that the tendency of web designers is not to construct faceted classifications complete with notation and schedules. It seems rather more possible that some website components such as those that promote navigation and access to site information may show evidence of the use of some form of facet analysis as embodied in FAST.

Several scholarly articles knit together the various definitions of the concepts central to FAST and attempt to provide more approachable descriptions of FAST than Ranganathan, whose language and examples are often impenetrable. A number of excellent books or primers on the subject are also available to those who are interested in more lengthy treatments of the subject– a list which is merely representative and by no means exhaustive.

Thus concludes the brief discussion of the early development of faceted analytico-synthetic theory and an introduction to the fundamental concepts of FAST as drawn from the canonical literature. By tracing the development of FAST from the early days of the UDC and Bliss classification to the complete explication of FAST as contained in Ranganathan's *Prolegomena* it can be seen that the theory has undergone extension and modification through application to practice by three groups, the LRC, CRG and CRSG. Because of the fact that multiple definitions currently exist for the central concepts of FAST, the operative definitions for terms used in the present study for coding and evaluative purposes will be drawn from traditional sources as represented by the glossary and as seen in the coding manual.

Chronological overview of developments in FAST

This part contains a description of the chronological development of FAST. It is notable that those who follow the framework of Ranganathan's faceted analytico-synthetic theory may accept similar definitions of central concepts like FA, but the end products of their work may seem remarkably dissimilar to one another, whether thesaurus, special classification, universal classification, or Web application.

This is not an attempt to exhaustively cover each system or theoretical development; rather, it will serve to indicate broad trends and to highlight representative developments and will be presented in decade increments. The dates for each part indicate the approximate beginning of each series of trends, but do not indicate that each development ends with the close of each decade.

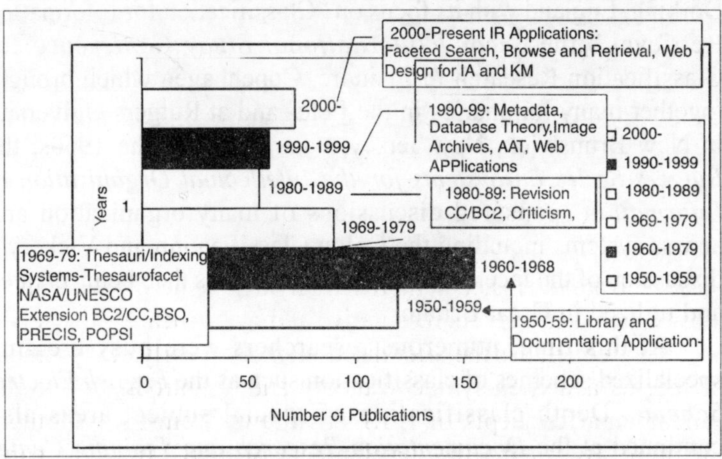

Fig. 4.1 Distribution of FAST Publications and Topic Themes 1950-Present [N=537]

Within the discipline of library and information science, FAST is considered a legacy system of information access and organization because researchers and practitioners throughout the years have continued to find value in the underlying theory and have utilized FAST in the creation of various applications. Given the variability of utilization, and resultant practices and applications, conducting a chronological survey of applications and research in this area provides an idea of the existence of trends, novel approaches, and well-trammeled areas.

Examples of the representative trends include FAST: as applied to IR as a set of design criteria, or as a conceptual framework to guide the design of schemes for knowledge or subject classification.

Beginning in Earnest-library and Documentation Applications: 1950-1968

As noted earlier, the 1950s through the end of the 1960s were periods of intense activity. Groups composed of scholars and practitioners in India, England and North America began to apply FAST theory to practice in a multitude of ways. This was the time of conferences which brought together researchers interested in the development and extension of FAST at such places as: Dorking, England with its focus on "Classification for Information Retrieval," the *Second International Study Conference* for Classification Research in Elsinore, Copenhagen which brought together many luminaries in the field- and at Rutgers University in New Brunswick, New Jersey, where through the 1960s, the *Rutgers Series on Systems for the Intellectual Organization of Information* sponsored discussions of many organization and access systems including the Colon Classification and Vickery's discussion of the faceted classification schemes then being created and utilized in Great Britain.

At this time, numerous researchers were busy creating specialized schemes of classification such as the *English Electric Scheme*. Depth classification of special subject areas also continued at the *Documentation Research and Training Center* (DRTC) in Bangalore. Richmond, the co-founder of the CRSG considered these kinds of classificatory activities to be essential as they filled the gap between theory and practice. The members produced original well-organized logical systems, applicable to new or revised needs of the communities which they served have managed to close the gap between universal classification systems and highly specialized ones.

It is especially important to note that although these groups began with FAST postulates and principles as described by Ranganathan, they freely experimented with FAST and sought to find flaws and limitations and to strengthen and augment the theory through practical engagement with it. Until his death in 1972, Ranganathan remained aware of these developments and encouraged them. The CRG rejected outright Ranganthan's notion that the universe of knowledge could be defined and broken into individual components. In seeking to extend FAST, they believed that the theory of integrative levels might provide a better framework for facet analysis than Ranganathan's own postulates and principles as detailed in the *Prolegomena*.

According to the CRG viewpoint:

* The world of things develops from the simple towards the complex by accumulation of new and divergent properties and that at certain points changes occur which transform the 'entity' from a member of one group or class into a member of a new group. The new entity has properties of its own, characteristic of the new level of organization within it, and behaves in a similarly new and characteristic manner.

The theory of integrative levels was not as fruitful for extending or augmenting FAST as hoped but it did lead the CRG to reconceptualize Ranganthan's five fundamental categories. Although Ranganthan postulated that facet analysis would be facilitated by application of these categories, and the CRG agreed that such a list of categories was a useful device for analysis, they posited that any such list of fundamental categories should never be used mechanically or imposed upon the subject.

Instead, the CRG believed that any listing of fundamental categories should only be used as a provisional guide when approaching a new field or group of entities to be organized, and that the component features of such a list might be more varied in scope than five. Other researchers, for example, Shera and Egan, and de Grolier, created provisional lists of fundamental categories.

Today there is general consensus about the importance of such provisional lists of "standard categories" and Aitchison, Gilchrist and Bawden have collocated these as a list of fundamental categories composed of 30 terms in five main categories:

* Entities, things and objects subdivided by characteristics and function
* Actions and activities
* Space, place, location and environment
* Time
* Kinds or types, systems and assemblies, applications and purposes

Throughout the 1950s and well into the 1970s, a number of experimental information retrieval applications utilized FAST, such as the *ASLIB-Cranfield test* of a faceted scheme for aeronautics and the American Institute of Physics AUDACIOUS project which utilized the UDC as a mechanized searching language. In the 1960s the *Center for Documentation and Communications Research* (CDCR) conducted a number of information retrieval experiments such as the *Aslib-Cranfield test of Metallurgical documents* using *English Electric Scheme*. Work at the CDCR also involved the creation of the *Semantic Code*: a linguistic factoring procedure for information retrieval heavily influenced by the colon classification and included hosting several information retrieval tests, including the *American Meteorological Society* tests of the mechanization of UDC for retrieval.

Thesaural Developments and Classificatory Extensions: 1969-1979

The use of FAST through the 1970s tended to involve the creation of thesauri and extension of existing classifications. Early discussions of the applicability of FAST to thesaurus construction began in the mid-1960s. Aitchison's work on Thesaurofacet, a faceted classification and controlled vocabulary for engineering and related subjects, was among the first to explicitly utilize FAST in this manner. Originally designed as the faceted *English Electric Scheme,* Thesaurofacet provided classification schedules as well as a controlled vocabulary for management and other scientific and technical subjects such as engineering. Integration of terms in both the classification schedule and thesaurus, resulted in the creation of a system that proved equally adaptable to early computerized indexing and information retrieval systems as well as to application in traditional library and documentation centers. Aitchison was also instrumental in the development of the UNESCO thesaurus in 1975 which assisted indexers and automatic retrieval of UNESCO documents and publications. Following Aitchison's lead, Anderson began work on a faceted classification and indexing system to be used to provide access to the contents of the MLA bibliography.

In the 1970s, a number of other special thesauri also developed using facet analysis and are still in use today, for example, the *British Technology Index*, the London Education Classification and the *London Classification of Business Studies*. More traditional applications utilizing FAST also continue to undergo revision and extension during this time. The members of the CRG, led by Jack Mills, pledged themselves to maintenance and continuing revision of the schedules of the now fully faceted and revised version of the *Bliss Bibliographic Classification*.

In a retrospective article Coates reviewed the developments in FAST in the twenty years after the Dorking conference and found that updating of the Universal Decimal and Colon classifications continued, but only the second edition of the Bliss Bibliographic Classification came closer to a working faceted classification than both Austin's PRECIS and the POPSI indexing systems developed in the early 1970s. Thomas' review of the impact of FAST on the teaching of subject analysis found that by the end of the 1970s, few ALA-accredited schools included instruction in the Colon classification and facet analysis but that instruction in other countries was far more comprehensive. Fewer special schemes were created during this time and if created, were most often used as access devices in information retrieval, examples include methods for the automatic encoding of chemical reactions and for faceted retrieval of linguistics information.

Revision, Criticism, Automation: 1980-1989

The 1980s were a time of revision and criticism of existing

schemes, and use of FAST in automated systems. Focus began to turn away from the creation of thesauri utilizing facet analysis to attempts to integrate a number of thesauri into a master file in order to use the resultant master-thesaurus as a switching language to support searching across databases. Similar work continued in other forms at the DRTC in India, as researchers there begin to experiment with the creation of computer-generated thesauri using the postulates and principles of facet analysis while still paying close attention to the creation of schemes of depth classification. Batty captured this shift in his discussion of the use of facet analysis as the basis of index language construction in his book *Life begins at forty: The resurgence of facet analysis.*

The BC2 attracted renewed attention at this time, not as a classification system, but as a "rich source of structure and terminology for thesauri covering different subject fields", even as its limitations are also being fully discussed. Some new faceted special schemes are still created, for specific reasons, to assist in the creation of finding aids, and to provide access to images. The 7th and final edition of the Colon Classification is published. Discussions of the role of a faceted approach to hypertext on the Web begin.

At the same time, FAST attracted the attention of software engineer Rueben Prieto-Diaz who created a faceted classification of software components and published his findings about the process. His groundbreaking work marked the first use of facet analysis and faceted classification in the construction of software component repository databases in order to support software component reuse. His facet analysis of software components yielded the following facets: function, objects, medium, system-type, functional area and setting thus enhancing understanding of the provisional nature of such lists of fundamental facets, while simultaneously expanding areas in which facet analysis had been successfully applied.

Databases, Interfaces and Retrieval Systems: 1990-1999

Work in the 1990s continued to focus on the applicability of FAST to database construction, and intensified the focus on the use of FAST in the design of information retrieval interfaces and systems. The *Art and Architecture Thesaurus* (AAT) is published.

Originally designed to classify terminology and to present faceted hierarchies of terms it can also function as a classified system for subject cataloguing.

AAT identified seven facets in the area of art and architecture: time and space; associated concepts; styles and periods; physical attributes; agents; activities; materials; and objects. This thesaurus currently exists in its second edition and is available on the Web. At this time, another more traditional application of FAST, the UDC, began to undergo revision and updating. The Universal Decimal Classification feasibility study began in 1993 with the directive to explore the potential for converting the UDC into a fully faceted system. This resulted in revisions and additions to the UDC throughout the 1990s.

A sharpening of focus in FAST-directed research throughout the 1990s resulted in many experiments which tested the utility of the theory as a theoretical underpinning for retrieval devices in online environments and knowledge bases. Ingwersen and Wormell's observations about the potential application of KO techniques such as FA/FC in information retrieval, thesaurus construction, and query negotiation/ formulation touch upon the most prevalent themes. In their view, FA/FC provided support for the creation of multiple access points and bootstrapped dynamic search procedures that might assist the user in finding the information being sought.

Ingversen and Wormell discussed the fact that FA/FC can improve access on several levels: physical, bibliographic, and intellectual. FAST can also facilitate IR by providing physical access through notational devices, while also providing intellectual access- on a deep conceptual level. Specific manifestations of work along these lines include using FAST as a means of improving information resources and interfaces and user friendliness and utilization of facet analysis as a way of assisting searches in the formulation of queries. Applicability of FAST to the design of databases is also a predominant theme and continues discussion begun in the 1970s by researchers such as Anderson.

FAST in Cyberspace 2000-2005

This part brings us to current developments. It is notable that over the years, researchers continue to refer to the historical impact of facet analysis and its potential in cyberspace:

* Meeting with S.R. Ranganathan in 1948 gave me a new view of classification as facet analysis plus traditional generic analysis and I applied this in schemes for Packaging, Occupational Safety and Health, and Education. This experience has suggested to me that facet analysis applied to any subject can reveal hitherto uncoordinated concepts - materials, processes, etc - and thus offer an indication of possible areas of future research. This could be a unique Information Science for the World Wide Web.
* The genius of Ranganathan is attested to by the very portability of his ideas across time, technology and cultures, simply because they address the very foundations of the business of effective information storage and retrieval. Perhaps in this respect, contemporary WWW developers might find themselves having more in common, or have more time for Ranganathan, than they appear to have for the current generation of IR researchers, despite their borrowings from IR, present us with research results in the form of search algorithms embedded in the various search engines. This is largely because contemporary IR research has developed within a particular historical paradigm, the assumptions of which may not fit well with the reality of IR on a widely distributed and disparate information source such as the WWW.

As in the 1980s, when discussions of FAST were not limited to researchers and practitioners in the field of information science, today FAST is being discussed widely. A recent Google Web search for "Faceted Classification" returned over eight thousand preponderantly relevant results. Five years ago, the same search returned only 100. "Facet analysis", another commonly used term on the web returned only a handful of results five years ago, and today returns 1500. This would seem to indicate that FC is the term favoured in many discussions about FAST or the facet analytical approach on the Web. Drawing conclusions about a topic using numbers of hits is disingenuous, but it does provide a rough means to take the pulse of a topic. Is it waxing or waning? Beyond search algorithm improvement, what accounts for this apparent eighty-fold growth in use of the term on various sites?

Today, it would seem that FAST has broad cross-over appeal. Web documents and discussion lists hosted by *Knowledge Management* (KM) specialists, and *Information Architecture* (IA) firms dominate the results of a Web search for faceted classification. The *Faceted Classification Discussion* (FCD) List, created December 2002, provides a forum for academic and business researchers interested in practical and theoretical discussions of FAST.

Often, attempts to find common ground are hampered by the task of translating practice into language that is understandable to all participants. Statements like these are seductive, "Faceted classification one of the most powerful, yet least understood, methods of organizing information". "Faceted classification serves up multiple 'pure' classification schemes rather than single 'motley' Taxonomy". What is FC? Where does the blogger or Web designer - someone with a casual interest in this latest hot topic - turn to find out about FC? Who holds the keys to the kingdom? The first three sites that turn up on Google search for FC are Phil Murray's website, KM Connection, geared for *Knowledge Management* (KM) enthusiasts; Peter Merholz's extensive discussion of "Innovation in classification"; and the Faceted Classification moderated by Peter Van Dijck, creator of XFML and Phil Murray, founder of KM Connection. References to scholarly articles about FA and FC in the IS literature are slowly beginning to appear in lists of Web links and Web logs alike.

At the recent ASIST Information Architecture Summit in Austin, Texas, FA was the topic of several talks: Grant Campbell used FA to improve access to information about marginalized communities, Miles Efron discussed the role of machine learning in automatic facet discovery and relation assignment, while Bradley Allen and Joseph Tennis discussed faceted metadata retrieval. One of the standard handbooks of Information Architecture devotes a part to a discussion of Ranganathan's FA and FC and how to use facets as an organizational mode.

The upcoming 2005 ASIST Information Architecture Summit will continue discussions of FAST with presentations that wrestle with creating a faceted classification for the website of the Canadian Government, a case study into the development of a faceted Web interface, and a panel discussion about how to create a faceted classification.

A vast and varied number of applications claim to utilize the facet analytical approach or FAST. There are several general categories of applications: Faceted metadata and data modeling or management applications that can involve software or guide the construction of website features such as *faceted search* (FS) or browsing. *Faceted metadata* is a common application. Peter Van Dijck's XFML: provides "an open XML format for publishing and sharing hierarchical faceted metadata and indexing efforts between websites." The main idea behind XFML is to provide support for automatic is two examples. Websites which are often cited as exemplars of faceted design include: Epicurious the "world's greatest recipe collection".

Other applications support *data modeling or management* such as Travis Wilson's Facet Map, "created to let users browse complex metadata while retaining a simple, familiar, menu interface." Facet Map consists of software which allows the browsing of visual data in a number of different formats by facets or conceptual categories. Similar to Facet Map but lacking the visualization and modeling features are *search and browsing systems* software that provides faceted search and browsing: Endeca and Adiuri's Waypoint products. The reasons for this are not clear, but they are the most frequent illustrations of FA/FC on KM and IA lists and Weblogs and made frequent appearances in presentations during the last three years of the IA Summit.

More traditional conceptualizations of FA and FC exist alongside these other applications. FATKS: Facet analytical theory in managing knowledge structure for humanities created a faceted classification system and easily automatable indexing tool for the humanities. Other projects include the Facet Project, which tested the efficacy of faceted thesauri for retrieval of multimedia collections. The Flamenco project which, by exposing faceted metadata, allows users to expand and organize search strategies in collections of art and architectural images, Pollitt's work with Interactive Information Retrieval based on a facet analytical approach that utilizes post-coordinated searching and a faceted thesaurus to generate different views of search results and recently, and semi-automatic construction of a faceted vocabulary for use as an organizational mechanism for web-based resources in the Classification-based Search and Knowledge Discovery project.

Review of Studies Similar to Proposed Research

A brief survey of studies that inform the proposed study follows. These research studies provide guidelines for the development of website component categories, analyse of the relative importance of various website components upon website usability or functionality, or look for evidence of FAST in website construction and design. A number of other studies investigate various website components, from different perspectives. A significant number of these are outside the academic literature or deal exclusively with graphic design issues. Further, a number of such studies instead directly address usability issues, which places their usefulness outside the scope of this study. The discussion which follows will cover studies which are directly relevant to the proposed study.

While there are many different types of website components, some have a greater potential to affect how readily a site visitor locates desired information. Library activities suggest the notion of "website flow" to describe the experience of using a website. Research indicates that one of the two most important dimensions of the online customer experience is website navigability, the other being customer service. Many researchers argue that navigation is critical to the success of a website. Library activities suggest that the functional utility of a website – defined in terms of the usefulness of content and the usability of the navigation - are the two most important components of a useful and usable website. The relative importance of organizational and access structures is also dependent on website type. A site that is more utilitarian will be more negatively affected by problematic navigation than will one designed primarily for entertainment.

Researcher conducted a global study of 1800 commercial websites. Although the research question involved assessing value-added features of e-commerce websites, the study provides a useful framework for website analysis with its three categories for site purpose, and four types of value creation. The study is limited by the sampling method, which relies on browser queries to identify the population of sites from which the sample was drawn. Each site was explored in sufficient detail so that all its value-adding features were identified and classified using the above framework, and the study found that most websites at the time of the study were primarily web "brochures" and that the content was primarily informational. This provides an example of a strategy for developing large sample of websites for analysis.

Another exploratory study of 100 purposively selected sites, sought to evaluate features which enhance or detract from website credibility, or the likelihood of site visitors to conduct a transaction or to return to the site in the future. This study clearly explicates guidelines and rationale for sample selection, but suffers from other methodological concerns. Study participants were randomly assigned to one content category and given randomly selected sites to view. Sites were not archived, and participants interacted with live sites. Constancy over time was not ensured, as the study took place over the period of one month, and participants used whatever computing equipment was available to them. Each participant was directed to visit a central website, to be assigned automatically and randomly to one content category. Next, participants were presented two URLs that were randomly selected from the category to which they had been assigned. Participants were asked to view the two sites, return to the central URL, and rate one as being more credible. No operational definition of credibility was provided, but participants were invited to enter comments about the sites in a Web form. This resulted in a rich data set of narrative responses. This study provides useful discussion of the issues involved with sampling on the web, and provides a series of negative examples of research design best avoided in the present study.

A survey of the use of faceted classification in website design served as the final impetus for the present study. A survey of 75 purposively selected e-commerce sites examined websites for the evidence of the use of faceted classification. Adkisson found that 52 out of 75 sites used some form of what she termed faceted classification. She indicated that faceted structures existed in both navigational and searching systems on the examined websites. Adkisson's work is not scholarly, peer-reviewed research, but is instead market research. It is notable in that it is a preliminary exploration into the existence of faceted structures on e-commerce websites. The proposed rigorous, academic study seeks provide explanations which may confirm or extend Adkisson's work.

PROPOSED RESEARCH PROCESS

An overview of the early development of FAST and definitions of the fundamental concepts, a digest of the chronological development through to the present, and recent studies related to the proposed research. Given the diverse understandings and various applications that claim to apply this theory, the proposed investigation of the use and utility of faceted analytico-synthetic theory is timely. This exploratory research seeks to uncover different types and kinds of practice in the construction and design of websites which will provide the potential for discovery, and highlight new developments that may well augment the traditional practice of FAST.

To restate the research questions:

* What types of access and organizational structures are used in websites?
* What is the evidence that there is use of faceted analytico-synthetic theory in website construction and design of website search tools?
* In what ways do the products of those Web designers who make explicit claims to utilize or be informed by faceted analytico-synthetic theory conform to or depart from the theory as described in LIS literature?

The proposed study into whether or not there is evidence of the use of FAST on the Web, and in the website construction and design practices of Is who explicitly invoke the language and forms of FAST will proceed in two phases:

Phase I relates to Research Questions (1) and (2) and Phase II relates to Research Questions (2) and (3).

Phase I:

* Craft a framework and criteria for sampling and analysis of websites.

* Conduct content analysis of websites to determine the extent to which organization and access structures are based on FAST. A second purpose of this study is to determine groupings by type of the sites identified as being based on FAST. This survey will include a random selection of sites in the DMOZ project. Wireframes of each site will be generated – fully described in a later part. Wireframes will serve to highlight commonalities and differences among websites.)
* Sites that show evidence of having been developed using FAST approaches will be further studied and subject to content analysis.

Phase II:

* Craft an interview instrument to elicit data from website designers in a semi- structured interview format. Topics to be discussed include types of structures created which utilize FAST and resources used by the designers to assist them with FAST oriented design.
* Interview a number of website designers who explicitly claim to use FAST. Identify their practices related to FAST by showing them selected wireframes and asking about their practices. Conducting semi-structured interviews will also serve to uncover how Web designers are extending and augmenting more traditional practices by de novo approaches.

Instrument development:

* Two sets of instruments will be developed for use in the proposed study. For Phase I, a coding manual will be prepared to enable training of coders for the purpose of intercoder reliability testing. It is in two parts, as the website capture and analysis will occur in two parts. First, all randomly selected websites will be captured during a short time period. During the first step of data capture, each website will be visited, assigned a unique number, the sitemap and page(s) of interest will be printed out, and a wireframe developed for each site. During the second step of data capture, the material gathered in step one will be revisited and examined for

evidence of faceted approaches using the guidelines established for analysis. Phase II of the study involves interviewing website designers using semi-structured interview techniques. Prompts consisting of wireframes will be drawn from commonly referenced websites and from the work of each designer interviewed.

CALL NUMBERS

Classification means the grouping together of items or people according to a feature they have in common. Most people have some classification systems in their home. In a kitchen, for example, many of us keep all the silverware together, all the canned food together, and all the pots together. Supermarkets provide another example of a classification system. Meats are together, dairy products are together, and fresh produce is in one place. Imagine trying to find what one needed if items were scattered randomly on the shelves, or if they were arranged alphabetically, placing apples next to beans next to cheese next to dog food.

In libraries, as elsewhere, having a classification system helps people find things. Books about a particular field of knowledge shelved together or near each other, whether that field is music, education or geology. This system helps the researcher find books by browsing, and also assigns specific locations for books on the shelf for easy access. Later as suggested, discuss strategies for finding materials that might fall into more than one discipline or subject.

Most libraries in the U.S. and many in other countries use either of two well-known classification systems, the Library of Congress system and the Dewey Decimal system. Like most academic libraries in the U.S., the Seattle Community College libraries use the Library of Congress system. Public libraries tend to use the Dewey Decimal system.

Library of Congress Classification System

As fields of knowledge have expanded and have increased in number to include relatively new areas such as computer science and space exploration, the Dewey Decimal system, with only ten major fields, has run out of room. In the 1970s, research and academic libraries started to use the Library of Congress system, which has twenty-one major fields and thus allows more subjects and more specialization. Fiction and biography are included in the classification system, which means those books have call numbers and are shelved with the rest of the collection.

* A General Works
* AE Fncyclopedias
* AG General reference works
* AI Indexes
* AS Societies, Academics
* AZ General history of Knowledge
* B Philosophy, Psychology, Religion
* B Philosophy
* BC Logic
* BD Metaphysics
* BF Psychology
* BH Aesthetics
* BJ Ethics
* BL Religions, Mythology
* BM Judaism
* BP Islam, Bahaism
* BR-BV Christianity
* BX Special sects
* C Auxiliary Sciences of History, Archaeology
* CB History of civilization
* CC Antiquities Archeology
* CJ Numismatics, Coins
* CN Epigraphy, Inscriptions
* CR Heraldry
* CS Genealogy
* CT Biography
* D History-General, Europe, Africa, and Asia
* D History
* DA-DQ Europe
* DR Turkey and the Balkan States
* DS Asia
* DT Africa
* DU Australia and Oceania
* DX Gypsies

* E-F History-Americas
* E Americas Indians of North America, United States
* F Canada, Central America, South America, Caribbean
* G Geography, Anthropology, Recreation
* G Geography
* GB Physical geography
* GC Oceanology and Oceanography
* GN Anthropology
* GR Folklore
* GT Manners and Customs
* GV Sports and Amusements, Games
* H Social Sciences
* H Social Sciences
* HA Statistics
* HB Economic Theory
* HC-HD Economic history and conditions
* HF Commerce, Employment
* HG Finance
* HM Sociology
* HN Social history, Social reform
* HQ Family, Marriage, Women, Gays
* HV Social and Public Welfare
* J Political Science
* JA Political Science
* JC Political theory
* JF Constitutional history and administration
* JK United States
* JL-JQ Other Regions
* JS Local Government
* JX International Law, Peace
* K Law
* KF Law: U.S. Federal and State
* KFW Law: Washington State
* L Education
* LA History of education
* LB Theory and practice, Teaching
* LD-LJ Universities and Colleges
* M Music

* ML Literature of music
* MT Musical instruction and study
* N Fine Arts
* NA Architecture
* NE Sculpture and related arts
* NC Graphic arts, Drawing
* ND Painting
* NE Engraving, Prints
* NK Art applied to industry, Decoration and ornament
* NX Arts in general
* P Language and Literature
* P Philology and linguistics
* PA Classical language and literatures
* PC Romance languages
* PD Germanic languages
* PE English language
* PG Slavic, Lithuanian-Lettish, Albanian
* PH Finno-Ugrian and Basque
* PJ Egyptian, Coptic, Hamitic, Semitic
* PK Indo-Iranian, Indo-Aryan
* PL Eastern Asia, Oceania, Africa
* PN Literary history and collections
* PQ Romance Literatures
* PR English Literatures
* PS American Literatures
* PT Germanic Literatures
* Q Science
* QA Mathematics, Computer Science
* QB Astronomy
* QC Physics
* QD Chemistry
* QE Geology
* QH Natural history
* QK Botany
* QL Zoology
* QM Human anatomy
* QP Physiology
* QR Microbiology

* R Medicine
* RC Internal medicine, Psychiatry
* RD Surgery
* RE Ophthalmology
* RM Pharmacology
* RT Nursing
* S Agriculture-Plant and Animal Industry
* S Agriculture
* SB Plant culture
* SD Forestry
* SF Animal culture
* SH Fish culture and fisheries
* SK Hunting sports
* T Technology
* TA Engineering, Civil engineering
* TC Hydraulic engineering
* TD Environmental technology
* TF Railroads engineering
* TG Bridges and Roofs
* TH Building construction
* TJ Mechanical engineering
* TK Electrical engineering
* TL Motor vehicles, Aeronautics
* TN Mineral industries, Mining and Metallurgy
* TP Chemical technology
* TR Photography
* TS Manufactures
* TT Arts and Crafts
* TX Home economics, Culinary Arts
* U Military Science
* V Naval Science
* Z Bibliography, Library Science, History of books, Printing

Call Numbers

In any library classification system, each book has its own call number-a unique combination of letters and numbers shown on the spine or on the front of the book. Books are arranged on the shelves by the call number, which serves as an address for the book. In the Dewey Decimal system, call numbers begin with a three-digit figure. In the Library of Congress system, call numbers begin with one or two letters.

Call numbers and library classification are intertwined because each field of study is represented by a call number. For example, in the Library of Congress system, the letter L represents education, the letter Q represents science, N represents the arts, and so forth. Each book in that field receives a corresponding call number-all books about education have a call number beginning with L and all books about science have a call number beginning with Q. In the Dewey Decimal system, all books about education have call numbers in the 370's and all books about science have call numbers in the 500's. This is why books about the same discipline are together on the shelf. Call numbers get longer as the subject represented become more specific.

Selective List of Academic Fields

Knowing the academic field in which your topic falls can help you decide where to browse in the library.

* *Agriculture*: The study of all the processes and services, both nonfarm and farm, involved in producing plants and animals and their produces and in getting them to the consumer.
* *Anthropology*: The science concerned with man, both normatively and historically, dealing with his physical characteristics, his racial, geographical, and historical distribution, classification, and relationships, and his cultural, environmental, and social development and relationship.
* *Arts, fine*: The pursuit of painting, sculpture, and architecture.
* *Astronomy*: A study of the celestial bodies, their composition, distances, motions, and the laws which control them.
* *Biology*: the study of living animal organisms.
* *Botany*: The study of plant life.
* *Business*: The study of commercial or industrial enterprises.

* *Chemistry*: The study of the composition, structure, and properties of matter and of changes in matter, including the accompanying energy phenomena.
* *Communications*: The study of the psychological, sociological, and physical components in the transmission, reception, and recording of verbal and nonverbal messages.
* *Economics*: The branch of social study that deals with the production, distribution, and consumption of commodities having exchange value and with the social phenomena arising from such activities.
* *Education*: The art of making available to each generation the organized knowledge of the past.
* *Engineering*: The study of the properties of matter and the sources of power in nature which are made useful in structures, machines, and manufactured products.
* *Geography*: The scïence of the earth, including a study of land, water, air, the distribution of plant and animal life, man and his industries, and the interrelations of these factors.
* *Geology*: The field of study dealing with the history of the earth, with those forces or agencies acting on the earth with certain types of rocks and minerals, and particularly with the evidences of such history as are revealed in rock formations and earth strata.
* *History*: The science or field of study concerned with the recording and critical representation of past events.
* *Home economics*: A discipline that draws from the biological, physical, and social science and the humanities the content needed to help people solve problems of food, clothing, shelter, and relationships and that deals with the development of the way of living of individuals, families, and community groups.
* *Language*: The faculty of verbal expression and the use of words in human intercourse.
* *Law*: The study of the binding custom or practice of a community.
* *Literature*: The study of the written or printed

productions of a country or a period, but more especially that written or printed matter which has high quality and style.

* *Mathematics*: The science which explains the relations existing between quantities and operations.
* *Medicine*: The science and art dealing with the prevention, cure, or alleviation of disease.
* *Military Science*: The study of methods of war oar armies.
* *Music*: The art and science of creating and delivering tomes expressive of, and stimulating to, human feelings.
* *Oceanography*: The study of the sea, embracing and integrating all knowledge pertaining to the sea's physical boundaries, the chemistry and physic of sea water, and marine biology.
* *Philosophy*: The science that seeks to organize an systematize all fields of knowledge as a means of understanding and interpreting the totality of reality; usually regarded as comprising logic, ethics, aesthetics, metaphysics, and epistemology.
* *Physics*: The branch of physical science that is concerned with mater and energy, including the study of phenomena associated with mechanics, heat, wave motion, sound, electricity, magnetism, light, and atomic and nuclear structure.
* *Political Science*: A field of social studies having for its purpose the ascertaining of political facts and arranging them in systematic order as determined by the logical and causal relations that exist among them; concerned with political authority in all its forms, and dealing with them historically, descriptively, comparatively, and theoretically.
* *Psychology*: The study of adjustments of organisms, especially the human organism, to changing environment.
* *Religion*: The study of encounters with that which is viewed as divine or as ultimate reality.
* *Sociology*: The science or study of human social

grouping and behaviour, regarded generally and collectively, and dealing particularly with the origins, development, purposes, functions, prob-lems, adjustments and peculiarities of human society.

* *Technology*: The study of the material culture resulting form the combination of logic, mathematics, and science.

LC Classification System and Call Numbers

Library of Congress call numbers combine letters of the alphabet and Arabic numerals to make a code, or call number that represents the subject of the work. Each book in the library has its own unique call number printed on its spine. Books are arranged on the shelf in a combined alphabetical and numerical order. Such an arrangement makes it very convenient for a researcher to browse in the desired subject area(s).

Knowledge of some basic principles may help you make the most of the classification system as a tool for finding the information you need:

* The classes In the Library of Congress Classification, like those In other classification systems, proceed from general to specific. General materials, such as dictionaries, handbooks, textbooks, directories, etc., are usually near the beginning of a class.
* Main classes are represented by a single letter:
* H Social Sciences
* Principle subdivisions are marked by an additional letter:
* HC Economic history and conditions
* HG Finance
* HJ Public finance
* HM Sociology
* HQ The family. Marriage. Woman
* HX Socialism. Communism. Anarchism.

Subject areas are divided further by the use of Arabic numerals filed in sequence:

* HQ 12-449 Sexual life.
* HQ 450-471 Erotica.
* HQ 503-1064 The Family. Marriage, including Child

study, Eugenics, Desertion, Adultery, Divorce, Polygamy and the Aged.

* HQ 1101-2030 Woman. Feminism. Women's clubs.

Because of the length and complexity of Library of Congress classification numbers, and because collections in which the system is used are generally quite large, the researcher can save time by beginning a search for books at the library catalog. The catalog will lead to the exact call number for a book in the subject area you want to find. Also, once you get a call number from the catalog, it becomes very easy to find a good place to begin your browsing.

Dates at the end of a call number usually Indicate the date of publication and are shelved in chronological order. The date is an essential part of the call number and should be copied down from the library catalog. All numbers before the decimal are arranged in ordinary sequence; all those following the decimal are read decimally. For example, the correct order for these call numbers would be:

GN	GN	GN	GN	GN
4	4	39.4	385	385.2
.F312	.F32	.F4	.F433	.G4

Call numbers appearing in the SCCC On-line Catalog look like this:

* PS647.E851 S62 1992, and correspond to a label on the spine of the book that looks like this:
* PS
* 647
* E851
* S62
* 1992

5

Library Classification Schemes

DEWEY DECIMAL CLASSIFICATION

Of modern library classification schemes, the *Dewey Decimal Classification* (*DDC*) is both the oldest and the most widely used in the United States. It also has a substantial following abroad. Such widespread use is a tribute to Melville Louis Kossuth Dewey, whose original plan was adaptable enough to incorporate new subjects as they emerged and flexible enough to withstand the changes imposed by the passage of time. Dewey was born on December 10, 1851, and graduated from Amherst College in 1874, where he became assistant college librarian. He actually began developing the first draft of his system for arranging books while working as a student assistant in the college library in 1873. He soon became a leader in American librarianship, helping to found both the *American Library Association* (ALA) and the first American library school at Columbia University. Being a man of many interests, he was also an advocate of spelling reform.

He shortened his forename to "Melvil", dropped his two middle names, and even attempted to change the spelling of his surname to "Dui". Throughout his career he promoted librarianship by his teaching, writing, and speaking. In recognizing and acting upon the need to systematize library collections for effective use, he knew of various previous attempts, but found them inadequate. Dewey never claimed to have originated decimals for classification notation, but earlier systems used them merely as shelf location devices with no significant relation to the subject matter. What Dewey did claim as original, and with some justification, was his "relativ index", compiled as a key to the "diverse material" included in his tables. His most significant contribution was perhaps the use of decimals for hierarchical divisions. Combined with the digits 0 to 9, decimals provide a pure notation that can be subdivided indefinitely. The first edition of Dewey's scheme, prepared for the Amherst College Library, was issued anonymously in 1876 under the title *A Classification and Subject Index for Cataloguing and Arranging the Books and Pamphlets of a Library*.

It included schedules to 1000 divisions numbered 000–999, together with a relative index and prefatory matter—a total of 44 pages. The second, "revised and greatly enlarged" edition was published under Dewey's name in 1885. Since that time 20 more full editions and 14 abridgments have appeared. The fourteenth edition, published in 1942, remained the standard edition for many years because an experimental index to the fifteenth edition, published in 1951, was unsuccessful. In 1958 the sixteenth edition appeared with many changes and additions, "Inorganic and Organic Chemistry." Since that time each successive edition has carried, besides other, less sweeping changes, totally new developments of one or more targeted portions of the system. The present twenty-second edition was published in 2003; the associated fourteenth abridged edition was published in 2004. *DDC* notations are assigned the tag 082 in *MARC 21* when they have been created for a particular item by the *Library of Congress* (LC) or other national cataloging agency.

A *DDC* notation created by a local library participating in a network is placed in MARC field 092. *DDC* complete call numbers are also placed in field 092, regardless of who assigned the *DDC* notation to the item involved. Closely related to *DDC* is the *Universal Decimal Classification* (*UDC*), which was based originally on *DDC*. It is discussed briefly at the end of this chapter.

DEWEY DECIMAL CLASSIFICATION SYSTEM

In 1876 Melvil Dewey divided all fields of knowledge into ten major categories. Fiction and biography aren't included in these categories and are shelved separately. Fiction books are on the shelves in alphabetical order according to the author's last name. Biographies are in alphabetical order according to the last name of the person who is the subject of the book. Many public libraries in the United States still use the Dewey Decimal System because this is the system they have historically used, and because it is an easy system to use and master.

It arranges the contents of a library based on the division of all knowledge into 10 groups, with each group assigned 100 numbers.

These 10 main groups are then subdivided again and again to provide more specific subject groups.

* 000 GENERALITIES
  - 010 Bibliography
  - 020 Library and Information Sciences
  - 030 General encyclopedic works
  - 040 General reference works
  - 050 General Serials and their indexes
  - 060 General organizations and museology
  - 070 News media, journalism, publishing
  - 080 General collections
  - 090 Manuscripts and rare books
* 100 PHILOSOPHY and RELATED DISCIPLINES
  - 110 Metaphysics
  - 120 Epistemology, causation, mankind
  - 130 Paranormal phenomena and arts
  - 140 Specific philosophical schools
  - 150 Psychology
  - 160 Logic
  - 170 Ethics
  - 180 Ancient, medieval, Oriental philosophy
  - 190 Modern Western philosophy
* 200 RELIGION
  - 210 Natural theology
  - 220 Bible
  - 230 Christian theology
  - 240 Christian moral and devotional theology
  - 250 Christian orders and local church
  - 260 Christian social history
  - 270 Christian church history
  - 280 Christian denominations and sects

- 290 Other and comparative religions

* 300 SOCIAL SCIENCES

- 310 General statistics
- 320 Political Science
- 330 Economics
- 340 Law
- 350 Public Administration
- 360 Social problems and services
- 380 Commerce
- 390 Customs, etiquette, folklore

* 400 LANGUAGE

- 410 Linguistics
- 420 English and Old English
- 430 Germanic languages
- 440 Romance languages
- 450 Italian, Romanian, Rhaeto-Romanic
- 460 Spanish and Portuguese languages
- 470 Italic languages
- 480 Hellenic languages
- 490 Other Languages

* 500 PURE SCIENCES

- 510 Mathematics
- 520 Astronomy
- 530 Physics
- 540 Chemistry
- 550 Earth sciences
- 560 Paleontology
- 570 Life sciences
- 580 Botany
- 590 Zoology

* 600 TECHNOLOGY

- 610 Medical sciences
- 620 Engineering
- 630 Agriculture
- 640 Home Economics
- 650 Management
- 660 Chemical engineering
- 670 Manufacturing

- 680 Manufacture for specific uses
- 690 Building

* 700 THE ARTS
- 710 Civic and Landscape arts
- 720 Architecture
- 730 Pottery, Sculpture
- 740 Drawing, decorative arts
- 750 Painting
- 760 Graphic arts
- 770 Photography
- 780 Music
- 790 Performing and recreational arts

* 800 LITERATURE
- 810 American literature
- 820 English literature
- 830 Germanic literatures
- 840 Romance Language literatures
- 850 Italian, Romanian, Rhaeto-Romanic literatures
- 860 Spanish literatures
- 870 Italic literatures
- 880 Classical Greek Literature
- 890 Literatures of other languages

* 900 GENERAL GEOGRAPHY and HISTORY
- 910 Geography and Travel
- 920 Biography and Genealogy
- 930 Ancient History
- 940 History - Europe
- 950 History - Asia
- 960 History - Africa
- 970 History - North America
- 980 History - South America
- 990 History - other areas

UNIVERSAL DECIMAL CLASSIFICATION

The *Universal Decimal Classification* (UDC) is a bibliographic and library classification developed by the Belgian bibliogra-phers Paul Otlet and Henri La Fontaine at the end of the 19th century. The UDC provides a systematic arrangement of all branches of human knowledge organized as a coherent system in which knowledge fields are related and inter-linked. Originally based on the Dewey Decimal Classification, the UDC was developed as a new analytico-synthetic classification system with a significantly larger vocabulary and syntax that enables very detailed content indexing and information retrieval in large collections.

In its first edition in 1905, the UDC already included many features that were revolutionary in the context of knowledge classifications.

* Tables of generally applicable concepts - called common auxiliary tables;
* A series of special auxiliary tables with specific but re-usable attributes in a particular field of knowledge;
* An expressive notational system with connecting symbols and syntax rules to enable coordination of subjects and the creation of a documentation language proper.

Although originally designed as an indexing and retrieval system, due to its logical structure and scalability, they UDC has become one of the most widely used knowledge organization systems in libraries, where it is used for either shelf arrangement, content indexing or both. UDC codes can describe any type of document or object to any desired level of detail. These can include textual documents and other media such as films, video and sound recordings, illustrations, maps as well as realia such as museum objects.

Since the first edition in French "Manuel du Répertoire bibliographique universel", the UDC has been translated and published in various editions in 40 languages. UDC Summary, an abridged Web version of the scheme is available in over 45 languages. The classification has been modified and extended over the years to cope with increasing output in all areas of human knowledge, and is still under continuous review to take account of new developments.

The Application of UDC

UDC is used in around 150,000 libraries in 130 countries and in many bibliographical services which require detailed content indexing. In a number of countries it is the main classification system for information exchange and is used in all type of libraries:

public, school, academic and special libraries. UDC is also used in national bibliographies of around 30 countries. Examples of large databases indexed by UDC include: NEBIS - 2.6 million records, COBIB.SI - 3.5 million records; Hungarian National Union Catalogue - 2.9 million records; VINITI RAS database with 28 million records; *Meteorological and Geoastrophysical Abstracts* (MGA) with 600 journal titles; PORBASE with 1.5 million records, etc. UDC has traditionally been used for the indexing of scientific articles which was an important source of information of scientific output in the period predating electronic publishing. Collections of research articles in many countries covering decades of scientific output contain UDC codes.

Examples of journal articles indexed by UDC:

* UDC code 663.12:57.06 in the article "Yeast Systematics: from Phenotype to Genotype" in the journal Food Technology and Biotechnology
* UDC code 37.037:796.56, provided in the article "The game method as means of interface of technical-tactical and psychological preparation in sports orienteering" in the Russian journal "Pedagogico-psychological and medico-biological problems of the physical culture and sport".
* UDC code 621.715:621.924:539.3 in the article Residual Stress in Shot-Peened Sheets of AIMg4.5Mn Alloy - in the journal Materials and technology.

The design of UDC lends itself to machine readability, and the system has been used both with early automatic mechanical sorting devices, and modern library OPACs. From 1993, a standard version of UDC is maintained and is distributed in a database format: UDC Master Reference File (UDC MRF) which is updated and released annually. The 2010 version of the MRF contains over 69,000 classes. In the past full printed editions used to have around 220,000 subdivisions.

UDC structure and Content

Notation

A notation is a code commonly used in classification schemes to represent a class, *i.e.* a subject and its position in the hierarchy, to enable mechanical sorting and filing of subjects. UDC uses Arabic numerals arranged decimally. Every number is thought of as a decimal fraction with the initial decimal point omitted, which determines the filing order. An advantage of decimal notational systems is that they are infinitely extensible, and when new subdivisions are introduced, they need not disturb the existing allocation of numbers. For ease of reading, a UDC notation is usually punctuated after every third digit:

Notation	Caption (Class description)
539.120	Theoretical problems of elementary particles physics. Theories and models of fundamental interactions
539.120.2	Symmetries of quantum physics
539.120.22	Conservation laws
539.120.222	Translations. Rotations
539.120.224	Reflection in time and space
539.120.226	Space-time symmetries
539.120.23	Internal symmetries
539.120.3	Currents
539.120.4	Unified field theories
539.120.5	Strings

In UDC the notation has two features that make the scheme easier to browse and work with:

* *Hierarchically expressive*: The longer the notation, the more specific the class: removing the final digit automatically produces a broader class code.
* *Syntactically expressive*: When UDC codes are combined, the sequence of digits is interrupted by a precise type of punctuation sign which indicates that the expression is a combination of classes rather than a simple class *e.g.* the colon in 34:32 indicates that there are two distinct notational elements: 34 Law. Jurisprudence and 32 Politics; the closing and opening parentheses and double quotes in the following code 91(574.22)"19"(084.3) indicate four separate notational elements: 913 Regional geography, (574.22) North Kazakhstan; "19" 20th century and (084.3) Maps (document form)

Basic Features and Syntax

The UDC is an anlytico-synthetic and/or faceted classification. It allows an unlimited combination of attributes of a subject and relationships between subjects to be expressed. UDC codes from different tables can be combined to present various aspects of document content and form, *e.g.* 94(410)"19"(075) History *(main subject)* of United Kingdom *(place)* in 20th century *(time)*, a textbook *(document form)*. Or: 37:2 Relationship between Education and Religion. Complex UDC expressions can be accurately parsed into constituent elements. UDC is also a disciplinary classification covering the entire universe of knowledge. This type of classification can also be described as *aspect* or *perspective*, which means that concepts are subsumed and placed under the field in which they are studied. Thus, the same concept can appear in different fields of knowledge. This particular feature is usually implemented in UDC by re-using the same concept in various combinations with the main subject, *e.g.* a code for language in common auxiliaries of language is used to derive numbers for ethnic grouping, individual languages in linguistics and individual literatures. Or, a code from the auxiliaries of place, *e.g. (410) United Kingdom*, uniquely representing the concept of United Kingdom can be used to express *911(410) Regional geography of United Kingdom* and *94(410) History of United Kingdom.*

Organization of Classes

Concepts are organized in two kinds of tables in UDC. Common auxiliary tables (including certain auxiliary signs). These tables contain facets of concepts representing, general recurrent characteristics, applicable over a range of subjects throughout the main tables, including notions such as place, language of the text and physical form of the document, which may occur in almost any subject. UDC numbers from these tables, called common auxiliaries are simply added at the end of the number for the subject taken from the main tables. There are over 15,000 of common auxiliaries in UDC.

The main tables or main schedules containing the various disciplines and branches of knowledge, arranged in 9 main classes, numbered from 0 to 9. At the beginning of each class there are also series of special auxiliaries, which express aspects that are recurrent within this specific class. Main tables in UDC contain more than 60,000 subdivisions.

Main Classes

* 0 Science and Knowledge. Organization. Computer Science. Information. Documentation. Librarianship. Institu-tions. Publications
* 1 Philosophy. Psychology
* 2 Religion. Theology
* 3 Social Sciences
* 4 vacant
* 5 Mathematics. Natural Sciences
* 6 Applied Sciences. Medicine, Technology
* 7 The Arts. Recreation. Entertainment. Sport
* 8 Language, Linguistics, Literature
* 9 Geography, Biography, History

The vacant class 4 is the result of a planned schedule expansion. This class was freed by moving linguistics into class 8 in 1960s to make space for future developments in the rapidly expanding fields of knowledge; primarily natural sciences and technology.

Common Auxiliary Tables

Common auxiliaries are aspect-free concepts that can be used in combination with any other UDC code from the main classes or with other common auxiliaries. They have unique notational representations that makes them stand out in complex expressions. Common auxiliary numbers always begin with a certain symbol known as a facet indicator, *e.g.* = (equal sign) always introduces concepts representing the language of a document; (0...) numbers enclosed in parentheses starting with zero always represent a concept designating document form. Thus (075) Textbook and =111 English can be combined to express, *e.g.*(075)=111 Textbooks in English, and when combined with numbers from the main UDC tables they can be used as follows:

2(075)=111 Religion textbooks in English, 51(075)=111 Mathematics textbooks in English etc.

* =... Common auxiliaries of language.

* (0...) Common auxiliaries of form.
* (1/9) Common auxiliaries of place.
* (=...) Common auxiliaries of human ancestry, ethnic grouping and nationality.
* "..." Common auxiliaries of time.
* -0... Common auxiliaries of general characteristics: Properties, Materials, Relations/Processes and Persons.
* -02 Common auxiliaries of properties.
* -03 Common auxiliaries of materials.
* -04 Common auxiliaries of relations, processes and operations.
* -05 Common auxilaries of persons and personal characteristics.

Connecting Signs

In order to preserve the precise meaning and enable accurate parsing of complex UDC expressions, a number of connecting symbols are made available to relate and extend UDC numbers. These are:

Symbol	Symbol Name	Meaning	Example
+	plus	addition	e.g. 59+636 zoology and animal breeding
/	stroke	consecutive extension	e.g. 592/599 Systematic zoology (everything from 592 to 599 inclusive)
:	colon	relation	e.g. 17:7 Relation of ethics to art
[ ]	square brackets	subgrouping	e.g. 311:[622+669](485) statistics of mining and metallurgy in Sweden (the auxiliary qualifiers 622+669 considered as a unit)
*	asterisk	Introduces non UDC notation	e.g. 523.4*433 Planetology, minor planet Eros (IAU authorized number after the asterisk)
A/Z	alphabetic extension	Direct alphabetical specification	e.g. 821.133.1MOL French literature, works of Molière

UDC Outline

UDC classes in this outline are taken from the Multilingual Universal Decimal Classification Summary released on the by the UDC Consortium under the Creative Commons Attribution Share Alike 3.0 licence.

COLON CLASSIFICATION (CC)

You have now studied in detail the Dewey Decimal Classification and Universal Decimal Classification schemes. This chapter attempts to familiarise you with the underlying principles of Colon Classification. The CC differs in several respects from the other two schemes, which you have already studied in this Block. S.R. Ranganathan, the author of CC, was well aware that a scheme of classification should be able to meet the challenge of ever rowing universe of knowledge and it should 'be able to accommodate, at an appropriate place, any new subject without disturbing the arrays already formed. The seventh edition of CC has succeeded to a large extent in fulfilling this objective;

Two basic strategies for number building in CC are:

* Subject analysis, and
* Synthesis.

The analysis of a given subject results in the facetisation of the subject, as treated in the document, on the basis of five fundamental categories and their manifestation in it. Synthesis consists of bringing together the facets manifest in a subject to represent, as completely as possible, the description of that subject. Synthesis also has another connotation. It consists of connecting to the core subject those other aspects, which it shares with other subjects. By dint of its capabilities of analysis and synthesis, CC is known as an analytico-synthetic scheme. It is also described as a Freely Faceted Scheme. Under a rigidly faceted scheme, each main class was given a facet formula and the numbers were coined with the help of a connecting digit, colon. The drawback under a rigidly faceted scheme, with a single connecting symbol, resulted from the cluttering of the connecting symbol, *i.e.*, whether a facet was present or absent, it had to be represented by a colon. With the introduction of 'separate connecting digits for personality, matter and energy facets in the fourth edition of CC, it became possible to represent only those facets in the number that are manifested in the subject treated in the document. Because of this facility, CC has since been called Freely Faceted.

Genesis of Colon Classification

Ranganathan was a mathematics lecturer. It was a mere accident that he was appointed Librarian of the Madras University Library in the year 1924. He was soon deputed to Britain for an observational tour of British libraries. While in Britain he also attended classes in the School of Librarianship, University of

London. Berwick Sayers, known as' the grammarian of library classification, was one of the teachers at the School. During his tour of Britain; Ranganathan visited several libraries and was quick to notice the lacunae in the classification schemes in use then. A chance visit to a departmental store in London gave Ranganathan a clue for evolving a scheme of classification. He saw the demonstration of a toy called meccano set.

The meccano set consists of several slotted strips, rods, wheels, screws, nuts and bolts with which several different models could be made. This gave him the idea that in a classification scheme there should be standard units that could be joined by connecting symbols. Ranganathan's standard units resembled the strips and his connecting symbols resembled the nuts and bolts of the meccano set. The standard units became the schedules. Thus, a class number could be constructed with the different elements enumerated in the schedules with a connecting symbol and he chose the colon as the connecting symbol. This was, dip, Ranganathan's conception of Colon Classification. The foundation of Colon Classification was laid in Britain in the year 1924. In 1925, his journey back to India gave Ranganathan ample time to work on the schedules. The library on the ship he was travelling in and the Madras University Library's book catalogue, which he was carrying with him served as the working equipment for him.

First Edition

On reaching Madras he took up the work of classifying the Madras University Library collection. The years between 1925 and 1932 were devoted mainly to the 'construction' of the schedules of CC. In 1929, he also established a library school at the University. Both teaching and library work at the University contributed immensely to the publication in 1933 of the first edition of Colon Classification. It had three distinct part: 127 pages of rules explaining the underlying principles, 135 pages of schedules and 106 pages of index. The notation was mixed, consisting of the 26 Roman capital letters denoting main classes, Indo-Arabic numerals and also Roman lower case letters. The colon (:) was used as the connecting symbol for joining facets. Each main class was provided with a facet formula.

Search for Theory

Ranganathan was aware of several inconsistencies in his scheme and did not fight shy of consulting subjects experts to know the gamut of each discipline. At the same time he tried to evolve a theory of library classification. The years from 1933 to 1939 were spent in working on the theory of classification. It was during these years that several Canons of Classification were formulated. The result was the publication of Prolegomena to Library Classification in 1937. Based on this theory, the second edition of Colon Classification was published in 1939. The changes from the first to the second edition were not substantial. In this edition, two new concepts of Octave principles and auto-bias device were introduced. A new main class 8 Spiritual Experience and Mysticism carne into being. The first edition, as already said, had three parts. A fourth part was added in the second edition. This additional part contained about 3,000 examples, which were illustrative of the rules given in the first part.

Subsequent Editions

In 1945, Ranganathan shifted to Banaras. He spent two years at Banaras Hindu University from 1945 to 1947. He was, however, bogged down in administrative work and all research came to a standstill. It was Sir Maurice Gwyer, the then Vice-Chancellor of Delhi University, who invited, Ranganathan to Delhi and gave him all facilities to devote himself to serious research. The eight years from 1947 to 1955 that he stayed at Delhi University were productive. Team research became possible, and a quarterly journal, Abgila, became the instrument to publish the research findings.

After a lapse of eleven years the third edition of Colon Classification appeared in 1950 without any major modifications. There were, however, a few changes in terminology. The findings of research at Delhi culminated in a dynamic theory of library classification. A major finding was that in any subject there could be only five ingredients. This gave rise to the Postulate of Five Fundamental Categories, which were stated as *Personality, Matter, Energy, Space and Time* (PMEST). The postulate further stated that these five fundamental categories; fall in the sequence of P M E S T. Each fundamental category was assigned an indicator digit as shown below:

Fundamental Category	Indicator Digit ‘
Personality	, (Comma)
Matter	; (Semi-colon)
Energy	: (Colon)
Space	. (Dot)
Time	. (Dot)

The indicator digit for time was later changed to a single inverted comma (‘). The ordinal value of the connecting symbols was also determined. These findings were included in the fourth edition of Colon Classification and the second edition of Prolegomena to Library Classification, published in 1957. The fifth edition appeared in the year 1957. The fifth edition had made several changes both in the rules and also in the schedules. Many Greek letters were introduced in the fourth edition to expand the base of the main classes. These were found to be irritants and were replaced in the sixth edition by empty and emptying digits. Some changes were also effected in a few main classes. In addition, the second level of space and time facets was introduced. Meanwhile, the sixth edition of Colon Classification, was published in 1960. At about this time, Ranganathan had shifted to Bangalore.

A new centre, *Documentation Research and Training Centre* (DRTC), was established by the Indian Statistical Institute with Ranganathan as its honourary professor. At DRTC, Ranganathan was assisted by a team of researchers. The DRTC brought out they several special schedules of classification based on the new research findings. In 1963, a reprint of the sixth edition was published with a few corrections and amendments. At that time an announcement was made that the seventh edition would be, brought out incorporating all the new findings. Unfortunately, Ranganathan passed away in 1972 and the work was delayed. The long awaited seventh edition of Colon Classification with substantial changes from the earlier editions appeared in 1987, without an Index.

Basic Principles in Colon Classification

The CC, like other schemes of classification, starts with a set of main classes which form the first order array of classes. Each main class is divided into facets. All facets are regarded as manifestations of five fundamental categories.

The terms are:

* Main classes,
* Array,
* Facet, and
* Fundamental categories.

Main Classes

The main classes in CC are like disciplines in DDC and theoretical subjects in UDC. They are the traditional subjects, which you are well acquainted with, like mathematics, physics, history, political science and soon. The number of main classes in CC is greater than those in DDC and UDC.

Array

The dictionary meaning of array is 'a systematic arrangement of numbers or symbols in an orderly manner.' In CC also, it means the same as its dictionary meaning. The arrangement, however, is referred to as the preferred sequence. The numbers, in a classification refer to a division of a subject on the basis –of a, single characteristic. For example, in medicine, the organs of the human body form the array of organs.

Facet

A facet is a characteristic by which 'a class is divided/ grouped, Each main class is divided into facets to signify the whole series of arrays based on, a set of related characteristics of division. In the main class Literature, all enumerated languages, after which the national literatures are known, constitute in DDC,, the language facet of that class. In the same class, all literary forms constitute another facet. It may also be stated here that within a facet an individual member is called a focus. Hindi literature, for example, is a focus in the language facet of the class Literature.

Fundamental Categories

To understand the basic principles of CC you have to first understand some of the rules framed by Ranganathan. He calls them postulates. One postulate states that there are five fundamental categories (FC), *viz.*, personality [P], matter [M], energy [E], space [S], and time [T], PMEST for short. A postulate is a presumption or assumption, which is never put to test. It is a basis for argument and hence one is not supposed to question the veracity of the assumption. That is the meaning of a postulate. According to Ranganathan, in any given subject, there may be a maximum of five fundamental categories. There can be less, but in no case more than five. They also come in the order of PMEST according to their decreasing concreteness. If you are able to identify the fundamental categories irk a given subject, you can classify any subject. Hence, you must have a clear perception of each of the five fundamental categories. As suggested, take up the five fundamental categories one by one for discussion in the reverse order.

Time and Space

These two have the usual meaning known to you. A century, a decade, a year, a month, a day, an hour are all indicators of time. If the subject is stated as Economic conditions of India in the 19th century, you can identify the time element in it. In some subjects, it may not be stated explicitly, *e.g.*, Economic conditions during the reign of Akbar. In this example, the fundamental category time is concealed, but still identifiable.

In the same way, it is fairly simple to locate the space element in a subject. In the title *Economic conditions of India in the 19th century*, you can find the space facet, *i.e.* India. Space is indicated by terms like continent, country, city, village, etc. All these come under the facet space.

Energy

The next fundamental category is energy. Energy refers to some type of action. In the subject medicine, diagnosis or treatment falls under the facet energy. It shows action. In agriculture, ploughing is energy, in education teaching is energy, and in sociology relief work is energy,and so on.

Matter

There is a major change in the seventh edition of CC in the case of the fundamental category matter. Up to the sixth edition, Matter was present only in a few main classes. There is a complete reversal in the seventh edition. In certain cases, what was considered energy now forms part of the matter facet. Besides, the fundamental category matter has undergone some other changes. It is distinguished as Matter Property [MP], Matter Material [MMt] and Matter Method [MM].

It is only matter property, which has almost replaced the fundamental category energy. To explain matter with a concrete example, in the class medicine, anatomy, physiology and diseases are viewed as manifestations of matter property. Similarly, in the main class agriculture, soil, manure, propagation, etc. are treated as manifestations of matter property. In the main class fine arts, under the class drawing, pencil drawing, ink drawing, and cartoon drawing are considered as a manifestation of matter method. In technology, product, and in biology substance are manifestation of matter material. Hence, in a given subject, it is not difficult to recognise the fundamental categories of time, space, energy and matter.

Personality

The fundamental category personality has evaded definition. Ranganathan found a way out to recognise personality by the method of residue, *i.e.*, when it cannot be any other fundamental category it is assigned to personality. However, experience in the design of depth schedules suggests that it is possible to identify a core concept in compound subjects going with a basic subject, such as, 'Human Body' in Medicine. Such a care concept is deemed to be a manifestation of 'Personality'.

Postulates of Basic Facet

Once you determine the different fundamental categories, they are to be attached to. a basic class in the order of P M E S T. A basic facet in the traditional meaning stands for a 16; class, *e.g.*, philosophy, psychology, chemistry, literature, history, etc. In CC, originally there were nearly 30 such main classes. This number rose to 47 in the sixth edition. You can find that many of the main classes listed in the seventh edition are not exactly basic subjects as you know them. If you take, for example, B Mathematics, the different subjects listed under it appear more like its extensions. Similarly properties of matter, sound, heat, electricity, magnetism etc., under C Physics are only adjuncts to the main class C. But in classifying, it makes a difference. In C6 Electricity, 6 is not a fundamental category, but is part of the basic class, and hence a separate facet formula had to be given for it.

Planes of Work

According to Ranganathan, there are three planes of work through which a scheme of library classification passes. The three planes are Idea plane, Herbal plane and Notational plane. A scheme of library classification has to first enumerate the Universe of Subjects, state their inter-relations and fix their order. This is done in the idea plane. The findings of the idea plane are to be represented in terms. This is -the verbal plane of work. Lastly, these terms are transformed into a notation. This last plane of work is known as the notational plane. There are thus three planes of work: idea, verbal and notational.

Rounds and Levels

Having identified five fundamental categories, it was found that some of them manifest themselves more than once in a subject, for example personality, matter and energy. This phenomenon was handled by the introduction of the postulates of rounds and levels. Take, far instance, a subject like Treatment of brain tumour by radium therapy. In this, we have the fundamental, categories brain FET tumour [A], treatment [ER], and radium therapy [El. 11 (E), thus, repeats itself. Such repetition of any of to three (R Ṁ and E) fundamental categories is called round of fundamental category. These rounds are indicated as [1PI], [2PI], [113], [2E],· [1Mi], [2M1] and so on.

Let us take another example: King Lear by Shakespeare. First you must find what fundamental categories are present in this subject. The basic class is, of course; literature. The isolates are, language, form of literature, author and his work. All these isolates, I under the fundamental category personality. They, therefore, belong to the personality facet. These occurrences are referred to as levels of personality and they all fall in the first round. They are therefore indicated as [1P1], [1P2], [1P3], [1P4]. They are read as first level; first round, second level; first round, third level; and first round, fourth level.

Postulates of Facet Sequence

We have been discussing so far five fundamental categories, their rounds and levels. The next question that arises is in what order are these to be arranged. This has been answered by Ranganathan by his postulates of facet sequence. He has given five postulates followed by some principles going with them.

Therefore, only the postulates are repeated here.

* *Postulate of first facet*: In any compound subject, the first facet should be the basic facet. It simply means that there should be a basic class or main class even if it is not stated explicitly in the title of the document. For example, if we take treatment of cancer as our subject, the badic facet is not stated. But, by implication, the basic facet in this case is medicine.
* *Postulate of concreteness*: The five fundamental categories appear in the sequence of PMEST only. This means they appear in the order of their decreasing concreteness. To explain this with an example, let us take a subject like Prevention of fungus diseases in oranges in Nagpur. Here, apart from supplying the basic facet we have to find out other fundamental categories and arrange them in the sequence of PMEST. Obviously, agriculture is the basic facet and the other fundamental categories are oranges [P], prevention [E], fungus diseases [M], and Nagpur [S]. To put them in order, according to the postulate, it will be

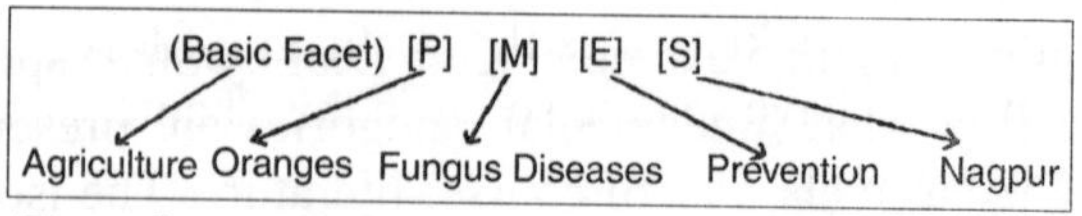

* *Postulate of facet sequence within a round*: In a compound subject, if any P, M and E occur in any

round, they should be arranged in the order of P, M, E. For example, Preparation of soil for growing grapes has agriculture as the personality facet. As per the postulate, the sequence of the facet will be:

- Agriculture (BF),
- Grapes [P],
- Soil [M], and
- Preparation [E].

* *Postulate of facet sequence within the last round*: The fourth postulate states that in the last round of facets of a compound subject, in which each of the fundamental categories other than energy may occur, and occur only once, the sequence of facets should be P, M, S and T. Take, for instance, a little like: A study of the emotions of adults in 20th century USA. Here the basic facet is psychology and the other facets are emotions (matter), adults (personality), 20th century (time) and USA (space). In this, there is no manifestation of energy. Hence, as stated in the postulate, the sequence should be:
  - Psychology (BF),
  - Adults [P],
  - Emotions [M],
  - USA [S],
  - 20th century [T].
* *Postulate of level cluster*: The last postulate for the sequence of facets states that different levels of the same fundamental category within a round should be kept together. Let us take an example like Succession rights of minors in Hindu law. In this, the facets, succession, minor and Hindu law are all manifestations of personality. When arranged, they will be Law (B F), Hindu law [1P1], Minor [1P2], and succession [1P3].

This postulate is known as the postulate of level cluster.

Whatever we have studied so far in this chapter can be put in a nutshell as follows:

* Because of facetisation, CC differs tan other schemes to a very great extent.

* Each successive edition of CC displayed improve-ment in analysis over the previous edition.
* The basic principles worked out in CC axe
* Three planes of work.
* Five fundamental categories.
* Rounds and levels.
* Facet sequence.

Notation

Ranganathan, in his theory of library classification, introduced the concept of three planes of work, which you are already familiar with. Of these, the notational plane is beset with several difficulties. It is in this sphere that much research has taken place and several innovations have been made. You already know the meaning of notation, its function and its kinds. As suggested, now turn our attention to the notation in CC.

Mixed Notation—Indicator Digits

CC uses a mixed notation. It consists of

* Indo-Arabic numerals, 1-9
* Roman alphabet -both capitals and lower case, A to Z and a to z.
* Parentheses (}
* Indicator digits

Table. 5.1 The Indicator Digits in the 7th Edition of CC

Digit/Symbol	Name of the Indicator Digit	Role of the Indicator Digit
*	Astenrisk	Indicates Agglomeration and Interpolation
←	Backward Arrow	Indicates backward range
"	Double Inverted Comma	Indicates Common Isolates
("The above three indicator digits have anteriorising value).		
&	Ampersand	Indicates phase relation
'	Single inverted Comma	Indicates phase relation

Table Contd..

.	Dot	Indicates Space Facet
:	Colon	Indicates Energy Facet
;	Semi-colon	Indicates Matter Facet
,	Comma	Indicates Personlity Facet
-	Hyphen	Indicates Specator of kind 1
=	Equal Sign	Indicates Speciator of Kind 2
+	Plus Sign	and Addition
→	Forward Arrow	Indicates Forward range

Note: For the arrangement of the class numbers, all the notations and digits used in the scheme have given values, and, in the ascending sequence, they stand in the following order

`) and ‵.;: - = ® a to z 01 to 9A to Z (Asterisk),+ (Plus),″ (Double Inverted Comma) and ←7- (backward arrow) have anteriorising value.`

Empty Digit

To increase the capacity of an array, CC has introduced what is called an empty digit. An empty digit has no semantic value, but it retains the ordinal value. Let us see the meaning of empty digit with the help of an example. If you are using the Indo-Arabic numerals, you can use a maximum of nine numerals. If a subject and to be divided, we can divide it only up to nine places and the tenth and subsequent divisions cannot be accommodated. To overcome this difficulty, CC uses numerals 1 to 8 only and 9 is left as an empty digit. It has no value by itself, but regains its full value when it is used in combination as 91, 92, 93... 98 or 991, 992, 993... 998 and so on. This method has given tremendous potential to increase arrays in any given facet. The same principle has been used while using a to z, or A to Z. In lower case letters, z is made an empty digit, and in capital letters, T, V and X are postulated as empty-emptying digits and Z as empty digit. Also, CC uses a number of devices for increasing hospitality and facilitating synthesis.

Devices

We have seen that new subjects always crop up and a classification scheme should be able to find appropriate places for such new subjects within its framework. Ranganathan provided a number of devices for this purpose. The purpose of such a device is to form a new isolate or to sharpen an existing isolate in an array. This method has considerably reduced the size of the scheme.

The four major devices used in CC are:

* Chronological device
* Geographical device
* Subject device
* Alphabetical device

Chronological Device

The purpose of this device is to sharpen a facet number. It can sharpen. an isolate or form a new isolate. This is done by employing a chronological number from the schedule of time isolates. All numbers for authors in the class Literature are derived through this device. It is impracticable to enumerate all authors. The chronological device has, however, taken care of such a contingency. To give an example, the number for Rabindranath Tagore is 0, 157,1M61. Here,-M61'stands for 1861, the year of birth of Rabindranath Tagore. This device has been used in several main classes like library science, mathematics, medicine, fine arts, psychology, education, economics, etc. This device can be used wherever warranted. The basic class of systems is derived through the chronological device.

Geographical Device

The purpose of all these devices, as stated earlier, 2 to form or to sharpen an isolate number in a schedule. Employing a geographical number from the schedule of space isolates is another mechanism of doing this. It has been used in library science, fine arts, religion, linguistics, history and in several other classes. The formation of an isolate using this device is as follows:

- 152 = d4437 means Rajasthani Hindi, where
  - 152 is Hindi
  - = is the connecting symbol
  - d is the symbol for dialect
  - 4437 is Rajasthan from the schedule of space isolates.
- Another example of the geographical device:

- Early Egyptian religion for which the number is Q,8677.
- Here, Q,8 is other religion, and
- 677 is Egypt from the schedule of space isolates.

Subject Device

Subject device is used to form or sharpen a facet by adding to it another class number from elsewhere in the scheme. This device has been used in several train classes. The part of the number derived by the subject device should be enclosed in parenthesis. For example, Medical college library is 2, J3 (L). In the example, in library science, 2,J3 represents college libraries to which is added (L) from the main class L Medicine to derive medical college library by subject device. Let us take another example of subject device. Hindu Law is Z,(Q,2) where Z is law and (Q,2) is Hindu religion from the main class Q Religion.

Alphabetical Device

Alphabetical device is also used to form or sharpen an isolate number. The device is used taking the first or the first two or three letters of the names of persons, or objects, or products widely accepted as such. The device can be used wherever warranted. The following are some examples where the device is used:

0, 157, 3M61,G	Gora, a novel by Rabindranath Tagore Here, G stands for Gora
0,157,3M61,H+W	Home and the World, a novel by Tagore. Here, the initial letters of the two words in the title are connected, using the plus sign (+). (H for Home and W for World)
D93CM	Maruti motor car. D93C is for motor cars and M stands for Maruti
J,381B	Basmati rice, where J,381 is rice' and B is for Basmati.

Phase Relations

Nowadays we come across several interdisciplinary subjects. This is the result of interaction between two or more subjects. For this purpose, CC has provided a device called Phase Relation. A phase relation may occur between two or more main classes; it may also occur within one and the same facet of a main class, or within one and the same array isolates. These three types are called inter-subject, intra-facet and intra-array phase relations respectively.

Besides, there are six kinds of phase relations indicated in CC. These six kinds are:

* General relation phase.
* Bias phase.
* Comparison phase.
* Difference phase.
* Tool phase:
* Influencing phase

The connecting symbol for a phase relation is composed of an ampersand and a relation indicator as shown in table 5.2:

Schedule of digits (CC 7 edition)

Kind of Phase Relation	Inter-subject	Infra-facet	Intra-array
General	a	j	t
Bias	b	k	u
Comparison	c	m	v
Difference	d	n	w
Tool	e	p	x
Influencing	G		

Following are a few examples to show the use of different kinds of phase relations in CC:

* A general study of special and university libraries - Type: intra-facet, Kind: general, No.2,14&jK
* Psychology for teachers - Type: Inter-subject, Kind: Nat, No.S&bT
* Comparison of Jainism and Buddhism - Type: intra-facet, Kind: comparison, No.61,3&m4
* Difference between undergraduate and postgraduate education Type: intra-array, Kidd: difference, No.T,181&w2
* Statistical analysis in library management - Type: inter-subject, Kind: tool, Nio.2:8&-ST

* Influence of music on literature - Type: inter-subject, Kind: influencing, No.O&gNR.

Systems and Specials

Up to the sixth edition of CC, systems and specials were enumerated along with the concerned main classes. In the seventh edition, they have been listed in the schedule of basic subjects. However, they have been separately defined.

Systems

The term system basic subjects denote a division of a main class expounded after a school of thought. A school of thought is a group, or succession of persons devoted to some cause or philosophy. The class number for a system is derived by the chronological device.

Some examples of system facets are:

* *B6-M8*: Hyperbolic geometry, where B6 is geometry and M8 means the 1880s. The number stands for a system of geometry expounded in the 1880s.
* *L-B*: Ayarveda. B is 999 to 1000 BC - a system of medicine that came into being prior to 1000 BC
* *S-N14*: Individualistic psychology. It means a school of psychology that came into being in 1914.
* *X-NI Communism*: The number stands for a system of economics that came into being in the 1910s.

Specials

The term special basic subjects denote a division of a main class in which the subject of study is restricted in some special manner. The class number of specials is derived by enumeration. Some of the examples of special basic subjects are:

Merits and Demerits of Colon Classification

Due to a sound theory and the provision of a hospitable notation, CC is capable of giving a unique number for almost every subject. The systematic order and the degree of detail due to analysis and synthesis are two great virtues of CC.

As a result, it has achieved two objectives:

1. Provision of a helpful order in each class, and

2. Facility in locating a given topic whether it is simple, compound or complex. It is claimed that CC can be effectively used in a computer-aided document finding system.

The major drawback of CC is that there exists no machinery to keep up the revision work as in the case of DDC and UDC. The guidance provided in the recently published seventh edition is not enough and lacks clarity at places. It calls for a manual with numerous examples to explain the application of various rules. It is far from simple, the virtue most cherished by the users.

6

Absolute Syntax and Structure of an Indexing and Switching Language

Switching from one information system to another would be convenient if the information languages – that is, the method of representation of subjects and other information content of discourse used in the systems are syntactically consistent, compatible with each other, and inter-convertible at a reasonable cost. In this connection, the development of an intermediate language through which the switching from one information language to another is an important consideration. An idea is a pattern, a gestalt, a form, a structure that one perceives. A subject of a discourse of an information source or of a user's query is a combination of ideas, that is, of structures; therefore, the structure of a subject representation that is, of a subject surrogate has a bearing on the user's 'perception' of the subject represented.

Some characteristic features of an information structure helpful to users, the problems of transformation of information structures, the linear structuring of subject surrogates, and some criteria for the choice of a 'standard format' or framework or model for such structuring are considered. Absolute syntax is defined as the sequence of the component ideas in a subject helpful and acceptable to a majority of users. The helpfulness of structuring of subject parallel to the absolute syntax is indicated, together with supporting information based on postulations and research on deep structure of languages, biocybernetics, syntax of knowledge, common structure in preserving messages in a set of transformations, etc. The generalised facet structure of subject representation obtained on the basis of the general theory of classification and the guiding principles for helpful sequence formulated thereof is found to be helpful and acceptable to a large number of users of information systems, and therefore, conjectured to parallel the absolute syntax. Work done in this regard and in the development of specific schemes for classification and for the fornulation of subject headings in different languages within the general framework is mentioned.

TERMINOLOGY

The following are the operational definitions of some of the technical terms used in this paper:

* *Idea*: An idea is a product of thinking, imagining, etc., got by the intellect, by integrating with the aid of logic, a selection from the apperception mass, and/or what is directly apprehended by intuition, and deposited in memory. Alternative term: Concept.
* *Entity*: An entity is any existent, concrete or conceptual that is, a thing or an idea.
* *Discourse*: A discourse is an expression of ideas, especially systematic or orderly expression in speech or writing.
* *Subject*: A subject is an organized or systematized account of a body of ideas, whose extension and intension are likely to fall coherently and comfortably within the intellectual competence and the field of inevitable specialization of a normal person.
* *Example*: A systematized account of "Conduction of heat" is a subject; and so may be deemed a systematized account of "Thermo-dynamics", and of the ideas in "Physics". But, not all the discourses embodied in the *McGraw-Hill Encyclopedia of Science and Technology*, taken as a whole can be deemed to be a subject; for, the totality of the subjects embodied therein cannot form an inevitable and convenient field of specialization of a normal person.

STRUCTURE AND PATTERN

The kind of pattern one perceives in a representation of an entity lies in the perceived structure. For instance, in a pictorial representation, the idea of "triangle" can be conveyed by 300 dots, or 30 dots, or 3 dots, as shown in fig. 6.1.

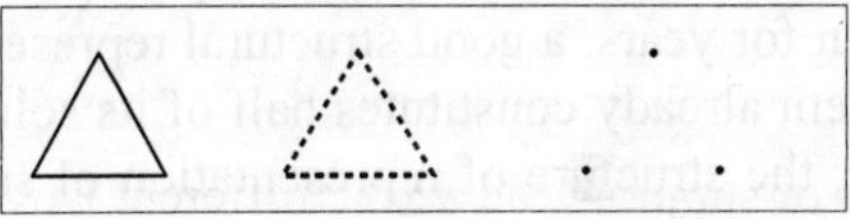

Fig. 6.1

Of these three representations, the last mentioned is deemed to be the most efficient, because it uses the fewest number of elements to convey the same amount of information as those using more number of elements. This indicates the important role of structure of a representation in relation to the perception of its "meaning". Structure is the way in which the components of an entity are put together. Researcher defines the concept of structure as "effective patterns of relationships in any situation". In a general sense, structure denotes logical form. The content of a logical form may be physical, musical, psychological, temporal, or in some other way non-physical. Anything that has structure has parts, properties or aspects, which are in some manner related to each other.

Thus, in every structure one can distinguish the relations and the items which are related. The items may be qualities, values, or any conceptually distinguishable feature called elements of the structure. An idea is a pattern, a structure, a gestalt, a form, a kind of picture that one perceives. A subject is constituted out of a combination of ideas that is, a combination of patterns. In understanding a complex structure, the human intellect finds it helpful to identify the substructures and categorize them. Such pattern recognition, pattern formulation, and categorization have been found to be involved in the human learning process and information handling.

Library activities point out that the representation of knowledge-structures is an important problem in cognitive psychology:

* "what are the primitive symbols or concepts, how are they related, how are they to be concatenated and

constructed into larger knowledgestructures, and how is this 'information file' to be accessed, searched and utilized. The choice of a representation is central, since how one handles this issue causes widespread effects throughout the remainder of his theoretical efforts. As computer scientists working on problem solving have known for years, a good structural representation of the problem already constitutes half of its sclution".

Therefore, the structure of representation of subject that is, surrogate of subject has a crucial role in conveying information about the subject denoted.

REPRESENTATION OF SUBJECT

An information system handles discourses. A discourse may be verbal as expressed in a query of a user of an information system. It may be in a recorded form as in a conventional document such as, a book, an article in a periodical, and a technical report or on magnetic tape, film, etc., all of which may form information sources. Finding information and/or documents containing information co-extensively matching the subject of a user's query may depend, in a good measure, on the capacity of the system to identify and specify coextensively the subjects of discourses that is, subjects embodied in queries and those embodied in information sources.

The representation of subjects expounded in discourses for example, subject headings, class numbers, data structures, algorithms or other kinds or surrogates may provide the first point of entry into an information retrieval system. An information system of this sort may form a node or component of a hierarchy of increasingly larger network of local, national, regional and global information systems. To facilitate the integration and collaborative functioning of the information systems developed in different contexts, it would be helpful if the "languages" used for representation of subjects in the different systems are syntactically consistent, compatible with each other, and inter-convertible at a reasonable cost. Thus, the representation of subject of discourses in the form of surrogates is central to the designing of information files for information storage and retrieval purposes.

PROBLEMS IN THE EFFICIENT USE OF THE LANGUAGE OF SURROGATE

The following are some of the factors which raise problems for the user of an information system in the efficient use of the language of the surrogate system. For various reasons, it may be difficult for the user to perceive precisely and express coextensively the subject of his interest at the moment. Therefore, the total semantic domain represented by the expression of the subject of his query may not be coextensive with the semantic domain of the subject of his interest as perceived by him.

The information scientist's perception of the semantic domain of the subject of interest of the user derived on the basis of the latter's expression of his interest at the moment, may not be coextensive with what the user purported to convey. A user may not and, perhaps, cannot be concentrating attention or work on at one and the same time on all the component ideas potentially falling in the subject of his interest, even if it be a narrow one. The recall value at the moment that is, the likelihood of being retained and recalled from memory for this component idea would be relatively greater than that for the other component ideas in the subject of his interest.

Therefore, he is more likely to bring up the name of this component idea in searching for information on the subject of his interest at the moment. The information scientists' knowledge and understanding of the subject of interest to the user may be inadequate.

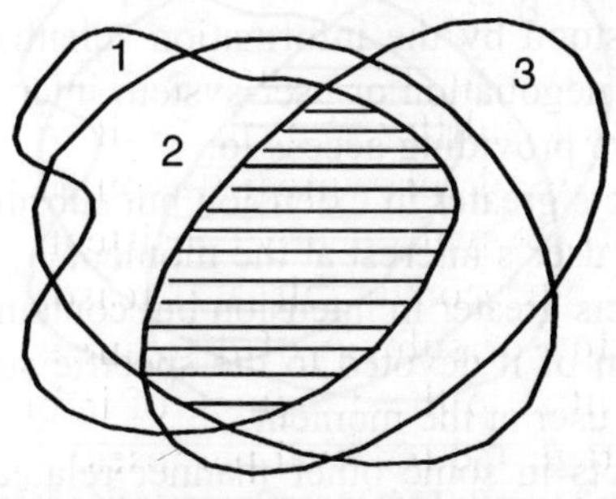

Fig. 6.2 Illustrates the Non-congruence of the Different Semantic Domains.

For various reasons, it would be difficult for the information scientist to perceive precisely and express coextensively the semantic domain of the subjects embodied in information sources. Therefore, the surrogate system prepared by him for representing the semantic domain of subjects embodied in information sources may not be coextensive with the semantic domain of the subject(s) purported to be described by the author of the work.

* User's perception of the semantic domain of his subject interest-at-the moment
* Actual semantic domain of the subject as expressed by user
* Librarian/Information Scientist's perception of the semantic domain of user's subject interest-at-the-moment

MINIMIZING THE CONSTRAINTS

Helpful Features of an Information System

Some of the features of an information system that may help in minimizing some of the constraints and difficulties are as follows:

* Providing access to information on the subject of interest to the user by the name of the component idea(s) he may bring up in using the surrogate system.
* Providing facility for browsing and selection of information to compensate for the dissimilarity and non-coextensiveness between the subject perceived and expressed by the user and the at perceived and understood by the information scientist at the time of query negotiation or user-system interfacing. This may involve providing access to:
* Subjects greater in extension but subsuming the subject of the user's interest at the moment.
* Subjects greater in intension but containing a substantial portion of it devoted to the specific subject of interest to the user at the moment.
* Subjects in some other manner related to the specific subject of interest to the user at the moment.

Intersystem Connection and Compatibility

In order to facilitate switching over or movement from one information system to another with the longrange goal of establishing system interconnection on a global scale, there are at least two approaches.

These are:

* To use the same or very nearly the same information storage and retrieval language in all the information systems; and
* To use an intermediate language or switching language through or by which one moves from one information system to another.

FRAMEWORK FOR REPRESENTATION

Problems of Transformation

The second one is the more practicable at present stage in the development of information systems throughout the world. However, in either of the methods, an important consideration relates to the framework elements, relations, and structure to be used for the analysis and representation of subjects of discourses that is, subjects embodied in information sources and in users' queries. This stage mentions some of the suggestions about a common knowledge structure and framework for representation of subjects and discusses one such framework. There are various methods of representing subjects, such as, class numbers, subject headings or strings of words, multi-dimensional arrays, tree-structures, etc.

These arise from the process of analysis of subjects of discourses into constituent elements; recognition of the relevant relations among the elements as they obtain in the context of the subject concerned; and assembling the elements in a preferred pattern so as to represent as coextensively as possible the subjects. Representation of subject by a subject heading or a class number is equivalent to transforming the n-dimensional configuration of the subject into a linear configuration. An arrangement of the component elements in each subject falling in a subject-field among themselves, in a sequence helpful to a majority of users requires keeping invariant every Immediate-Neighbourhood relation among all the subjects while transforming or mapping the n-dimensional configuration of subjects on to a line.

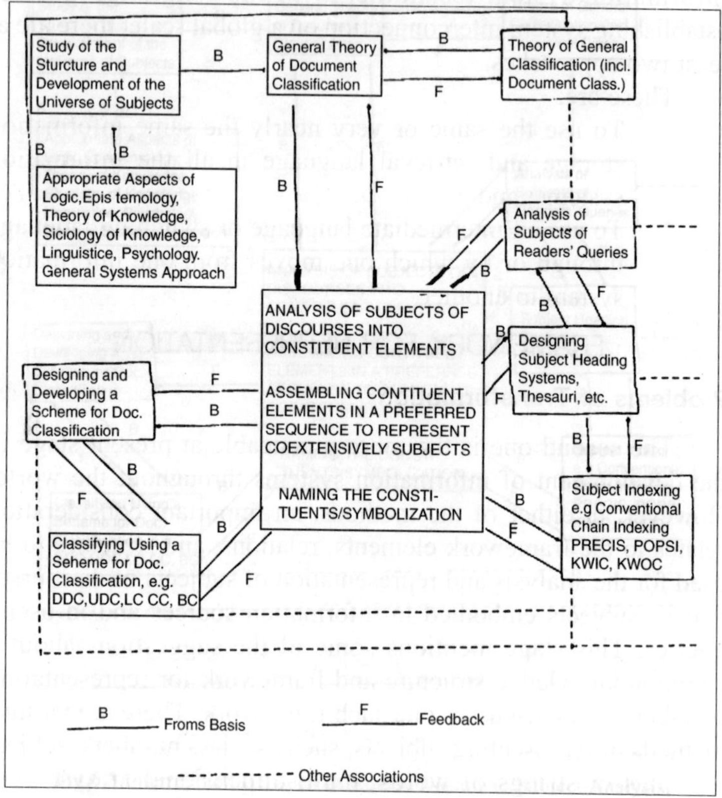

Fig.6.3 Interrelation Between Discourse Discourse/Subject Analysis, Classification, Subject Indexing, Subject Heading Work, Thesauri, etc.

The number of subjects falling even in one subject-field is quite large and continues to increase rapidly such that it is difficult to arrange them in a helpful sequence consistently without the aid of guiding principles. In the transformation, only one of the many Immediate Neighbourhood relations can be kept invariant. Determining which should this be, and which components should come respectively as remove 2, remove 3, etc., with respect to a reference component is a difficult decision. To depend, for this purpose, on the conjecture of different classificationists as to what is helpful to a majority of users may not yield a consistent pattern of arrangement of components of all subjects. But, such a consistency in pattern is helpful and necessary to the users, as well as the designers of the information system.

Criteria for Choice of Frame Work

The problem of transfer and trans- formation of knowledge-structures, are as follows.

* The long-term task is not merely to analyse the problems but to design methodological instruments for carrying out practical researches into problems of communication. These may be treated as problems of mapping. Given an original territory of factual phenomena how does this territory become mapped in the brain of the investigator? How does this map become transformed into a verbal or symbolic expression a linguistic map? How is this map transformed again into a language adopted to the needs of the ultimate recipient, the learner? Finally, how is this third map introjected into the learner's brain to form a pattern of knowledge? If we can establish a cartography for these maps, we can formulate "projective equations" leading from one map to the next. Each map will be a pattern of definable variables under appropriate controls and observing changes in the next map, the equations can be solved and laws of projection may be discovered.

Anderson and Bower have listed the following considerations deemed helpful in the choice of a "standard format" for representing information:

* The representation should be capable of expressing any conception which a human can formulate or understand.
* The representation should allow for relatively efficient search for and retrieval of information. That is, specific information should remain relatively accessible even when the data-files grow to encyclopedic proportions.
* The representation should saliently exhibit the substantive information extracted from a given input.

It should not be influenced by the peculiarities of the particular natural language in which that information was communicated. This hope for language-invariance amounts to a wish for a universal interlingua in which any conception in any language could be expressed, but for which the format would not be specific to a particular language...

* For reasons of parsimony, the representation should involve a minimum of formal categories. That is, it should make a minimum of formal distinctions at the outset; more complex distinctions would be built up by the construction rules for concatenating primitive ideas.
* The representation must allow for easy expression of concatenation operations, by which "duplex ideas" can be constructed out of "simple ideas". This means, for example, that the representation should allow easy expression of conceptual hierarchies, or multiply embedded predications, or allow one to predicate new information on any old information- structure".

ABSOLUTE SYNTAX

A Postulate

At the International Conference on Scientific Information, S. R. Ranganathan suggested that.

* To help in the establishment of a fairly longlived helpful scheme for classification, a team of epistemologists, psychologists, linguists, reference librarians, classificationists and statisticians should investigate the way in which the human mind thinks that is, the Syntax of Facets that will give the greatest satisfaction to the greatest number of readers".

In 1966, in his valedictory address to the Maryland Symposium on Relational Factors in Classification, Ranganathan postulated such a syntax of facets and named it as Absolute Syntax. Absolute syntax in the sequence in which the component ideas of subjects falling in a subject-field arrange themselves in the minds of a majority of normal intellectuals, for instance when they think and communicate about the subject. Ideas are largely products of intellection. Intellectual activity is known to be controlled by brain. There is considerable similarity in the structure and, therefore, in the functioning of the brain in a majority of normal human beings.

Thus, a majority of normal human beings have more or less a similar mode of thinking and learning that is, in forming ideas and in combining them to build knowledge-structures. It is further stated that biologically man has not changed to any appreciable extent since the emergence of Homo sapiens; for, the structure of the genetic material has not appreciably changed since then that is, for some 500,000 years although we have changed culturally. Therefore, the probability of a sudden change that is, a mutation in the mode of thinking and learning of a majority of normal persons in the immediate future is quite low.

Hence, if the syntax of the representation of the component ideas of subjects is made to conform to, or parallel to, the Absolute Syntax, then the pattern of linking of the component ideas that is, the resulting knowledge structure is likely to be:

* Helpful to majority of normal intellectuals;
* Consistent in pattern in subjects falling in different subject-fields;
* Relatively more stable and continue to be helpful to a majority of normal intellectuals so long as there is no mutation in their mode of thinking;
* Free from the aberrations due to variations in linguistic syntax from the use of the verbal plane in naming subjects;
* Capable of representing and indication of subjects co-extensively with a minimum number of variety of component elements;
* Helpful in recognizing the less explored and unexplored regions in the universe of ideas; and
* Helpful in probing deeper into the pattern of human thinking and modes of combination of ideas.

Analogy from Search for Linguistic Universals

It was pointed out that the formulation of a generic framework for structuring subjects has a parallel in the search for universal linguistic forms such as that expounded, and the generative grammarians. Birnbaum suggests a multi-layered syntactic structure between the deepest of the deep structures and the surface structure. As a result of the general trend towards a generative semantic framework, a new slightly modified model of generative grammar seems now to be taking shape.

This model can be thought of as comprising three independent components:

* A Semantic Component which will define the relations obtaining between semantic units or, rather hierarchically ordered clusters of semantic features such as:
  - (Thing),
  - (Concrete),
  - (Countable),
  - (Animate),
  - (Human),
  - (Personal),
  - (Male),
  - (Adult);
  - (Predication),
  - (Agent),
  - (Definite),
  - (Action),
  - (Patient – Oriented),
  - (Time-Determined),
  - (Aspect – Determined), etc.,
* A Transformational Component which will convert the semantic deep structure representations into surface structure representations.
* A Phonological Component.

Fillmore points out that:

* "There may also be some psychological reasons that argue for the use of predication as a data-base language in a model of memory... Perhaps 'thinking' represents operations at the level of the semantic base structure, before it has been transformed into actual sentences through the application of syntactic rules".

The case categories suggested the following:

* "*Agentive* (A), the case of the typically animate perceived instigator of the action identified by the verb.
* *Instrumental* (I), the case of the inanimate force or object causally involved in the action or state identified by the verb.
* *Dative* (D), the case of the animate being affected by the state or action identified by the verb.
* *Factitive* (F), the case of the object or being resulting from the action or state identified by the verb, or understood as a part of the meaning of the verb.
* *Locative* (L), the case which identifies the location of spatial orientation of the state or action identified by the verb.
* *Objective* (O), the semantically most neutral case, the case of anything representable by a noun whose role in the action or state identified by the verb is identified by the semantic interpretation of the verb itself.."

Vleduts and Stokolova also propose structures – standard phrases at different levels for subject - representation in different disciplines. Leibniz's ideal language and the Whorfian hypothesis that "Every language contains terms that have come to attain cosmic scope of reference that crystallize in themselves the postulations of an unformulated philosophy.. such are our words 'reality, substance, matter' and.. 'space. time, past, present, future", are worth noting here.

Biocybernetic View

In his book on Systems Philosophy, Ervin Lazlo mentions about "basic modes of thinking".

> "..It is also becoming evident that all men, regardless of the culture they happen to belong to, have basically similar nervous systems, are equipped with analogous sense receptors, command like patterns of response, and use patterns of thought which obey very similar laws or regularities. In other words, there appear to be some "universal" traits underlying cultural cognitive relativities: Chomsky could locate "linguistic universals" and Kluckholn discovered a number of" universal categories of culture.

"Finding such universals is rendered difficult if not impossible, by arguing out of one's own culturally or individually relativistic categories. In that light, every other world-model becomes but a special case of one's own, and is forced into the latter's structural scheme. But, in using the neutral frame work of a cybernetic mode, one is no more arguing out of his own culturecategories than out of that of a thermostat. Conceptualizing the cognitive process with such categories, we can reach universal structures, for we are not dealing with particular contents. Regardless of whether a person conceives a sensory pattern as trees, meaning "standing peoples, in whom winged ones built their lodges and reared their families" or interprets the very same pattern as obstructions to be cut down and burnt; he is using a construct which endows his perceptual input with meaning. And the development of constructs and gestalts obeys some general regularities, already manifest in biological evolution and set forth in cultural development".

Lazlo further points out:

* Regardless of the genetically and empirically induced differences, however, basic modes of thinking characterize all human beings, and indeed all higher biological species. These are rooted in, and explained by, the fact that all such organisms are self-maintaining open systems using a specific mode of reproduction, and forming part of some similarly specific social structure. The mental capacities needed to maintain such systems in their environments are adaptive functions; they crystallize as cognition in the more evolved species, and culminate in man.

The most immediately pertinent to human cognition make up an ascending ordering of categories, universally human in principle but variously evolved in different real individuals.

These categories may be listed as follows:

* Gestalt (invariant patterns with established meanings to which the input patterns are assimilated);
* Rational constructs (theoretic entities postulated through abstract reasoning and connected to the input patterns

by means of some established rule of correspondence); and

* Aesthetic construct (non-discursive meanings discovered in the input and illuminating some part of the knower's "felt experience"). These are the types of constructs which represent the limits of human cognition, given the kind of perceptions, cognitive organizations and effective output channels at our disposal. I argue that many forms of human experience do not constitute disjunctive culture conditioned categories, but a set of universal structures which transcends individual and cultural differences and relativities, and accommodates as subclasses, the many varieties of cognitive patterns as environment mappings and constructions of natural cognitive systems on the specially human level of nature's hierarchy"

Syntax of Knowledge and Epistemics

Meredith suggests the existence of a "syntax of knowledge". The argument runs as follows:

* "At a multi-lingual conference with a community of disciplines, experience and thought, the translators have no difficulty in transforming, virtually instantaneously, the most elaborate syntactic forms of one language into the quite different forms of another whilst reserving the essential structure of information and conceptualization in the speech. Thus, there is a 'syntax of knowledge' which, even if not entirely independent of the particular languages, can and does, in practice, follow its own course alongside the syntactic sequence of language. It may serve to sharpen the difference if, provisionally, we think of the latter as governed by temporal relations (by the sequence of words in the sentence) and the 'syntax of knowledge' as primarily a spatial structure only shredded into temporal filaments in order to conform to the sequential character of speech.
* "This is a big step forward. Even though the syntax of language cannot be entirely divorced from the syntax of

knowledge, we can pragmatically separate them by treating the one as a temporal sequence and the other as a spatial pattern. But, it may be objected, what about the temporal character of knowledge itself? Our knowledge of history, our under- standing of sequential operations, of industrial processes, of astronomical events etc., all of which involve time. Two points may be noted here:

* Even though in a narrative the sequence of paragraphs normally follows the time-sequence of the events narrated, this correspondence scarcely holds at all within the limits of a single sentence. And what is called linguistic syntax is largely based on the analysis of the single sentence. 'The assassin shot the President at the end of his speech'. In the actual event, the speech came before the shot; in the sentence after it. Thus, 'epistemic time' and 'linguistic time' are partially independent.
* We speak a sentence sequentially, that is, at the beginning we have not yet spoken the end but what we are talking about even though it may be temporal event, is known to us throughout. 'Epistemic time' is in fact 'dead' time, the completed past history, fossilised, and hence not "time" at all in the linguistic sense. It has a discernible sequence but no flow. Our knowledge of it is a geometric knowledge of evidence spread out in space or held in memory".

Common Structure

Arturo Rosenbleuth postulates a "common structure" in preserving the message received through a set of transformations:

* "When a person hears a symphony, the messages sent by the orchestra reach the listener as air vibrations. These vibrations stimulate mechanically the receptors of the organ of corti, and these receptors set up nerve impulses along the fibres of the VIIIth nerve. It is clear that at this stage the physical events that are taking place are of an entirely different kind from those occurring in the instruments of the orchestra. Yet the message is

preserved because there are similarities in certain features of the two series of events sounds emitted by the orchestra and nerve impulses traveling over the auditory nerves. The existence of these similarities of relations is precisely what is called a common structure. The mental decoding, which is the perception of the symphony, again preserves the corresponding relations. A common structure thus implies the quantitative preservation of the relations that exist between the independent constituents of an event or message through a set of trans- formations".

Logic of Exposition and Linguistic Syntax

Rosenbleuth also comments on syntax of thought and linguistic syntax thus:

"As a further example of the fundamental difference between the mental events and the correlated neuro-physiological processes, let us consider the processes that would develop in my brain if I presented verbally a specific relatively complex, argument on three different occasions in Spanish, English, and French, respectively. Although the neurophysiological correlates corresponding to the logic of my exposition might be similar or identical in the three cases, clearly those corresponding to the selection of words and their syntactical organization, a very important aspect of the presentation of the argument would be absolutely dissimilar. If I should want to use dictionaries to translate from the language of the introspective data to that of the physical processes, I would need in this instance three different dictionaries, and more, if I were capable of using fluently other languages."

Concept and Conception

Suzanne Langer points out that the psychological context of our thoughts may be private and personal. Therefore, two persons talking about the same thing may perceive it in different ways. They are then said to have different conceptions. But, if they understand each other, then their respective conceptions embody the same concept. A concept is an abstracted form. Abstraction is the consideration of logical form apart from content.

GENERALIZED FACET STRUCTURE FOR SUBJECTS

Analysis into constituent ideas and structuring of several thousands of subjects in a variety of subject fields for the purpose of designing and developing of schemes for subject classification, preparation of feature headings and subject headings, and for indexing of subjects have helped in:

* Categorizing the constituent elements in a subject into three types: Facet, Modifier, and Relations.
* Sub-categorizing each of the three types of constituent elements into a few kinds.
* Developing a typology of Basic Subjects, the modes of formation of Basic Subjects, and the arrangement of Basic Subjects.
* Developing a typology of Modifiers for basic facet and for isolate facet in different subject-fields.
* Recognizing the relative strength of bond between the first context specifying element and other types of facets in subjects.
* Formulating principles for helpful sequence among
* Facet s of a subject
* Spectators to a facet
* Compound subjects falling in a particular subject-field
* Subjects falling in different subject-fields.
* Developing a Generalized Facet structure of subject, with specific models for different subject-fields.

The main developments are briefly outlined in a recent FID/CR report. Subject structuring obtained using the Generalized Facet Structure has been found to give a co-extensive representation of subjects and arrangement of subjects helpful to majority of users.

The chart in fig. 6.4 shows the interrelation between subject-structuring, designing a classification scheme, generation of subject indexes, etc. Depth classification schemes for over a hundred subject-fields have been designed and several hundreds of articles, technical reports etc., have been classified using these schemes in each subject-field. The structuring of subjects and the sequence in which the subjects get arranged have been found to be acceptable to a large number of users. In a small-scale experiment, subject-headings each with several components, structured in the manner, were presented to about a hundred persons for indication by them of the subject that each of them perceived in the structuring.

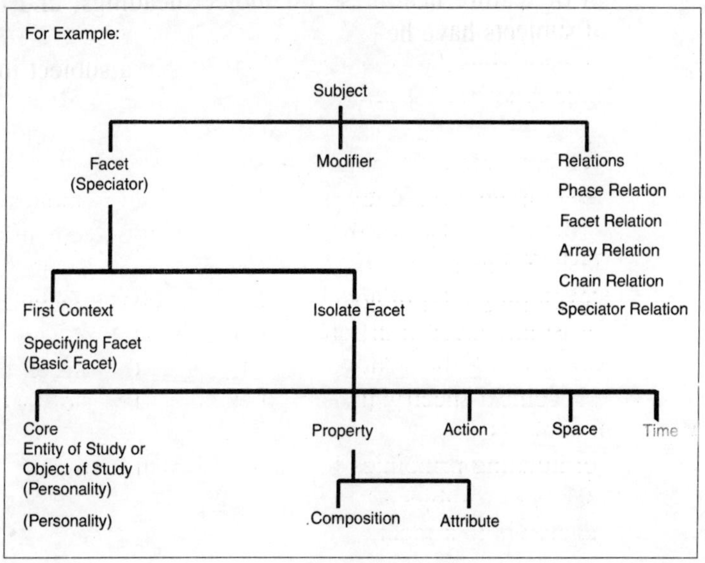

Fig. 6.4.

Although there were more than one way of representing each subject in the natural language, the subject perceived was the same in all the cases. That is, there was no homonym. Large scale experiments with other types of structuring of subjects has been planned. Translation of the subject heading terms into different natural languages did not give rise to any difficulty in interpreting the subject represented by persons knowing the language concerned. The facility of rearrangement of given terms into the preferred sequence and synthesis of class number given the descriptors, using computer, have been demonstrated.

These experiences indicate that the structuring of subjects conforming to the model developed according to the General

Theory of Classification:

* Helps to secure a facet syntax parallel to that of the absolute syntax;
* Gives a "standard format" for representing information considered helpful by Anderson and Bower; and
* Provides a frame work for an intermediate or linking language that is helpful and consistent.

7

Hidden Roots of Classification

Points out that a twofold infinity characterises the design of classification-the infinity in the diverse purposes of the readers and that in the dimensions of the universe of subjects. Illustrates the risk in basing the design of classification on conjecture and suggests basing it on the results of a sound statistical study. With the aid of the analogy of roots of flames shows an alternative helpful method to be basing classification on postulates and principles inherent in the near-seminal level. Describes with illustrations a set of postulates and principles. Points out that classification is equivalent to mapping the multi-dimensional universe of subjects along a single dimension and that the crucial problem in such a mapping is, determining which of the many immediate neighbourhood relations among facets to the Basic Subject, should be kept invariant. The Wall-Picture Principle is shown to give the best result in this matter. This Principle fixes the syntactical relations among facets. Raises the issue whether there is an Absolute Syntax, and whether the syntax of facets implied in the Wall-Picture Principle is equivalent to it. Suggests the investigation of this problem by a team of Linguists, Psychologists, Classificationists, Reference Librarians and Statisticians.

PLIGHT OF CLASSIFICATIONIST

The problem to be faced by the Designer of a scheme for the depth classification of nascent micro-thought, gushing forth from the minds of the hundreds of research workers in each of thousands of narrow subject fields and getting embodied in millions of articles published from year to year the-gravity of the problem of the Classificationist is not easily realised. Because, his design work concerns an invisible, intangible commodity called Thought or Idea. Therefore, I shall use the analogy of design work in a field where what is designed is visible to the eye.

Plight of Architect

Imagine the plight of an Architect designing a satellite township for a City Extension Board. Imagine one member after another of the Board suggesting changes day after day. Imagine the building material to be used having to be changed several times during the period of design and even during construction. Imagine also the sudden unexpected floods and earth tremors the first within living memory in the locality forcing a redesign of the foundation at an advanced stage. Imagine further the machinery and the tools for construction having to be changed frequently.

Greater Precariousness

The plight of classificationist is even more precarious than that of the Architect. For, in the universe of ideas turbulent changes are becoming frequent, unpredictable, and violent. The disturbance caused in the universe of ideas by eruptions such as those of Electrons, Laser, Plastics, Statistical Analysis, and Breaking of the Atom are now straining the schemes for classification and even breaking some of them, The purpose of the consumers of ideas is infinitely more varied than those in the case of township. Each reader wants it all his own way. In fact, the Classificationist has to reckon with a far greater number of factors than the Architect almost tending to infinity.

TWO-FOLD INFINITY

As a matter of fact, a two-fold infinity characterises the domain of Depth Classification. Firstly, there is infinity inherent in the purposes of readers and consequently in their approaches to a collection of documents in the stack or their main entries in the catalogue. Secondly, there is infinity in the dimensions of the universe of ideas to be organized by the Classificationist. Let us leave infinity alone. Let us confine ourselves to large numbers.

PROBLEM OF CLASSIFICATIONIST

The problem of a Classificationist is as follows:

Different readers have different purposes; and even the same reader has different purposes at different times. But the Classificationist cannot provide a different scheme for classification to suit each of the large number of purposes. He cannot simulate the old man of Aesop's, going out with his son and the donkey. Classificationist is obliged to use the statistical idea "Mode". He has to design the scheme to suit the most dominant purpose prevailing among readers. How to single out one out of many purposes as the most dominant one?

METHOD OF CONJECTURE

We cannot deal with a situation involving large numbers in the way followed for small numbers. In dealing with situations involving large numbers, humanity depended, for a long long time, on mere conjecture by persons rich in experience and intelligence. That is what Classificationists are doing till now.

METHOD OF CONJECTURE AND COLON CLASSIFICATION

This gave an insight into the varying purposes and approaches of readers. It also helped us to conjecture the sequence of the facets in a subject, that would serve the dominant purpose and approach of the readers. On this conjecture was based the sequence of facets in subjects going with each Main Subject. In other words, this conjecture helped us to lay down our Facet Formula for different Main Subjects. I began with a library of about 30,000 volumes. By the end of 1928 it grew to about 50,000 volumes.

All these volumes were classified on the basis of the different Facet Formulae constructed according to the conjecture about the dominant purpose and approach. On the whole, the arrangement of books appeared to give satisfaction. Author began to write out the First Edition of the Colon classification in 1929. While developing the different Facet Formulae, if used to experiment upon the way in which the different students preferred the Facet Sequence. However, as a student of Statistics, I was aware of the limitation of conjecture. Therefore, before completing the press copy of the book, I made an intensive experiment with the senior readers.

RISK IN CONJECTURE

In compound subjects going with the Main Subject Law, we often have two facets. Our Law Collection was very meagre. Only a few students of the Law College used it. They had to read mostly Indian Law. They also read British Law to some extent. The Indian Law of those years was largely based on the British Law. This made the students always approach the subject from the angle of the Problem Facet instead of the Community Facet. In other words, the Problem Facet was the first that they would bring up. The Community Facet was quite secondary to them.

This had led me to use the Facet Sequence:

Law as helpful to the dominant purpose and approach of the readers. To check up the validity of this conjecture, I invited some Members of the Bar, Judges of the High Court, and experienced Jurists.

We used to take them into the Law Gangway. We learnt from them that the Facet Sequence should be the very opposite namely:

Law

This was confirmed by most of the senior readers. They attributed the students' approach, resulting in the false conjecture, to the faulty method of teaching Law. Students were made to know only of the modern Indian and British Laws, which were alike; and they were not told that each country had its own system of Municipal law. We had also a similar experience with Chemistry. In these two Main Subjects all the books had to be reclassified and the class numbers had to be altered in all the places of their occurrence — in several places in the book itself, in the catalogue entries, shelf register, and accession register. This is the price to be paid when risk asserts itself in conjecture. Fortunately, in most of the other subjects the conjecture turned out to be correct. But it is the exception that highlights the "Risk in Conjecture" wherever large numbers are involved.

STATISTICAL METHOD

To minimize the risk of conjecture, the determination of the dominant purpose of readers must be based on a statistical study. This in its turn should be based on extensive observations in libraries of all standards — public, academic, and specialist — and in libraries of all countries. This will be far too expensive. At any rate, this has not been done. The result is that a certain amount of risk is taken by most of the schemes for classification by basing themselves on conjecture. It is not easy to make a statistical study of the problem of dominant approach of readers, the most helpful sequence of facets, the most helpful succession of characteristics within each facet, and the most helpful sequence of isolates within each array. The library profession has yet to clarify its own ideas in formulating such problems needing statistical study. The precautions to be taken in statistical observation in these cases have yet to be formulated. There is every probability for the digestion of the observed statistical data demanding new statistical techniques. In spite of the immaturity and infancy of this line of statistical approach to classification, We hope that some rich Foundation will arrange for this statistical determination of the dominant purpose and approach of readers. Again, this may have to be repeated in different epochs to find out the change that might occur.

LARGE NUMBER OF DIMENSIONS IN THE UNIVERSE OF IDEAS

The statistical negotiation of the large number of purposes and approaches of readers with statistical methods will take long. Depth classification cannot wait till then. Let us therefore turn our attention to the large number of dimensions of the universe of ideas. Let us see whether we can find an a priori method for organizing the idea-masses-from Macro through Micro to Spot Idea-in a helpful way and thereby find methods for the design of depth classification. The aim and end of classification is to arrange ideas scattered in many dimensions, along a line - in a linear sequence. How are we to do it?

ANALOGY OF ROOTS OF FLAME

The scatter of the tongues of flame shooting up from a pile of logs cannot be changed to our liking and brought into a line by catching the tongues of flame and rearranging them. The right method will be to manipulate the logs forming the root of the flames. So it is with classification of the universe of subjects — that is, the arrangement of subjects. The universe of subjects is dynamic. It throws forth subjects in a turbulent manner. It is doing so incessantly in our times. The scatter of the subjects so thrown forth is in many dimensions and is unhelpful. To anticipate the subjects and arrange them in advance in a helpful sequence would prove as futile and maddening as manipulating the tongues of flame. Because the subjects will not burn us, we are often tempted to secure a helpful classification of subjects by directly manipulating them.

The result is frequent break-down and even the desperate declaration that classification is impossible and alphabetical arrangement by names of subjects is the only sensible way. The subjects are the tongues of flame. They belong to the phenomenal level. It is tiring and ineffective, if not futile, to manipulate the subjects directly and arrange them as desired. It is best to manipulate their roots at the near-seminal level at which all the subject-proliferations are traceable to a few roots. The roots of subjects, are hidden even at the near-seminal level. They are hidden in the sense that they cannot be reached by intellectual analysis. They will have to be apprehended with intuition.

If intuition is functioning cent per cent the roots can be unerringly and permanently located. Hardly anybody is found with cent per cent intuition. Further, in the scale of values of anybody worth cent per cent intuition, classification may find itself very near the bottom. Therefore, we have to depend upon whatever can be got through the play of a momentary flash of intuition in some person or other essentially intellectual. Postulates and Principles are usually disclosed by such momentary flashes. They may go a long way though not the full way. When they cease to be helpful, they may be replaced by another set of Postulates and Principles that may be disclosed at that time.

POSTULATES

We have now a set of postulates to guide the design of classification. The attributes "True" and "False" do not apply to postulates. The only attributes applicable to them are "Helpfulness" and "Unhelpfulness". The following set of postulates have proved helpful.

Postulate of Fundamental Categories

There are five and only Five Fundamental Categories — *viz.*, Time, Space, Energy, Matter, and Personality. These terms and the ideas denoted by them belong strictly to the context of classificatory discipline. They have nothing to do with their use in Metaphysics or Physics. In our context, their significance can be seen only in the statements about the facets of a subject — their separation and their sequence. This set of fundamental categories is, for brevity, denoted by the initionym PMEST.

Time

Perhaps the fundamental category "Time" gives the least difficulty in its identification. It is in accordance with what we commonly understand by that term. The usual Time Isolate Ideas such as millennium, century, decade, year, and so on - are its manifestations. Time Isolate Ideas of another kind - such as day and night, seasons such as summer and winter, time with meteorological quality such as, wet, dry, and stormy - are also taken as manifestations of the fundamental category "Time".

Space

The fundamental category "Space" comes next to "Time" in difficulty in its identification. It is in accordance with what we commonly understand by that term. The surface of the earth, the space inside it, and the space outside it, are manifestations of the fundamental category "Space". The usual Geographical Isolate-Ideas such as continents, countries, and counties-and water formations-such as oceans and seas are taken to be its manifestations. Physiographical Isolate-Ideas such as desert, prairie, rain-forest, plateau, mountain, river, and lake-are also taken to be manifestations of the fundamental category "Space".

So also an area occupied by a population-cluster-such as a city, a town, and a village-is taken to be a manifestation of the fundamental category “Space”.

Scope For Comparative Study

Both CC and UDC give schedules of Time and Space Isolates. Therefore, there is some material for comparative study. On the basis of this study, it has been possible to cultivate the region of classificatory discipline falling within the purview of the fundamental categories “Time” and “Space”. The other schemes have not developed this region to a sufficient degree. CC is the only scheme with distinctive and consciously enumerated schedules of the three fundamental categories “Energy”, “Matter”., and “Personality”. The “Analytical Subdivisions” of UDC are of a casual nature. They are also mixtures of the manifestations of all the three fundamental categories. Therefore, there is no good scope for comparative study in respect of the manifestations of these three fundamental categories. In the circumstances, as the only meagre scope for comparative study, we have to use different editions of CC.

Energy

Even otherwise, the identification of the fundamental category “Energy” is a little more difficult than that of “Space” or “Time”. Generally speaking, its manifestation is an action of one kind or another. The action may be among and by all kinds of entities-inanimate, animate, conceptual, intellectual, and intuitive. Till now, we have been taking Morphology, Physiology, Disease, Ecology, Hygiene, and some other isolate ideas also as manifestations of the fundamental category “Energy”.

It was difficult to see any “Action” in them. Therefore, we enumerated them in a schedule and labelled them as Energy Isolates. We were led into this position by a sheer accident. This was the use of the term ‘Problem’ to denote these isolates ideas from-Ed 1 onwards of the Colon classification. This gave rise to a blind tradition of thirty years’ standing. Wrong traditions die hard. With the rush of preoccupation with many other ideas in classification and in other branches of library science, hardly any time or inclination was found to look at these 'Problems' critically. But the time has now come to give up this tradition. These isolate ideas are no longer taken to be manifestations of the fundamental category "Energy". Edition 7 of CC will incorporate this change.

Matter

The identification of the fundamental category "Matter" is more difficult than even of "Energy". Its manifestations are taken to be of two kinds-Material and Property. It may look strange that property should be taken along with material. But let us take a table as an example. The table is made of the material, timber or steel, as the case may be. The material is intrinsic to the table, but is not the table itself. Moreover, the same material can figure also in several other entities. So also, the table has the property of being two and a half ft. high and the property of having a soft top or a hard top. The property is intrinsic to the table, but not the table itself. Moreover, the same property can figure also in several other entities. Each of the isolate ideas Morphology, Physiology, Disease, etc., mentioned in the preceding part and now being excluded from the manifestations of the fundamental category "Energy", admit of being looked upon as Property. As such, they are now regarded as manifestations of the fundamental category "Matter".

Personality

The fundamental category "Personality" presents the greatest difficulty in its identification. It is too elusive. It is ineffable.

Method of Residues

If a certain manifestation is easily determined not to be one of "Time" or "Space" or "Energy" or "Matter" it is taken to be a main- festation of the fundamental category "Personality". This is the Method of Residues. For, according to the postulate, there are five and only five fundamental categories. Therefore, any entity, which is not a manifestation of "Time" nor of "Space" nor of "Energy" nor of "Matter", should be a manifestation of "Personality".

The application of this Method of Residues may not be easy in certain cases. But experience will lead to the establishment of reflex action in recognizing the fundamental category manifesting itself in any isolate idea, even as experience leads to the establishment of a reflex action in recognizing Chinese, Indians, Egyptians, Italians, French, Germans, and Russians. This does not amount to saying that there is no difficulty at all. There are still some areas of doubt in distinguishing between manifestations of the fundamental categories "Energy", "Matter", and "Personality". These difficult areas do not turn up very often. Therefore, we can get along, in spite of this difficulty, for the time being, and solve it in due course as experience increases. We cannot give up the proven advantage of Classification Guided by Postulates and Principles, and say, "We shall begin to use them only when all the difficulties about them are finally solved".

POSTULATE OF BASIC FACET

Every Compound Subject has a Basic Facet. This is implied in the very definition of the term 'Compound Subject'. A subject may have two or more basic facets. Then it will be a case of phase relation between the basic facets themselves or between the compound subjects of which they are the respective basic facets or a case of one of the subjects figuring as an isolate facet in a compound subject going with the other basic facet.

Recognition of the Basic Facet

S.No	Title	Basic	Facet
1	Explicit	1.1 Treatise on coal mining	Mining
		1.2 Agricultural diseases	Agriculture
		1.3 Text-book of Indian History	History
		2.1 Structure of proteins	Chemistry
2	Implicit	2.2 Care of cows	Animal husbandry
		2.3 Income-tax	Economics

To recognize the Basic Facet of a Compound Subject, a general knowledge of the schedules of Basic Subjects is necessary. Most of the Schemes for Classification give roughly similar schedules of them. The indication, by the title of a document of the Basic Facet of its subject may be either.

Absence of Indication

If the title does not express the subject at all but is oblique or fanciful, the contents page and even the whole document may have to be perused to determine the Basic facet. Most of the Works in Literature and many Classics in diverse subjects come under this group.

POSTULATE OF ISOLATE FACET

Each isolate facet of a compound subject can be deemed to be a manifestation of one and only one of the five Fundamental Categories. It is generally easy to identify isolate ideas that are manifestations of the fundamental categories: Time, Space, Energy, and Matter. A idea, not found to be a manifestation of any of these four categories, has a good chance to be a manifestation of the fundamental category "Personality". Its manifestation can also be directly sensed in some cases. Some examples are given in the succeeding parts.

Biological Sciences

* In the Subjects in Botany Plant Group. Plant.
* In the Subjects in Agriculture-Cultivar Group. Cultivar.
* In the Subjects in Zoology Animal Group. Animal. Organ.
* In the Subjects in Animal Husbandry Animal. Organ.
* In the Subjects in Medicine-Human Body. Organ.

Social Sciences

* In the Subjects in Education-Child. Adolescent. Adult, Genius. Imbecile. Blind.
* In the Subjects in History and Political Science Head of the State. Executive. Legislature. Party. Public. Local Body. Judiciary. Civil Service.
* In the Subjects in Sociology-Rural Folk. City Folk. Professional Group. Working Class. Royalty. Aristocracy. Middle Class. Military Class. Nomadics. Aryans. Semetics. Hindus. Christians. Muslims. Indians. Chinese. British.

* In the Subjects in Law Legal Personality. State. Association. Property. Contract. Treaty. Tort. Crime. Cause of Action. Court.

Humanities

* In the Subjects in Linguistics-a Language. Phoneme. Syllable. Word. Phrase. Clause. Sentence. Piece of Composition. Punctuation.
* In the Subjects in Religion-Vedic Religion. Hinduism. Vaishnavism. Saivism. Jainism. Buddhism. Christianity. Islam. Shintoism. Sikhism. Zoroastrianism. Sacred Book. Church. Sects.
* In the Subjects in Psychology Child. Adolescent. Adult. Genius. Imbecile. Blind.
* In the Subjects in Literature Poetry. Drama. Fiction. Author. Work.

Mathematics

* In the Subjects in Arithmetic Prime Number. Partition of Numbers. Arithmetical Function.
* In the Subjects in Theory of Equation-Simple Equation. Quadratic Equation. Abelian Equation.
* In the Subjects in Higher Algebra Binary Form. Linear Form. Cremona Transformation.
* In the Subjects in Differential Equation-Linear, Quadratic, Cubic, Quartic, Quintic, Sextic. First Order. Second Order. Third Order. Fourth Order. Fifth Order. Sixth Order.

Physical Sciences

* In the Subjects in Properties of Matter-Solid. Glass. Crystal. Liquid-Surface. Liquid. Gas.
* In the Subjects in Sound-Audible Sound. Infra Sound. Ultra Sound.
* In the Subjects in Radiation-Light. Ultra-Violet Ray. X-Ray. Gamma Ray. Infra-Red Ray. Hertzian Wave.
* In the Subjects in Electricity-Current. Direct Current. Alternating Current. Weak Current.

* In the Subjects in Magnetism-Dia-Magnetism. Para-Magnetism. Terrestrial Magnetism.
* In the Subjects in Nuclear Physics Neutron. Nutrino. Proton. Beta Ray. Meson. Cosmic Ray.
* In the Subjects in Chemistry-Inorganic Substance. Hydrogen. Calcium. aluminum. Carbon. Bismuth. Oxygen. Fluorine. Iron. Metal. Non-Metal. Alloy. Basic Oxide. Acid. Salt.
* Organic Substance. methane. Phenophthalene. Carbohydrate. Starch. Aromatic Compound. Benzene. Heterocyclic Compound. Alkaloid. Amino Acid. Protein. Vitamin. Hormone. Chlorophyll. Enzyme.

Recognition of Isolate Ideas

The indication, by the title of a document, of the isolate facets of its subject may be either:

* Explicit, or
* Implicit in the context, or
* Hidden within a derived composite term, or
* Absent.

The basic subject of the document will be of help in sensing the absence of the indication of a necessary facet of the compound subject. Experience will develop the capacity for sensing this. In that case, the contents page or even the whole document should be perused to find the absent isolate ideas, if any. Again, experience will develop the capacity to sense the derived composite terms in a title and to break it into its fundamental constituent terms. In each example, against each isolate idea appropriate symbol is given to indicate the fundamental category of which it can be deemed to be a manifestation.

Symbols used:

* (BF) = Basic Facet
* [S] = Space Facet
* [E] = Energy Facet
* [P] = Personality Facet
* [M] = Matter Facet
* [T] = Time Facet

S.No.	Indication	Title	Basic and Isolate Facets
1	Explicit	1.1 Coal washing	Mining (BF). Coal [P]. Washing [E].
		1.2 Control of virus diseases of the stem of rice plant in the winter of 1967 in Madras	Agriculture (BF). Control [E]. Virus disease [M]. Stem [P]. Rice plant [P]. Winter [T]. 1967 [T]. Madras [S].
	Explicit	1.3 Election of the President of the Congress Party in India in 1967	History (BF). Election [E]. President [P]. Congress Party [P]. India [S]. 1967 [T].
2	Implicit (The implied facetsare in italics)	2.1 The structure of protein and electron microscope	*Chemistry* (BF). Structure [M]. Protein [P]. Determination [E]. Electron microscope [M].
		2.2 X-ray diagnosis in cow farming	Animal husbandry (BF). X-Ray [M]. Diagnosis[E]. Disease [M]. Cow [P].
		2.3 Tape-record andprotection of the folksongs of the Todas	Sociology (BF). Taperecord [M]. Dying out [M]. Protection [E]. Folk songs [M]. Todas [P].
3	Hidden within a Derived composite term (the hidden facets are in italics)	3.1 Phthisis	*Medicine* (BF). Lungs [P]. Tubercular disease[M].
		3.2 Indian franchise in 1967	*History* (BF). India [P]. Citizens [P]. Franchise[M]. 1967 [T].
		3.3 Birth control essential in India today (1966)	Sociology (BF). Overpopulation [M]. Prevention [E]. Birth control [M]. India [S]. Today [T].

POSTULATE OF ROUNDS FOR ENERGY

The fundamental category "Energy" may manifest itself in one and the same subject more than once. The first manifestation is taken to end Round 1 of the manifestation of the three fundamental categories "Personality", "Matter", and "Energy". The second manifestation is taken to end Round 2. And so on. We shall denote the manifestations of the fundamental category "Energy" in Rounds 1, 2 etc., by the respective names Round 1 Energy Facet, Round 2 Energy Facet, etc. We shall represent them by the respective symbols [1E], [2E], etc. Which manifestation of the fundamental category "Energy" should be deemed to be the Round 1 which the Round 2 will be determined by the Wall-Picture Principle.

POSTULATE OF ROUNDS FOR PERSONALITY AND MATTER

Each of the fundamental categories "Personality" and "Matter" may manifest itself in Round 1, Round 2, and so on. We shall denote the manifestation of the fundamental category "Personality" in the Rounds 1, 2 etc., by the names Round 1 Personality Facet, Round 2 Personality Facet, etc. We shall represent them by the respective symbols [1P], [2P], etc. So also we can have Round 1 Matter Facet, Round 2 Matter Facet, etc. We shall represent them by the respective symbols [1M], [2M], etc.

POSTULATE OF ROUND FOR SPACE AND TIME

Ordinarily, any of the fundamental categories "Space" and "Time" may manifest itself only in the last Round in a subject. We shall represent them by the respective symbols [S], [T].

POSTULATE OF LEVEL

Any of the fundamental categories "Personality" and "Matter" may manifest itself more than once in one and the same Round within a subject; and similarly with "Space" and "Time" in the Last Round. The first manifestation of a fundamental category within a Round will be said to be its Level 1 Facet in that Round. Its second manifestation within that Round will be said to be its Level 2 Facet in that Round. And so on.

Personality and Matter

We shall call the successive manifestations of the fundamental category "Personality" in the Round 1 by the respective names Round 1 Level 1 Personality Facet, Round 1 Level 2 Personality Facet, etc. We shall represent them by the respective symbols, [1P1], [1P2], [2P1], [2P2], etc. Similarly, [1M1], [1M2], [2M1], [2M2], etc.

Space and Time

Since Space and Time Facets can occur only in the last round of a subject, there is no need to indicate the Round in their names or their symbols. It is sufficient if we represent them by the respective symbols [S1], [S2], [T1], [T2], etc.

Energy

The fundamental category "Energy" can occur only once within a Round. Therefore, no Level in its case.

POSTULATE OF FIRST FACET

In a Compound Subject, the Basic Facet should be the first facet. Every Compound Subject, should have a Basic Facet. Again, Isolate Facets can form a subject, if and only if they are attached to a Basic Facet. Helpfulness requires that all the Compound Subjects going with a Basic Facet should be arranged together. To secure this, the Basic Facet should be given the First Position among the facets of a Compound Subject.

POSTULATE OF CONCRETENESS

The five fundamental categories fall into the following sequence, when arranged according to their decreasing concreteness: P, M, E, S, T. This Postulate conforms to what the majority of persons think in respect of the relative concreteness of the isolates which are manifestations in each of the five respective fundamental categories.

POSTULATE OF FACET SEQUENCE WITHIN A ROUND

In any Round of Facets of a Compound Subject in which each of any of the first three fundamental categories occurs only once, their sequence should be: Personality Facet, Matter Facet, and Energy Facet.

POSTULATE OF FACET SEQUENCE WITHIN THE LAST ROUND

In the Last Round of facets of a Compound Subject, in which each of the fundamental categories other than Energy occurs only once, the sequence of the facets should be Personality Facet, Matter Facet, Space Facet, and Time Facet.

POSTULATE OF A LEVEL CLUSTER

Facets of different levels of the same fundamental category within a Round of facets in a Compound Subject should be kept together.

ALTERNATIVE SETS OF POSTULATES

It will be helping the cause of classification, if an alternative set of postulates is forthcoming. This will happen when the present set of postulates begins to prove unhelpful. This conjecture is based upon the history of science and upon the formulation of fundamental laws such as Postulates, Canons, Principles, and Hypotheses.

WALL-PICTURE PRINCIPLE

If two facets A and B of a subject are such that the concept behind B will not be operative unless the concept behind A is conceded, even as a mural picture is not possible unless the wall exists to draw upon, then the facet A should preceded the facet B.

* In "Cure of Disease" the concept behind the term 'Cure' is not operative unless the concept behind the term 'Disease' is conceded. Therefore, when expressed in transformed skeleton form, we shall have 'Disease. Cure'. In this case, the application of the Wall Picture Principle has determined that the Round to which the concept 'Disease' should be assigned as the one preceding the Energy Facet 'Cure'.
* In "Prevention of Disease" also, the concept behind the term 'Prevention' is not operative unless the concept

behind the term 'Disease' is conceded. Therefore, when expressed in transformed skeleton form, we shall have 'Disease. Prevention'. Thus, the application of the Wall-Picture Principle has determined that the Round to which the concept 'Disease' should be assigned as the one preceding the Energy Facet 'Prevention'.

* A comparison of examples 1 and 2 leads to an important warning in applying the Wall- Picture Principle. In example 1, 'Disease' actually comes in before 'Cure' begins. But in example 2, 'Disease' does not come in at all. Indeed, 'Prevention' is to secure that it does not come. In the former the concept as well as what is conceived are conceded before 'Cure' begins. In the latter, the concept 'Disease' alone is conceded, but not 'Disease' itself, before 'Prevention' begins. Thus, in applying the Wall Picture Principle it is only the concept that should be conceded, but not the correlate of the concept existing outside the mind.
* In "President of India", the concept behind the term 'President' is not operative unless the concept behind the term 'India' is conceded. Therefore, when expressed in transformed skeleton form, we shall have 'India. President'. In this case, the application of the Wallpicture Principle has determined the respective Levels to which the concepts 'India' and 'President' should be assigned.
* Consider "Release of Contract in India". The concept behind the term 'Release' is not operative unless the concept behind the term 'Contract' is conceded. Further, the concept behind the term 'Contract' is not operative unless the concept behind the term 'India' is conceded. Therefore, when expressed in a transformed skeleton form, we shall have 'India. Contract Release'. In this case, the application of the Wall-Picture Principle has determined the respective Levels to which the concepts 'India', 'Contract'. and Release' should be assigned.
* Consider "Hamlet by Shakespeare, the English Dramatist". The concept behind the term 'Hamlet' is

not operative unless the concept behind the term 'Shakespeare' is conceded. Again, the concept behind the term 'Shakespeare' is not operative, unless the concept behind the term 'Drama' is conceded. So also, the concept behind the term 'Drama' is not operative unless the concept behind the term 'English' is conceded. Therefore, when expressed in transformed skeleton form, we shall have 'English. Drama. Shakespeare. Hamlet'. In this case, the application of the Wall-Picture Principle has determined the respective Levels to which the concepts 'English', 'Drama', 'Shakespeare', and 'Hamlet' should be assigned.

* Supplementary to Postulates. The Wall-Picture Principle and the Postulates for Facet Sequence will produce the same result wherever they are both applicable. In those cases, we need not invoke the aid of the Wall-Picture Principle. But in the examples, the Postulates by themselves cannot determine the Round and the Levels indicated. Thus, the use of the Wall-Picture Principle is supplementary to the use of the Postulates. The former is more versatile than the latter.

WHOLE-ORGAN PRINCIPLE

If, in a subject, facet B is an organ of facet A, then A should precede B. Consider "The Public Accounts Committee of the Parliament of India". The Facet 'Public Accounts Committee' is an organ of the facet 'Parliament'. The facet 'Parliament' itself is an organ of 'India', When expressed in a transformed skeleton form, we shall have 'India. Parliament. Public Accounts Committee'. This sequence of Levels can also be inferred directly from the Wall-Picture Principle. However, the Levels shown for a subject in Law, and the Levels shown for a subject in Literature, are not in the relation of 'Whole' and 'Organ'. Therefore, those Levels can be inferred only by directly invoking the Wall-Picture Principle.

COW-CALF PRINCIPLE

If a facet A and another facet B belonging to the same subject are not to be separated though they are distinct from each other and thus separable, A and B should be kept together in the same Round, even as a milch cow and its unweaned calf are not separately sold out though they are distinct entities and thus separable, but are kept together in possession of the same owner. Consider "Enforcement of the Functions of the President of India". Here, the three facets 'India', 'President', and 'Functions' are not to be separated and puf into different Rounds, although they are separable. They should all be put together in Round 1 that is, before the Energy Facet, 'Enforcement' or after it. We cannot put any one of them in Round 1 and the other two in Round 2. The Cow-Calf Principle determines only that all the three facets should be put in one and the same Round. To decide which Round it should be, we should invoke the direct aid of Wall-Picture Principle. This Principle would definitely assign them to Round 1. Therefore, when expressed in transformed skeleton form, we shall have 'India. President. Function. Enforcement'. We can also get the same result by repeated applicauon of the Wall-Picture Principle.

ACTAND-ACTION-ACTOR-TOOL PRINCIPLE

If, in a subject, facet B denotes action on facet A by facet C, with facet D as the tool, then the four facets should be arranged in the sequence A, B, C, D. Consider "Charkha Cotton Spinning by Girls". Here, the Action is 'Spinning'; the Actand is 'Cotton'; the Actor is 'Girls'; and the Tool is 'Charkha'. Therefore, when expressed in transformed skeleton form, we shall have 'Cotton. Spinning. Girls. Charkha'. This result can also be got by the repeated application of the Wall-Picture Principle.

LINEAR ARRANGEMENT OF SUBJECTS AND ITS NECESSITY

The human mind is, after all, at a very early stage in its evolution. Although we can speak of many dimensions, it usually works, more or less, in one dimension. Even mathematicians have to work "bit by bit along the line". There may be exceptions; but most serious thinkers have to think out one thing at a time in succession. In particular, the documents in the stack and their main entries in the catalogue have to be in linear sequence. The search for any one document or its entry has to be made by scanning along the line. But the universe of subjects has many dimensions. Let us say, n dimensions, where n is a large positive integer. The subjects in the Universe of Subjects have to be arranged in a line for the convenience of readers.

MATHEMATICAL TRANSFORMATION AND MAPPING

To state this in mathematical terms, we have to transform the n-dimensional space into one-dimensional space. In other words, we have to map an n-dimensional space on a one-dimensional space. This is the problem in classification.

INVARIANT AMONG IMMEDIATE-NEIGHBOURHOOD-RELATIONS

Consider the five points spread out on a plane.

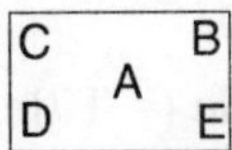

Here B, C, D, and E each claims Immediate-Neighbourhood-Relation with A. Let us arrange all the five points in one line. Let us put A at the left end. Then there can be only one Immediate-Neighbourhood- Position after A.

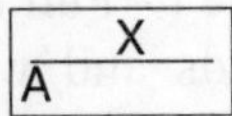

We can give that position only to one of B, C, D, and E and not to all. To which shall we give that position? In other words, which of the four Immediate-Neighbourhood-Relations should be kept invariant while arranging the five points along a line? Consider the points as subjects. This lays bare our inescapable problem in classification. It is a mischief created by the mathematics of transformation and mapping. If we begin to ask which of B, C, D, and E should be given the benefit of keeping invariant its Immediate-Neighbourhood-Relation with A, the chances will be equal to all the four elements. This tantalising problem attains colossal dimensions when we have to arrange millions of micro-subjects.

DESCENT TOWARDS THE SEMINAL LEVEL

In the phenomenal world there are millions and millions of subjects. We do not know which of the Immediate-Neighbourhood-

Relations should be kept invariant in arranging the subjects in a helpful way along a line. A suitable method would be to descend from the phenomenal level nearer to the seminal level. According to the Postulate of Fundamental Categories, we should descend down and down, and down and down, and allow the various subjects and ideas to become absorbed and reassembled, reabsorbed, and again reassembled, and so on, until we find only five ultimate generic ideas-seminal ideas, Fundamental Categories-standing out.

PRACTICAL CLASSIFICATION

STEPS IN PRACTICAL CLASSIFICATION

Classifying a document consists of the following steps in succession.

* *Step 0.* — Raw Title (= Title as found in the document).
* *Step 1.* — Full Title (= Title expressing each of the relevant basic and isolate ideas in the subject of the document, got by filling up all the ellipses in the Raw Title).
* *Step 2.* Kernel Title (= Full title minus all the auxiliary or apparatus words and with each composite term denoting a composite idea replaced by the fundamental constituent terms denoting its fundamental constituent ideas).
* *Step 3.* — Analysed Title (= Kernel Title with each kernel term marked by a symbol, denoting the fundamental category of which the idea denoted by the term is a manifestation and also the round and the level to which it is assigned in conformity to the Postulates of Classification).
* *Step 4.* — Transformed Title (= Analysed Title with the kernel terms rearranged according to the symbols of analysis attached to them).
* *Step 5.* — Title in Standard Facet Terms (= Transformed Title with the kernel terms replaced, wherever necessary, by their respective equivalent terms as given in the appropriate schedules).

- * *Step 6.* — Title in Facet Numbers (= Title in Standard Terms with the kernel terms replaced by their equivalent numbers from the schedules).
- * *Step 7.* — Class Number (got by removing the symbols of analysis and inserting the appropriate Connecting Symbols between the facet numbers in accordance with the Rules).

This work amounts to the analysis of the subject into facets and the determination of the sequence of the facets. This is done in the idea plane. The work in Step 7 amounts to synthesis of the facet numbers in the notational plane. The work in the idea plane deals in reality with the Syntax of the Facets; and this is reflected in the notational plane also.

ANALYTICO-SYNTHETIC CLASSIFICATION

By 'Analytico-Synthetic Classification' is meant a scheme for classification involving analysis and transformation in the idea plane and synthesis in the notational plane according to stated postulates and principles.

ADVANTAGE OF POSTULATES AND PRINCIPLES

Practical classification based on the stated postulates and principles bypasses the work of thinking about all the subjects at one and the same time, analysing each of them in a helpful sequence in such a way that, in the finally resulting sequence of subjects, the intended Immediate-Neighbourhood-Relation remains invariant. The ad hoc decision of these for each document is tantalising. Nightmare is often the result. For example, the number of the possible sequences of the facets in the diverse subjects, out of which one and only one is to be chosen consistently, is very large.

EXAMPLE OF TANTALISATION

Let me illustrate with a small fringe of the problem. Consider the subject "Agriculture of Wheat". It has only two facets — Basic Facet "Agriculture" and Isolate Facet "Wheat". The sequence of these facets does not give much trouble. Maintaining deeper consistency in such cases is quite easy. But, consider the micro-subject "Leaf virus of wheat and spraying of chemicals from aeroplane in the coastal areas of Florida during the wet summer months in the present decade".

This has 14 facets. The following 11 facets are explicitly mentioned in the title:

* Leaf.
* Virus.
* Wheat.
* Spraying.
* Chemicals.
* Aeroplane.
* Coastal area.
* Florida.
* Wet.
* Summer.
* Present decade.

The following three facets are implied in the title:

* Agriculture.
* Disease.
* Cure.

There are 87,178,297,200 possible sequences in which these can be arranged. How are we to select the most helpful of these eighty-seven thousand million sequences? How are we to be consistent in their selection-consistent also at a deeper level, at which the same pattern of sequence of facets is followed in diverse subjects? An ad hoc decision of this in each case is tantalising.

BYPASSING THE TANTALISATION

But step 5 in practical classification-secures consistency without undue strain to the mind-without being tantalised. Further, when all the subjects are given their respective class numbers and are arranged by their class numbers, they all fall automatically into a helpful sequence. This is the advantage of using an Analytico-Synthetic Classification guided by Postulates and Principles.

HELPFULNESS FOR THE MAJORITY OF READERS

The sequence secured by the postulates and principles is found to be helpful to the majority of readers. This has now been tried out not only in the arrangement of books and of their main entries in libraries, but also in the arrangement of the main entries in documentation lists of current articles in about a hundred very specialised subjects, such as Production Engineering of Screw, Production of Diesel Engine, and Nuclear Medicine. The concerned expert specialists have expressed satisfaction with the sequence secured by this classification.

MINORITY GROUPS AMONG READERS

No minority group, however, should be left without help. The formation of special collections in the stack room is one form of help to a single minority in a particular library. But to meet the needs of several minorities, the catalogue can be pressed into service. A separate guide-card giving the interest of each minority may be inserted in the alphabetical part of the catalogue. Behind the guide-card for a particular minority may be inserted a duplicate set of the main entry cards of all the documents of interest to that minority. These duplicate main entry cards should be arranged in the classified sequence. This is only an aside. We shall now resume our main line of thought.

SEARCH FOR THE HIDDEN ROOTS OF CLASSIFICATION

SYNTAX OF FACETS

My wish is that in our search for hidden roots of classification, we should not stop with the postulates and principles at the near-seminal level. These form only a first approximation. What pleased me most was the announcement that this Seminar intended to dive deeper still, to find the very tip of the tap-root in the intellect, so to speak. In analytic synthetic classification, one of the vital steps is the determination of the helpful sequence of the facets of a subject. This means the Syntax of Facets. This in its turn means a harmonious sequence of the facets, that gives satisfaction to the human mind. Webster quotes the following passage to show the power of a good syntax:

"His mind moved in a rich erudite and complex Syntax
That turned all opposition into admiration".

The syntax of facets in classification based on the postulates and principles gives satisfaction to the majority of readers.

QUEST FOR THE REASON FOR SATISFACTION

What is the reason for the Syntax of Facets given by the postulates and principles being satisfactory to most people? The reason should be searched in the minds of the readers. This will lead us to the roots of classification hidden far deep in the intellect-in-action. In this behalf, a suggestion, that to help in the establishment of a fairly long-lived helpful scheme for classification, a team of epistemologists, psychologists, linguists, reference librarians, classificationists, and statisticians should investigate the way in which the human intellect works today that is, the Syntax of Facets that will give the greatest satisfaction to the greatest number of readers. Probably, the time was not then ripe for it.

ABSOLUTE SYNTAX

By 'Absolute Syntax' is meant the sequence in which the facet ideas of a subject arrange themselves in the minds of the majority of persons. Linguistic Syntax is the Syntax of Words that is, the sequence in which the words stand arranged in a sentence or in the name of a subject in a natural language. The Linguistic Syntax may vary with the language; often it does. The result in Step 5 in the steps in classifying a document corresponds to Absolute Syntax that is, Syntax of Facets. In it, the kernel terms in the name of a subject stand rearranged according to the Syntactic Principles governing the sequence of the facets denoted by the respective kernel terms. On the other hand, the result in Step 3 corresponds to Linguistic Syntax. In it, the kernel terms stand arranged in the same sequence as the one in which these terms are found in the name of the subject in the natural language used.

Here is an example.

* Consider the Subject

* "The Heart of the Frog".

This is Step 0. the full title in Step 1 will be

* "The Heart of the Frog Zoology".

In Step 2, where only the kernel terms are retained, we shall have

* "Heart. Frog. Zoology".

This sequence is according to the Linguistic Syntax of the English language. According to the Linguistic Syntax of the Tamil language, the kernel terms will stand arranged in Step 2 as follows:

* "Zoology. Frog. Heart".

In step 5, the kernel terms will stand arranged as:

* "Zoology. Frog. Heart".

This represents the Syntax of Facets. It happens that the Linguistic Syntax of the English language differs from the Syntax of Facets; while the Linguistic Syntax of the Tamil language agrees with the Syntax of Facets.

There may be languages in which the Linguistic Syntax may give respectively

* "Zoology. Heart. Frog

* Frog. Heart. Zoology

* Frog. Zoology. Heart

* Heart. Zoology. Frog" respectively

The number of variations of Linguistic Syntax from the Syntax of Facets will increase with the number of the kernel terms in the name of the subject which is the same as the number of the facets in it.

ABSOLUTE SYNTAX AND FACET SYNTAX

In general, the number of Linguistic Syntaxes for the name of a subject, in the different natural languages all taken together, can become as great as factorial n, where n is the number of kernel terms in the name of the subject. But, there is only one Syntax of Facets for the subject. For this reason, it is conjectured that the Syntax of Facets is the same as the Absolute Syntax. This implies that the Absolute Syntax is the one conforming to the Postulates and Principles guiding the design of an Analytico-Synthetic Classification.

Problem for Investigation

The problem for investigation is, "Is there an Absolute Syntax governing the sequence of the facets of a subject, inherent in the human intellect-in-action as it is today?" This investigation should be made by a team of specialists in Epistemology, Psychology, Linguistics, Reference Service, Design of Classification, and Statistical Analysis.

Removal of Encrustation

It is not expected that the Absolute Syntax will be inherent in the minds of one and all the adults, without any exception. For, from childhood onwards the Linguistic Syntax of the mother tongue makes an incessant impact on the mind of a person. It is too much to expect that the encrustation formed by this incessant impact would not have become too hard and opaque for the inherent Absolute Syntax to become operative. On the other hand, I only expect the Absolute Syntax will be operative with the majority of persons.

Frequency Study

While investigating the problem, the Team of Specialists would use the same assortment of subjects. They should examine a reliable random sample of persons drawn from each of most of the natural languages. Probably, it will be helpful to have three sets of random samples one for children, one for adolescents, and one for adults. The investigation may have to be done in five stages. In the first instance, without any suggestion whatever being made by the Team, the sequence of facets naturally preferred in the various facets by the different persons should be found out and recorded. Thereafter, an attempt should be made to break gently the encrustation of the Linguistic Syntax in the minds of the people. The degree of success in this work will throw the people into several groups. At the third stage, the sequence of facets in the subjects, preferred by each of the groups, should then be found out and recorded.

The work in the fourth stage will fall largely to the share of the Statisticians. They will have to construct the necessary and possible frequency tables and curves, and the correlation tables and curves and surfaces; and they should also furnish all the necessary statistical constants emerging from the study of the problem. In the fifth stage, it may be possible to find out, from the results tabulated by the Statisticians, whether there is an Absolute Syntax, and if so, what it is; and in particular, it can be verified whether the Syntax of Facets based on the Postulates and Principles for an Analytico-Synthetic Classification is the same as or at least a good approximation to the Absolute Syntax.

Help to Classificationist

The final findings of such a team of specialists will enable the classificationists to build schemes for classification on fairly firm foundations. At present, a good deal of professional energy and time get dissipated in discussing problems in classification guided solely by conjectures and conflicting opinions based on insufficient data. This wastage should be avoided. I wish that the deliberations of this Seminar leads to the solution of this problem along objective and scientific lines by Teams of Specialists, probing into the hidden roots of classification. The results will be of help in the study of absolute linguistics also. This piece of tiny research deserves to be provided for by a Foundation.

8

Library Classification System of U.S. Geological Survey (USGS)

INTRODUCTION

The newly revised classification system presented in this report is designed for use in the U.S. Geological Survey (USGS) Library and other earth science libraries. Prior to the administration of Fred Boughton Weeks, 1903-1908, the library lacked a classification scheme. The Dewey Decimal system for geologic material was not sufficiently developed to accommodate the range of specialized material collected at the USGS Library, and The Library of Congress Classification System had not yet been published. The library staff and patrons were concerned about continued development of the collection without an acceptable classification scheme. Mr. Weeks and bibliographer John M. Nickles of the library staff, with the assistance of three consultants from the New York Public Library, developed the USGS classification system designed specifically for an earth science library.

Seven schedules were created:

* *General subject collection*: Consists of disciplines in the earth sciences, such as geology, petrology, mineralogy, paleontology, and biology. The pure sciences are included insofar as they augment the earth sciences, for example, physics, chemistry engineering, mathematics, and computer sciences. The schedule allows for integration of general works throughout.

* *Geological survey collection*: Contains the monographs, periodicals, and monographic series issued by the geological surveys of the world. The notation for this schedule consists of numbers enclosed by parenthesis, (XXX).
* *Earth science periodical collection*: Contains publications issued by earth science societies, associations, and earth science departments of universities. The notation for this schedule is identified by a uppercase G and a geographic number, G(XXX).
* *Government documents collection*: Contains periodicals and monographic series issued by federal, state, provincial and local governments throughout the world. The notation for this schedule is identified by an uppercase P and a geographic number, P(XXX).
* *General science periodical collection*: Contains science periodicals issued by societies, associations, and universities throughout the world. The notation for this collection is identified by an uppercase S and a geographic number, S(XXX).
* *Earth science map collection*: The notation of the map collection consists of an uppercase M followed by a geographic number and a subject number, M(XXX)X.
* *Geographic schedule*: Consists of numbers enclosed in parentheses that can be combined with notation from the other schedules. The geographic number is highly visible throughout the classification system and thus immediately recognizable when scanning the system for a particular locale. For example, the number 203 represents the subject geology. When the geographic number for the United States, (200), is added to the number 203, *i.e.*, 203(200), the resulting number represents a study on the geology of the United States. Using a similar methodology, studies on earthquakes in California would be 240(276), and mineral resources of Russia 403(570).

SUBJECT CLASSIFICATION SCHEDULE

The subject schedule has three main divisions: general works, earth sciences, and pure sciences. The collection consists chiefly of monographs but includes those periodicals that are narrow in scope, international in scope, or those issued by an international agency.

GENERAL OUTLINE OF THE SUBJECT CLASSIFICATION SCHEDULE

General works:

* 001-095: Science, computer science, information systems, bibliographies, directories, dictionaries, and biographies.

Earth sciences:

* 101-190:Mineralogy and petrology
* 201-298:General geology, geologic hazards, tectonics, geodynamics, structural geology, geophysics, and geochemistry.
* 301-371: Historical and stratigraphic geology.
* 401-471: Mineral resources, mineral industries, mines and mining, and groups of minerals.
* 501-590: Geography, geomorphology, meteorology, landforms, oceanography, and environmental sciences.
* 601-699:Paleontology, paleoecology paleogeography.

Pure sciences:

* 701-795: Mathematics, astronomy, engineering, geodesy, surveying, cartography, and hydrology.
* 801-895: Physics and chemistry.
* 901-999: Biology, ecology, evolution, botany, agriculture, forestry, and zoology.

Constructing Call Numbers

Call numbers consist of a classification number, shelf list number, title mark and date.

Classification Number

The classification number consists of numbers 001-999 taken from the subject schedule.

Geographic Notation

To add a region to a call number, consult the geographic schedule and choose the appropriate parenthetical number, (000)-(995), for the geographic locale represented in the study.

Example:

- *Title*: China's energy and mineral industries/ by J.P. Dorian, 1988.
- *Class no.*: 403
- *Geographic no.*: (610)
- *Complete class no.*: 403(610)

Shelf List Number

The shelf list number contains information about the main entry of the piece being classified and also provides the work with its singular location on the shelves or in the library online system. The first part of the number consists of an upper case letter and usually a three digit number representing either an author or a title main entry. The number for an author main entry is unique for each author.

The shelf list number for an author main entry is completed by lower case letter representing the title of a work and is called a title mark. The title mark allows the various works of an author to be arranged in alphabetical order after the unique three digit number.

The shelf list number for a title main entry is usually complete with an uppercase letter and a three digit number. If the shelf list number duplicates another number, add a title mark to make it unique. Titles beginning with numbers are treated as words when creating shelf list numbers. If the title consists of one word, construct the shelf list number from successive letters within that word. A shelf list number is needed. The shelf list number has three elements.

Examples:

Call number with author main entry and no region:		
* Title	:	Multivariate geostatistics/ H. Wackernagel, 1995
* Class no.	:	208.2
* Shelf list no.	:	W323
* Title mark	:	m
* Date	:	1995
* Call number	:	208.2 W323m 1995

Table Contd...

Call number with author main entry and a region:

*	Title	:	Expert witness guide for scientists and engineers/ A.E. Surosky, 1993
*	Class no.	:	760
*	Region	:	(200)
*	Shelf list no.	:	S976
*	Title mark	:	e
*	Date	:	1993
*	Call number	:	760(200) S976e 1993

Call number with title main entry and a region:

*	Title	:	China's energy and mineral industries edited by J.P. Dorian, 1989.
*	Class no.	:	403
*	Region	:	(610)
*	Shelf list no.	:	C442
*	Date	:	1989
*	Call number	:	403(610) C442 1989

The first element, an uppercase letter, is taken from the first letter of the first word of the main entry. The second element, a three digit number, is taken from Library of Congress shelf listing tables. The final element is the title mark taken from the title, or in case of a title main entry, from the next distinctive word in the title.

Dates in Call Numbers

Current classification policy has a date added to the end of monographic call numbers. In previous years a date was used only for successive editions. The date is usually taken from the imprint. Call numbers for congresses, however, use the date of the congress rather than the year of publication.

Example

Multi volume sets that are published with different edition dates for various volumes are classified without a date. Call numbers that would duplicate an earlier edition that was published in the same year are made unique by adding a, b, c, etc., to the date for successive versions.

Monograph with date:			
*	Title	:	Estimation of building vulnerability.../ G.C. Hart, 1988.
*	Class no.	:	240.2
*	Shelf list no.	:	H377e
*	Date	:	1988
Congress with date:			
*	Title	:	Mineral resources of Russia: diamonds and gold: proceedings of the Second
*	International Symposium "Mineral Resources of Russia"	:	held 1994, St.
*		:	Petersburg (published 1995)
*	Class no.	:	401(570)
*	Shelf list no.	:	I573m
*	Date	:	1994

Size in Call Numbers

Due to restricted space at the Reston Library, publications are grouped according to size. The sizes are:

*	Octavo	up to 28 cm.
*	Oversize (quarto)28.1 to 33 cm.	
*	Folio	33.1 to 46 cm.
*	Superfolio	46.1 up

Prior to July 1999, oversize materials were designated by the addition of a lower case letter in front of the shelf list number: q (oversize), f (folio) or ff (superfolio). These designations are no longer used. Instead, shelf location is indicated using a size designation label above the call number.

Translations

Translations by Publishing Houses

Translations by publishing houses are given the call number of the original with a capital letter representing the language of the translation added to the end of the title mark. If the bibliographic information of the original is unknown the call number is based on the bibliographic information of the translation. A capital letter is added to the end of the title mark for the language of the translation.

Example

*	Original	:	Wirbellose Tiere der Vorzeit/ U. Lehmann.
*	Call number	:	610 L528w
*	Translation	:	Fossil invertebrates/ U. Lehmann.
*	Call number	:	610 L528wE

Translations by USGS Translators or Translation Services

These translations are not classified or cataloged. Instead, they are kept in folders in the library's Translation file.

Restricted Material

All reports with the note: "for administrative use only," "for official use only," or similar notes are treated as restricted materials and designated by a "RESTRICTED" label above the call number. Prior to July 1999, restricted materials were designated with a * (star) in front of the classification number.

Example:

*	Title	:	Mineral summaries
*	Note	:	"for official use only"
			Restricted
*	Call no.	:	403(271) M562 1990

GEOLOGICAL SURVEY SCHEDULE (XXX)

The geological survey schedule contains monographs, periodicals and monographic series issued by the geological surveys of the world. These works are classified according to the location of the geological survey issuing the publication and therefore the classification number consists of the geographic number for that region.

CONSTRUCTING CALL NUMBERS FOR MONOGRAPHS

Call numbers for monographs in the geological survey schedule consist of a geographic number, a shelf list number, and a date.

Example

*	Author main entry	:	
*	Title	:	Ground-water resources of the Surman area.../ by William Ogilbee.
*	Class no.	:	(200) for USGS
*	Shelf list no.	:	O344 for author
*	Title mark	:	g for title
*	Issuing date	:	1989 imprint date
*	Call no.		(200) O344g 1989
*	Title main entry		
*	Title	:	Characterization of organic contaminants and environmental
*			samples associated with Mount St. Helens/ by W.E. Pereira....
*	Class no.	:	(200) for USGS
*	Shelf list no.	:	C472 for title
*	Issuing date	:	1980 for imprint
*	Call no.		(200) C472 1980

CONSTRUCTING CALL NUMBERS FOR PERIODICALS AND MONOGRAPHIC SERIES

Current practice uses the title main entry as the basis for the shelf list number. An exception to the current practice are serials issued by the U.S. Geological Survey, Water Resources Division.

EARTH SCIENCE PERIODICAL SCHEDULE G(XXX)

This schedule includes periodicals and monographic series issued by geologic societies, associations, organizations, and geology departments of universities, and publishers' series on economic geology, geodynamics, geology, historical geology, mineralogy, paleontology, petrology, physical geology, and structural geology. Periodicals and monographic series on paleontology and natural history issued by university paleontological departments and laboratories, local government departments of paleontology, or museums of natural history are classified in 602 followed by a geographic number.

CONSTRUCTING CALL NUMBERS

* The classification number is composed of an uppercase "G" and a geographic number. The geographic number usually esents the place of publication. There are two exceptions:
* Publications that report research in one region exclusively, but are published elsewhere, are given the geographic number for the research area.
* Periodicals of national associations and societies are usually given the geographic number for the country in which they are located, rather than the local region in which they are issued.

Example: American Association of Petroleum Geologists

*	Class no.	:	G(200) for United States
*	Not	:	G(244) for Tulsa, OK

Shelf List Number and Title Mark

Shelf list numbers are based on the name of the issuing agency. The title mark is based on the series title.

Example:

*	Title	:	Annual meeting and field trip guidebook/ National Association of Geology Teachers.
*	Class no.	:	G(200)
*	Shelf list no.	:	N376
*	Title mark	:	aft
*	Call number	:	G(200) N376aft

Publishers' series are the exception. Shelf list numbers are based on the title main entry.

GOVERNMENT DOCUMENTS SCHEDULE P(XXX)

This schedule contains periodicals and monographic series issued by federal, state, provincial, and local governments. In the past, monographs were also classed here. The current policy is to class monographic government documents in the subject schedule.

Exceptions:

* Monographic and serial publications of geological surveys are classified in the geological survey schedule.
* Publications of all mining and mineral resources bureaus are classified in the subject schedule under the classification number 402.

CONSTRUCTING CALL NUMBERS

The classification number is composed of an uppercase "P" and a geographic number. The geographic number represents the country, state or province in which the issuing government agency is located.

The shelf list number is constructed from the name of the government agency issuing the work. Title marks are from the title of the publication.

Example:

*	Title	:	Report to the Governor and the General Assembly/ by Georgia Nuclear Advisory Commission.
*	Class no.	:	P(233) for Georgia
*	Shelf list no.	:	N466 for Nuclear Advisory Commission
*	Title mark	:	r for report
*	Call number	:	P(233) N466r

GENERAL SCIENCE PERIODICALS SCHEDULE S(XXX)

This schedule contains periodicals issued by universities, societies, associations, and publishers' series on the following topics: archaeology, astronomy, biology, chemistry, computer science, earthquakes, engineering, geography, geomorpho-logy, geophysics, geothermal resources, geysers, glaciology, hydrology, mathematics, metals, mineral industries, mineral resources, mines and mining, natural resources, oceanog-raphy, ore deposits, petroleum, physics, pollution, precious stones, sedimentation, seismology, and volcanoes.

Classifications numbers are constructed with an uppercase "S" and a geographic number representing the place of publication. The same exceptions found in the earth science schedule also apply to this schedule. Shelf list numbers consist of an uppercase letter representing the issuing body, a three digit number, and a title mark. Shelf list numbers for publishers' series are based on the title main entry.

Example:

*	Title	:	Ohio Journal of Science/ by the Ohio Academy of Science.
*	Class no.	:	S(251)
*	Shelf list no.	:	O346
*	Title mark	:	o
*	Call number	:	S(251) O346o

MAP AND NON-MAP MATERIAL CALL NUMBERS

CONSTRUCTING MONOGRAPHIC MAP CALL NUMBERS

Classification Numbers

Map classification numbers are composed of three elements: the capital letter "M," a geographic number, and a truncated subject number if needed.

Shelf list Numbers

The three digit number in the map shelf list is constructed from C.A. Cutter's author's tables. Shelf list numbers for a monograph are constructed with two or three elements:

Shelf List Numbers with Three Elements

A three element shelf list number is composed of a capital letter representing a subregion, quadrangle, valley, basin, or area; a three digit number taken from the Cutter tables; and a work letter representing the main entry. Later editions of the same map will have a date on the third line of the call number.

Shelf List Numbers with two Elements

When the contents of a map represents an entire region, the shelf list number is composed of the imprint date and a work letter representing the main entry. If the item was published over several years only the initial publication year is used.

MAP SETS CLASSIFICATION

Definition

Map sets: Multiple maps, issued simultaneously or over time, intended to form a single group covering a given geographic area. Classification numbers for map sets consist of four elements: capital letter "M" for map, geographic number for the region, an abbreviated subject number, and lower case "s" for map set. Map set shelf list numbers are constructed according to two alternatives:

Scale

If all the sheets of the set use one scale, use an abbreviated form of the scale as the shelf list number according to the following procedures: Delete the initial "1" and the colon following it and the three zeros from the end of the scale. Enter the remaining number in the shelf list line. Add a work letter to the shelf list number to resolve conflicts with identical call numbers. If the conflict is not resolved, add a title mark for title of the map set.

Region/Scale

When the region given on the map is a subregion of the geographic number found in the classification number, the abbreviated scale in the shelf list number is preceded by two letters, the first uppercase and the second lower case, representing the subregion.

Cutter Numbers

Map sets without a constant scale among the various sheets are given shelf list numbers which include a three digit number from the Cutter tables:

CLASSIFICATION OF MAP INDEXES

In order to locate the indexes next to the maps, their call number is that of the map set/series except that the ending "s" is replaced by an "i":

*	Set	:	M(276)58s
*	Index	:	M(276) 58i

When an index covers maps of several scales, the smallest scale only will appear in the shelf list numbers of the index:

*	Set	:	M(276)58s 100
*	Index	:	M(276)58i 100

NON-MAP MATERIALS CLASSIFICATION NUMBERS

Classification numbers for non-map materials (posters, tables, etc. that are stored in map cases) are constructed with three elements: uppercase letter "M", a parenthetical expression (NMM) for non-map material, and a subject number.

SPECIAL FORMAT CALL NUMBERS

The U.S. Geological Survey Library has found it desirable to distinguish the call numbers of special formats from printed materials. This has been done by adding a special format uppercase term to the end of a standard call number. The following is a list of special formats and the appropriate call number symbols:

	Format	Call Number
*	Audiocassettes	Audioc
*	Audio CD-ROM	Audio CD
*	CD-ROM	CD-Rom
*	Computer cassettes	Compc
*	Computer disks	Disk
*	Games	Game
*	Globes	Globe
*	Internet documents	Internet
*	Kits	Kit
*	Microfiche	Fiche
*	Microfilm	Mfilm
*	Videocassettes	Videoc
*	Video CD-ROM	CD-Rom

REGIONAL LIBRARY CALL NUMBERS

The USGS Library has branches in Denver, CO, Menlo Park, CA and Flagstaff, AZ. These libraries will sometimes have additional notations as part of the classification number.

DENVER LIBRARY

Call numbers for publications preceded by an upper case "L" indicate that they are locked in a case. Special collections use "FR" for field records and "PH" for photograph collection. These designations precede the call number.

SHELF LIST TABLES

The U.S. Geological Survey Library uses the Library of Congress shelf list tables to construct shelf list numbers. The tables are designed in a simple format, which is basically self-explanatory. A few points may need clarification. The USGS Reston Library generally uses three digit shelf list numbers. The regional libraries may use 4 digits.

The shelf list number begins with an upper case letter representing the main entry.

* Using the surname "Smith", the shelf list number will begin with the letter "S".
* Select the first number from table 1, 2, 3, or 4 depending on the uppercase letter.

Use table:

* If the upper case letter is a vowel.
* If the upper case letter is a "S".
* If the upper case letter is a "Q".
* If the upper case letter is a consonant.

9

Fundamental Categories, Facet Analysis and Facet Sequence

FUNDAMENTAL CATEGORIES

In mapping the universe of subjects, different systems of classification have adopted different methods and approaches. Ranganathan adopted a systematic procedure based on certain assumptions which we have called Postulates. The process of division that Ranganathan followed recognises that every subject has a basic facet, *i.e.*, the first context-specifying facet and represented by the concept/term called *basic subject* (BS), to which one or more isolate ideas may he attached. He postulated these fundamental ideas by the term 'Fundamental Categories'. By going to a dictionary and finding out the meaning of each of the two component terms 'Fundamental' and 'Category' and then combining the meanings, one cannot understand what the *Fundamental Categories* (FC) are. The word-group forming the term FC is an unbreakable one and can be defined by enumeration only.

POSTULATE OF FUNDAMENTAL CATEGORIES

According to this postulate "There are five and only five fundamental categories - *viz.*, Time, Space, Energy, Matter and Personality." Explaining these, Ranganathan emphasises that these terms and the ideas denoted by them belong strictly to the context of the discipline concerned. Their significance, in our context, can be seen only in the context of the discipline concerned. This set of FC is, for brevity, denoted by the initionym PMEST.

After identifying basic subjects, the analysis of isolate ideas going with basic classes has also to be done in a systematic and logical way to produce the desired result. An examination of subjects will reveal that every subject has its different aspects and together all these present a coherent account of the subject. For example, consider the following six terms in the subject of chemistry:

1.	Alcohol	1.	Substance
2.	Liquid	2.	State
3..	Volatility	3.	Property
4.	Combustion	4.	Reaction
5.	Analysis	5.	Operation
6.	Burette	6.	Device for

It can be seen that each of the isolate terms in the left column belongs to a corresponding category in the right column. Here, substance means all substances and state mean all states. It, therefore, follows that each of the above terms is a category of ideas and can be regarded as a facet of the subject chemistry. Indeed we can discern this type of organisation of ideas in any subject. Table illustrates this. This table lists some basic subjects and the type of facets that go with each of them respectively.

While designing Colon Classification, Ranganathan discerned that although different subjects have facets special to them, there is an underlying unity of ideas when these facets are examined in depth. In each one of the subjects, there is a core set of ideas that are central to every aspect of the study of that subject. This underlying of ideas led Ranganathan to postulate the Fundamental Categories.

FIVE FUNDAMENTAL CATEGORIES

There are five and only five Fundamental Categories.

These are:

* Personality [P]
* Matter [M]
* Energy [E]
* Space [S]
* Time [T]

Table. 9.1 Matrix of Basic Subjects and Their Corresponding Facets.

Basic	Facets					
1	2	3	4	5	6	7
Library	**Type of**	**Materials'**	**Activity**	**City**	**year**	
Science	Library Library) (Research	(Documents)	(Classification)	(Delhi)	(1997)	
Chemistry	Substance (alcohol liquid)	Property (Volatility)	Reaction (Combustion)	Analysis (Ope- ration)	Device (Burette)	
Botany	Natural of Plants (Flowering plant)	Property (Colour,	Structural (morpho- logy)	Country (India)	Year (1986)	
Agriculture	Crops (Rice)	Property (protein content)	Operation (Harves- ting)	Machinery (Tractor)	Country (Burma)	Year (1985)
Medicine	Organs (Lungs)	Structural (Anatomy)	Disease (Cancer)	Treatment (Oral)	Drug' (Strepto- mycin)	
Education	F.ducand (Children)	Subjects (Maths)	Teaching Techniques (Question Answer)	Equipment (Slide Projector)	City (Delhi)	Year (1987)
History	Community (Indians)	Activities (Freedom Struggle)	Period (1910-1947)			
Sociology.	Social Groups (Labour Class)	Activities (Marriage)	Welfare (Flood- Relief)	Country (Pakistan)	(1987)	Year

Note:

Words given under each facet in brackets are isolates of the respective facets.

Let us loop at Table—again in the light of the five Fundamental Categories. Each of the facets, going with the basic subjects, can be regarded as a manifestation of one or the other of the five Fundamental Categories. Figure 9.1 graphically represents this idea. PME are the categories that operate in a space-time configurations.

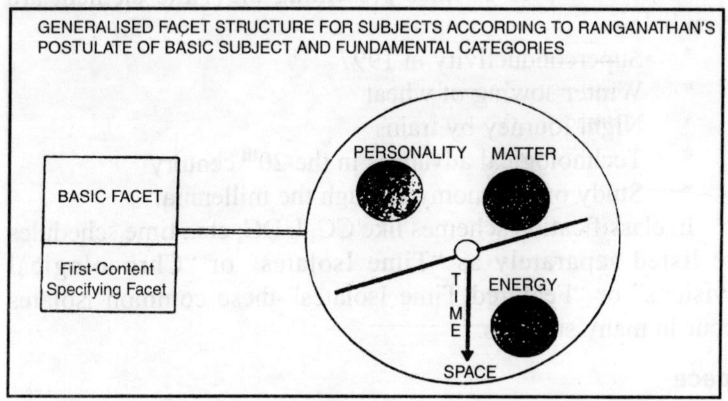

Fig. 9.1

For example let us consider a wooden table in relation to the basic subject furniture manufacture. Here. "table" with its distinct shape, volume, utility, etc., is the core idea and is central-to every other idea that goes with it. Hence, it i. s to be regarded as a member of the facet furniture, which in turn can be regarded as P. The wood, that has gone into the making of the table can be regarded -as the manifestation of M. The processe4 and activities that ace necessary to get the finished product could be. regarded as the manifestation of E. That the table is in the premises of IGNOU in Delhi represents the concept space and therefore facet S and. it is, there in 1997 which represents the facet T. Although this, example is an over-simplification of the method of analysis, it explains the basic ideas of Fundamental Categories fairly clearly. Let us now try to get a formal explanation of *Fundamental Categories* (FCS).

Time

The FC "Time" gives the least difficulty in identification. It is used in accordance with what we commonly understand by the term. The usual Time isolate ideas such as millennium, century, decade, year and so on are its manifestations. Time isolates of another kind - such as, day and night, seasons such as summer and winter, and time with meteorological quality such as wet, dry, snowy, stormy, etc., are also taken as a manifestation of the FC "Time".

Some examples of titles presenting the Time element are given below:

* Superconductivity in 1997
* Winter sowing of wheat
* Night journey by trains
* Technological advances in the 20th century
* Study of astronomy through the millennia.

In classification schemes like CC, UDC, etc., time schedules are listed separately as "Time Isolates" or "Chronological divisions" or "Featured Time Isolates" these common isolates occur in many subjects.

Space

The FC "Space" comes next to "Time". Normally, there is no difficulty in its identification and is representated in most schemes of classification. It is in accordance with what is commonly understood by the term. It includes geographical isolate ideas like continents, countries, states, districts, taluks, cities, towns, villages; water formation and physiographical isolate ideas such as oceans and seas, deserts, prairie, rain-forest, plateau, mountain, rivers, canals; climatological zones, tropics; areas occupied by population clusters, such as city, town, etc.A,ll these are taken to be a manifestation of the FC "Space".

The following are examples of titles wherein Space Isolates are present.

* Textile industry in Canada
* Mountain ranges of India
* Airconditioning in the tropics
* Public library services in village
* Political conflicts relating to the Indian Ocean
* The Ganga cleaning project.

It is clear that the manifestation of FCs Time and Space can be easily understood and present no difficulty, generally, in their identification. In many cases, they can be identified from the titles of documents themselves.

Energy

The manifestations of Energy are generally actions. They connote dynamic actions, such as, "doing", "changing "evaluating "determining", "forecasting", "analysis", etc. The action may be among and by all kinds of entities - inanimate, animate, conceptual, intellectual, and intuitive. The identification of the FC "Energy" is a little more difficult than that of "Time" or "Space". As matter of fact, the distinction between the manifestation of "Energy" isolate and "Matter Property" isolate poses problems mainly due to action-associated ideas. It has been found that two groups of attributes can be deemed to be manifestations of Matter (Property). They are:

Isolate idea denoting a "static" attribute that is an action-associated attribute doing some characteristic function-general or specific - or a behaviour of an.entity or a system. For example, "Function", "Physiology" and "Control". On this basis an isolate idea such as "Control occurs as a facet in the subject "Management" because, it denotes a function of management. But, on the other hand, the isolate idea "Control" occurring as a facet in the subject of "Control of the diseases of the human body" is deemed to be a manifestation of Energy. Here "Control" does not denote a function of anyone deemed to be a dynamic attribute of the core entity. Thus, it is not a manifestation of Matter.

The following are examples of Energy Isolates:

*	Preparation	Focusing	Separation
*	Generation	Reflection	Diagnosis
*	Operating	Scattering	Extraction
*	Collecting	Discussing	Distillation
*	Investigation	Warming	Fusion

Examples of titles carrying Energy Isolates are:

* Preparation of sulphuric acid
* Generation of knowledge in R&D laboratories

* Operating diesel engines
* Scattering of lights
* Warming of seafood
* Estimation of Chlorine in water for drinking

Matter

The identification of the FC "Matter", is more difficult than even "Energy", Its manifestations are taken to be of two kinds - Matter-Material and Matter-Property. Viewed from the angle of Classification, Matter-Material ranges from chemical elements or raw materials from one end to finished products at the other end. There is a series of intermediate stages, connecting these two ends. For example, cotton is a raw material in the context of garment manufacture which is a finished product. Cotton fabric is at the intermediate stage. Cotton, however, is the ultimate crop product in the context of agriculture.

According to Ranganathan's school of thought, properties of things, persons, etc., are also deemed to be manifestations of Matter. Isolates such as variance, intensity, wave length, height, weight, volume, etc., are regarded as manifestations of Matter.

Here, are some examples of titles displaying Matter Isolates.

* Density of solid
* Ink quality in printing
* Rubber quality in the manufacturing of mattresses
* Electric current resistance of superconductors

Personality

The Fundamental Category "Personality" presents the greatest difficulty in identification. It is too elusive. Therefore, Ranganathan had suggested adopting the Method of Residues for identifying Personality Isolate in the facet analysis of a Compound Subject. If a certain manifestation is easily determined not to be one of "Time", "Space", "Energy", or "Matter", it is deemed.to be a manifestation of the FC "Personality". This is so, as according to the Postulate of FCs, there are five and only five FCs. The application of this method of residues, however, is not infallible. But experience will lead to the establishment of reflex action in recognising this FC manifesting in any isolate idea.

Nevertheless, later developments have suggested that it is helpful to recognise the manifestations of FC "Personality" first and then the manifestation of the other FCs. Experience in the design of depth schedules suggests that it is possible to identify a core concept in compound subjects going with a basic subject, such as "human mind" in psychology, "human body" in medicine, etc. Such a core concept is deemed to be a manifestation of FC "Personality". The attributes of such a core concept can be several. A concept helps to determine the pattern of sequence of concepts. It helps in determining the relative degree of affinity of subjects going with different basic subjects. Greater weightage will have to be given in relation to the affinities among core concepts, The core concepts in their role as manifestations of the FC "Personality" act as leading parts of the system. Thus, to search for this leading part core concept should be the best method of recognising the manifestation of the FC "Personality"

In other words, "Personality" is a central part of the whole subject, encompassing a range of related ideas. Crops in agriculture, natural groups of plants in botany, animals in zoology, the Community of people in history, substances in chemistry, and social groups in sociology are some of the best examples to understand and comprehend the FC Personality.

Examples of tides displaying Personality Isolates are:

* Quantitative analysis of Organic Compounds
* Economics of Steel Industry
* Cotton bleaching in hydrogen peroxide
* History of Indian people
* Cancer of Lung
* Study of anger in Women
* Sugarcane yield in Uttar Pradesh

FACET ANALYSIS

Subject Analysis Using Facet Analysis

A facet is an aspect of a subject. Facet analysis means an analysis of a subject into its aspects obtained on the basis of a systematic application of a set of characteristics. Facet analysis of a subject results in the formation of groups of classes. Let us illustrate this with an example: In analysing the subject "Toy

Manufacture", we can discern that "'Toys", being the ultimate product manufactured, is one of its facets; the "Materials" used in the making of toys is another facet and the "Process of manufacturing toys" is yet another facet. Thus, the Toys facet will contain a number of groups and subgroups; similar is the case with the "Material" facet and "Process" facet. Chart 9.1 given here will further clarify this:

Chart 9.1

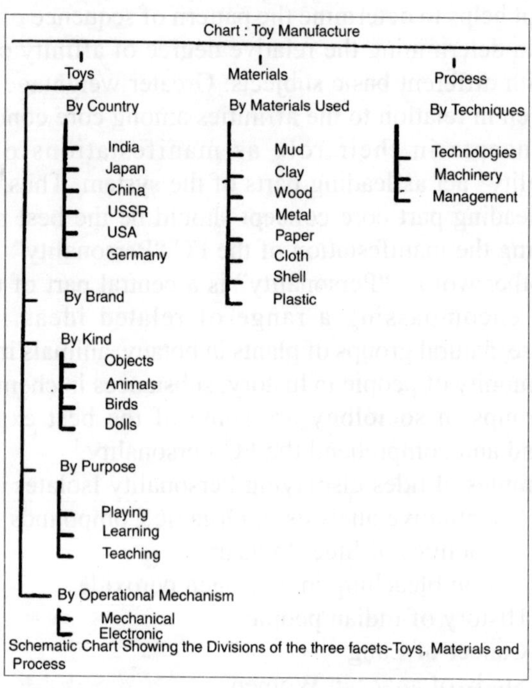

Schematic Chart Showing the Divisions of the three facets-Toys, Materials and Process

We have divided "Toys" into a number of subgroups on the basis of the application of a set of characteristics; similarly "Materials" used in the making of "Toys" have been divided to produce a number of subgroups and so also the "Process" of manufacture of "Toys" has been divided to result in a number of subgroups. Each of these subgroups could be further divided to form sub-subgroups till a point is reached when no more division would be possible, These subgroups and the sub-subgroups as well as the members of each one of these groups are all arranged systematically in a helpful order and displayed in a classification schedule which serves as a tool for classification.

It is clear from the example that all subjects can be broken up into their facets applying appropriate characteristics for the purpose of division. We should also note that facet analysis is independlent of any system of' classification The purpose of such division of subjects into their facets is to obtain a helpful order in classifying documents on the basis of their subject contents for organising them on library shelves, in catalogues and in bibliographies and such other tools of storage and retrieval of information.

Thus, facet analysis, according to Ranganathan, is "Analysis of a subject into facets according to the postulates and principles stated for the purpose". In the words of Palmer and Wells it ". . . means the analysis of a specific subject into facets produced by the application of characteristics".

The earlier schemes of classification were enumerative in nature and the entire universe of subjects was systematically divided into classes and sub-classes and resulted in readymade class numbers. In contrast, Ranganathan adopted the faceted approach wherein, instead of enumerating all subjects of past, present and anticipatable future, it would be better to enumerate the basic concepts or elements or descriptors. At the time of classification of documents depending on the subject concerned - simple, compound, complex - the concepts/descriptors can be analysed and then synthesised in an appropriate manner resulting in class numbers representing the subject(s) discussed in' the documents. While the facet analysis approach is adopted by the classificationist in desigring classification schemes, the classifier adopts it for classifying document.

Let us.now see the application of facet analysis in:

* Colon Classification (CC),
* Dewey Decimal Classification (DDC), and
* Universal Decimal Classification (UDC) schemes.

Colon Classification and Facet Analysis

Among the systems of library classification, it is in Colon Classification that we see the explicit application of facet analysis in full measure. Ranganathan developed his postulate of Fundamental Categories from the rigorous analysis of subjects into their facets. In fact, in the first three editions of Colon Classification, the Fundamental Categories of PMEST had not featured. After carefully studying the kinds of facets in different subjects, Ranganathan was able to establish that they could be accommodated in Five Fundamental Categories, despite their apparent surface differences.

In subsequent editions of CC, the Postulate of Fundamental Categories has been used to design schedules for every, basic subject. CC is regarded as a Freely Faceted Classification System because it is the nature of subjects that determines their facets which are fitted into the framework of postulates and not based on any predetermined facet structure. The enumeration of isolates for each class, the common isolates, the space and time isolates, the language isolates, etc., - all these have emerged using the Principle of Facet Analysis.

Applying the postulate of Fundamental Categories of Ranganathan to the subject 'Toy Manufacture' we may regard

* Toys as a manifestation of Personality
* Materials as a manifestation of Matter
* Manufacture as a manifestation of Energy
* Space and Time can be added when warranted

If the title "Treatment of Lung Disease in India in 1997", is analysed, it results in the following facets:

*	Basic Subject	:	Medicine
*	Personality	:	Lung
*	Matter	:	Disease
*	Energy	:	Treatment
*	Space	:	India
*	Time	:	1997

DEWEY DECIMAL CLASSIFICATION AND FACET ANALYSIS

In Dewey Decimal Classification, there is clear indication of the implicit use of Facet Analysis for the design of the classification system. In the Editor's Introduction to the 19th edition of DDC, it is stated, "In all classes (002-029, 069, 079.1-.9, 090, 100-700, 900), unless a different sequence is prescribed, arrangement is first by most specific discipline and most specific subject under it, then by area of specification, then by time specification if the schedules permit then by form of presentation" For example, a work on the Native snakes of Texas is classified as follows:

Discipline	Science	5
	Zoology	9
	Cold-blooded Vertebrates	7
	Reptiles	9
	Snakes	6
Area	(Sign of Geographic concept to follow)	0
	North America	7
	South Central U.S.	6
	Texas	4
Thus, 597.960 976		4

Discipline Science 5 Zoology 9 Cold-blooded Vertbrates 7 Reptiles 9 Snakes 6 Area (Sign of Geographic conceptto follow) 0 North America 7 South Central U.S. 6 Texas 4 Thus, 597.9609764.

Works of Shakespeare is classified as follows:

*	Discipline	Literature	8
*	Language	English	2
*	Form	Drama	2
*	Period	Elizabethan period 1558-1625	3
*	Works	Shakespeare's Works	3
*	Thus, 822.33		

The facets that divide the work Native snakes of Texas, are "Discipline", Zoology is one of the divisions of this facet; "Subject" representing a natural group of animals, snakes being a member of this facet; "Area" is the Space Facet, Texas being a member of this facet. In the second example, the facets are "Discipline" "Language", "Form", "Period" and "Works". Although DDC does not indicate explicity the method of facet analysis in the schedules, it should be clear from these two examples that the method of facet analysis has been the basis of its design. It should be noted that DDC does not enumerate in its schedules "Facet Isolates" as is done by CC, but display combinations of "Facet Isolates" representing a compound subject. The standard subdivisions, the area table, the time schedules applicable to certain subjects, etc., are given separately which can he added to any class when needed.

In addition, throughout its Schedules, DDC had given copious notes to divide a particular class by a set of divisions given elsewhere in its schedule, indicating thereby that the principle of facet analysis could be applied to any subject when required. For example:

All these examples will have to be studied with DDC Schedules:

* *Jews in India*: This is analysed into the following facets: Social Stratification (305.6), Religious Groups, Jews. Under Social Stratification by Religious groups (305.6); the following note is given. Add to Base number 305.6 the numbers following 2 in "Persons" notation 21-29. The number for Jews in table is 296. The final class number is 305.696
* *Migration of Birds*: This is analysed into the following facets: Bird, Migration Under a note given at 598.21-.28 (General Principles) at Birds, the instructions are given to "Add to base number 598.2 the numbers following 591 in 591.1-591.8" and the number for migration is 591.525. The final class number is 598.252 5
* *Sacred places of Jainism*: This is analysed into the following facets. Jainism, Sacred places. The Note given at 294.41-.48 "Add to base number 294.4 the numbers following 291 in 291.1-291.8" and the number for sacred places is 291.35. The final class number is 294.435 These are examples where there is a clear indication of facet analysis and synthesis.

Universal Decimal Classification and Facet Analysis

The *Universal Decimal Classification* (UDC) has adopted the basic structure of DDC but has developed on its own philosophy, policies and principles. The facet structure of UDC is much more explicit than it, is in DDC.

Some of its faceted features are given below:

* Common auxiliaries of Place, Race and Nationality, Time, Points of View, etc.;
* Facet indicators Colon (:) Square Buckets ( ) Double Colon (::) to 'combine two or more facets;
* Special auxiliaries to introduce facets peculiar to a given basic· class with specific facet indicative;
* Availability of a facet division for application to any class which warrants such division. This is somewhat similar to the provisions in DDC.

Some examples of the application of Common auxiliaries and Special auxiliaries are given below (The words in bold face represent the respective common auxiliary):

FACET SEQUENCE

We have so far been discussing an analysis of subjects into their facets. But the purpose of such analysis is to synthesise the facets-in a chosen order to be helpful for document storage and retrieval. So the end objective of analysis is to establish an order of synthesis of the facets. Without this rigorous analysis, it would be difficult to establish a rational order of synthesis. Indeed facet analysis and facet synthesis are the two sides of the same coin, the one has no purpose without the other.

The question now arises is what should be the sequence of facets? Is there any single order by which the sequence of facets could be established which is most helpful for the purpose of document storage and retrieval? Ire the example "Toy Manufacture", we identified three facets', *viz.*, Toys (A), Materials (B) and Process (C).

The following are the six ways of arranging these three facets:

a	Toys, Materials Process	ABC
b	Toys, Process, Materials	ACB
c	Materials,Toys, Process	BAC
d	Materials,Process,Toys	BCA
e	Process, Toys, Materials	CAB
f	Process, Materials Toys	CBA

If there are only two facets, there are two ways of arranging them *viz.*, AB or BA. If there are three facets, there are six ways of arranging them. If there are four facets, there are 24 ways of arranging them. If there are five facets, there, are 120 ways of arranging them. Obviously we have to choose only one among the various choices.available, as we cannot have all of them. How to choose one order among the many is the question.

We shall study in the succeeding part how this problem is handled in CC, DDC and UDC.

Facet Sequence in Colon Classification

After determining the various facets cc-curing in a Compound Subject, one should arrange them in a helpful sequence. For this purpose, Ranganathan enunciated five postulates.

These are:

* Postulate of First Facet
* Postulate of Concreteness
* Postulate of Facet Sequence within a Round
* Postulate of Facet Sequence with the Last Round
* Postulate of Level and Level-Cluster

Postulate of First Facet

In a compound subject, the basic facet should be the first facet As stated fir, every compound subject should have a Basic Facet and one or were Isolate Facets. To achieve helpfulness requires that all compound subjects going with a basic facet should be arranged together. Hence, the basic facet should be given the first position among the facets of a compound subject.

For example: Treatment of Lung Cancer. In this example, the basic facet is implicit, *i.e.*, Medicine.

The other isolate facets of the compound subjects are:

* Treatment [E]
* Lung [P]
* Cancer [M]

The sequence of facets should be:

* Medicine [BF],
* Lung [P],
* Cancer [M],
* Treatment [E]

At this juncture, it may be worthwhile mentioning that the indication of the basic facet in the title of document may be either explicit or implicit or absent. In the absence of any indication, the information professional would do well to read the contents page and/or the whole document.

Postulate of Concreteness

The postulate is stated thus:

The Five Fundamental Categories fall into the following sequence, when analysed according to their decreasing concreteness: P,M,E,S,T. This sequence of the FCs according to their relative concreteness conforms to the approach of the majority of readers.

Consider the following titles:s

- * Library Science in the 1980s: BS (Basic Subject) and T (Time) are specified.
- * Library Science in India in the 1980s: BS, T, and S (Space) are specified.
- * Classification in India in the 1980s: BS, T, S, E (Energy) are specified.
- * Classification of microforms in India in the 1980s: BS, T, S, E and M (Matter) are specified.
- * Classification of i-nicroforl iis in special libraries in India in the 1980s:- 11S, 11 (Peronality), M, E, S and T are specified.

All aspects of library science in the 1980s are discussed in item (a). Item (e) however, discusses a very specific area, *viz.*, Classification of microforms in special libraries in India in the 1980s. In other words, as we run down from (a) to (e), the contents are becoming increasingly concrete and move in the ascending order of concreteness. This is obtained by fixing a sequence an the Fundamental Categories which is in decreasing -concreteness if we move frorn P to T, or in increasing concreteness if we move from T to P. The intellectual organisation of subjects would command this arrangement of moving from the general to the specific and would be acceptable to the majority of users.

Postulate of Facet Sequence within a Round

In any Round of facets of a compound subject in which each or any of the Fundamental Categories - Personality, Matter, Energy - occur only once, their sequence should be: Personality Facet, Matter Facet, and Energy Facet.

Subject	Facet Sequence
1) Prevention of Diseases in Rice Plant	Agriculture [BF]
	Rice Plant'[IP1]
	Disease [1141]
	Prevention [I E]
2) Treatment of Lung Cancer	Medicine [BF]
	Lung [IPl]
	Cancer [1M1]
	Treatment [1 E]

Postulate of Facet Sequence within the Last Round

In the last Round of facets of a compound subject, in· which each of the Fundamental Categories other than Energy may occur and occurs only once, the sequence of the facets should be Personality Facet, Matter Facet, Space Facet, Time Facet.

The postulate implies that there can be more than one Round. The question then is - what is a Round? In order to explain the manifestation of Fundamental Categories more than once in the form of facets, Ranganathan formulated the Postulates of "Rounds and Levels".

According to the Postulate of Round, "The FC Energy may manifest itself in one and the, same subject more than once. The first manifestation is taken to end Round I of the manifestation of the three FCs Personality, Matter and Energy. The second manifestation is taken to end Round 2, and so on."

Similarly, the FCs Personality and Matter may get manifested itself in Round I and Round 2 and so on.

Depending on the Round to which they belong, Personality and Matter are represented as [1P], [2P], [IM], [2M], etc.

However, in regard to the FCs "Space and Time", they manifest themselves only in the last of the Rounds in a subject.

Example: Assessment of ultra-violet treatment of bone cancer in Karnataka in'1997

An analysis of the title using the Postulate of Basic Facet, Fundamental Categories, Rounds, etc.,

Gives rise to the following facet sequence:

* Medicine [BF];

* Bone [1P];
* Cancer-[IM];-
* Treatment [IE];'
* Ultra-violet Ray [2P];
* Assessment [2E];
* Karnataka [S]; 1997.[T].

Note

While the FC "Personality" occurs twice as [I P] and [2P], "Matter" occurs as [IM], and "Energy" twice as [IE] and [2E], "Space" and "Time" occur once as [S] and [T]. It may be observed that [S] and [T] occur only in the last Round of the compound subject. At this juncture, it may be appropriate to mention that with the introduction of the concept of speciator in the General Theory of Classification, speciation of the FC "Energy" was allowed. This has resulted generally, in the elimination of the concept of Rounds as far as the FCs "Personality and Matter" were concerned. Consequently, [2P], [2N ~, [3P], [3M] and so on have become speciators to the FC "Energy" depending on whether it is [1E],[2E], etc. However, in some special cases they may occur. For example, the concept of "side effects" of treatment may occur as [2M].

Postulate of Level

This postulate states that "Any of the Fundamental Categories 'Personality' and 'Matter' may manifest itself more than once in one and the same Round within a subject; and similarly with 'Space' 'Time' - in the last Round. This first, manifestation of the FC within a round is known as Level 1 and a similar second manifestation within a Round as Level 2".

Postulate of Level-Cluster

This postulate is stated thus:

Facets of different levels of the same Fundamental Category within a Round of facets in a compound subject should be kept together:

* Consider the following titles:
  - Criticism of Shakespeare's Hamlet.
  - Hindu law of property.
  - Diseases of leaves of flowering plants and their treatment by chemical spray.

– Quality of cotton fabrics for designing shirts.

We can see a cluster of isolates that can be deemed as manifestations of the FC Personality. In the first title, English, Drama, Shakespeare and Hamlet are deemed to be manifestations of Ps and criticism is an energy isolate. The sequencing of the personality isolates is to be on the basis of Wall-Picture Principle. The sequence of facets, according to the Wall-Picture principle would be language, farm, author and work. In the second example, Hindu law is followed by property, both being Ps. In the third example, the sequence of the FC' Personality in the first round would be flowering plants and then leaves.

In the fourth example, the terms quality and cotton fabrics can be regarded as manifestations of M and the sequence would be cotton fabrics preceding quality. "Classification of documents according to their contents should be done with the help of facet analysis and synthesis. One must bear in mind that we must be sensitive to the postulates and-principles that would help us in arriving at a sequence of helpful and logical teams, for storage and retrieval". It must be remembered that the FCs will operate only after the basic class is identified. All facet term's will follow the basic class in their respective order of arrangement.

Sample Exercises in Facet Analysis and Sequencing

Following are some examples in facet analysis and sequencing. Each title is analysed, the terms representing the subject content are derived and then are ordered according to the postulates and principles.

* Criticism of Shakespeare's Drama:	
– Literature, English, Drama,	
– Shakespeare, Hamlet, Criticism	
– Literature	BS
– English	[IP1]
– Drama	[1P2]
– Shakespeare	[IP3]
– Hamlet	[IN]
– Criticism	[E]
* Hindu law of property:	
– Law, Hindu, Property	

Table Contd...

–	Law	BS
–	Hindu	[1PI]
–	Property	[1P2]

* Diseases of leaves of flowering plants and their treatment by chemical spray:

–	Botany, Flowering plants,	
–	Leaves Diseases, Treatment	
–	Botany	BS
–	Flowering Plants	[1PI]
–	Leaves	[1P2]
–	Diseases	[1MPI]
–	Treatment	[1E]

Facet Sequence in Dewey Decimal Classification

Dewey Decimal Classification (DDC) does not specify any facet sequence in its schedules of compound subjects, although it uses implicitly the principle of facet analysis. But, extensive rules have been provided throughout its schedule for classifying documents, which demand a treatment of using facet analysis and synthesis. Let us see how this is done.

Agriculture and Related Technologies have been divided first by crop production, then by plant injuries, diseases, pests and then by individual crops as given below:

* 630 Agriculture and related technologies
* 631 Crops and their production
* 632 Plant injuries, diseases, pests
* 633 Field crops
* 634 Orchards, fruits, forestry
* 635 Garden crops

Now, a document on Harvesting of Peaches could either be classed in 631.55 giving preference to Harvesting or under 634.25, giving preference to Peaches. But the specific subject of the document requires a combination of the two, *viz.*, the particular crop and harvesting. Rules given under 634.25 (Add as instructed under 633-635) precisely indicate that the two facets could be combined, drawing the subdivisions of 631 representing harvesting to arrive at 634.255 which stands for Harvesting of

Peaches. In this way, throughout the schedule, rules have been provided to combine facets directly without any connecting symbol or with a connecting symbol of Zero (0). But the citation order is set by the system and is not necessarily based on any stated principle.

In addition to the set of rules prescribed at various places in the Schedules, DDC suggests a Citation Order Formula when no rule has been provided.

The facets and the sequence or citation order suggested are given below:

* Things
* Kinds of things
* Parts of things - 29 Analysis and Facet Sequence.

Materials from which the Things, Kinds and Parts are made, Properties of the Things, Kinds, Parts, Materials Processes within the Things, Kinds, Parts, Materials Operations upon the Things, Kinds, Parts or Materials Agents performing such Operations. This is given as Rule 4 under 8.55 Citation Order in the Editor's Introduction on page 57. The rule says: "Apply the Citation Order Formula which will generally prove to be reasonable and helpful.

Facet Sequence in Universal Decimal Classification

That UDC has many more facet features than DDC. Although there is no specific citation order or facet sequence given in UDC, either in its introduction or anywhere in the Schedules of classes, a Citation Order has keen recommended by Jack Mills in his Guide to Universal Decimal Classification which is as given below:

Things, Kinds, Parts; Materials:

* Properties;
* Processes;
* Operations;
* Agent.

The Common and Special Auxiliaries with their specific facet indicators provide full scope to apply facet synthesis wherever necessary.

Particularly the relation signs Colon (:), the Square Brackets [ ] and the Double Colon (::) facilitate combination of facets: For example, for classifying a document "Virus diseases and indoor plants", the schedule provides separate places for "virus diseases" and "indoor plants", as 635.91 and 632.38. But they can be combined by the relation sign colon (:) to get a class number as 635.91:632.38. This can be reversed as 632.38:635.91, making "virus diseases" the first facet and "indoor plants" the second, if a library prefers this sequence. But if a Double Colon (::) is used for the combination, the reversing device would not be allowed.

Square Brackets [ ] as a facet combinator is used to indicate a particular chosen order of facets. For example: Indoor animones (animones are a kind of indoor plants) get the class number 635.91:582.675.1(582.675.1 standing for animones), But if a library wants to gather everything on particular plants together, under the general heading. 'Horticulture", it might change the above number to 635.91 [582.675.1] to make the main facet the individual plant (in this case Animones) with "indoor" as a secondary facet. This principle is known as Flexibility in facet citation. This is acclaimed as a strength but it could also be viewed as an undersirable feature if libraries using UDC chase different facet sequences.

The Special Auxiliaries also give scope for facet combinations. There are three types of special auxiliaries which are using facet indicators [Hyphen (-) Point Zero (.0) and the Apostrophe]. The Hypen and Point Zero are used to introduce a facet peculiar to a given basic class.

Examples:

*	62-31	Reciprocating valve gear parts
*	820-31	English novels
*	621.3.066	Electrical switch mechanism
*	66.066	Clarification, etc., Chemical Engineering

The apostrophe, is at present used with a rather different meaning in chemistry and similar subjects where it is used to indicate synthesis of material elements as well as notational.

Examples:

*	546.33	Sodium
*	546.13	Chlorine
*	546.33' 13	Sodium Chloride

SOME GENERAL OBSERVATIONS

We can discern from the above study on facet analysis_ and facet sequence that Colon Classification is backed by a theoretical basis for fixing the facet structure of its schedules. While this theoretical basis may be subjected to criticism (as it has been), it is essential to have a theoretical basis without which the order of arrangement of classes would suffer. Framing ad hoc rules for using facet analysis and synthesis, both DDC and UDC are not able to get a most desirable filiatory sequence of classes, The policy of DDC, while recognising its weak structure, is not to introduce any basic structural changes which might endanger its use by several thousands of libraries throughout the world, but meet the problem by providing rules for facet analysis wherever necessary.

UDC, having a greater facility for facet analysis and synthesis, suffers from its adaptation of DDC's structure which restricts its scope of the use of the facet principles of analysis and synthesis. In recent times there developed a generation gap among the three classification systems. With DDC or UDC, it is not possible to make any drastic change to meet the expanding demands of bibliographic classification. Future classification systems would benefit from Ranganathan's contribution to theoretical foundation to library and bibliographic classification.

SUMMARY

This chapter has.

* Described briefly Ranganathan's Five Fundamental Categories with examples;
* Defined and explained,the concepts and techniques of facet analysis and facet sequence and their application in the classification of document in a library; and
* Explained the postulates and principles of facet sequence and their application in CC, DDC and UDC.

10

Isolates

INTRODUCTION

One of the very notable features of the ever expanding Universe of Knowledge, seen particularly in the past 50 years, is the emergence of interdisciplinary subjects. These newly emerging subjects naturally call for newer techniques for classifying documents of such nature and organising them in a helpful sequence for storage and retrieval. Ranganathan identified the formation of these new subjects, and called them Complex Subjects in which two subjects are interrelated.

In this Unit, we shall study the theoretical principles and techniques associated with classifying complex subjects which have two phases of either basic or compound subjects. Analogous to facet analysis and synthesis, this technique is known as phase analysis and synthesis.

We shall study the different types and kinds of phase relations and the principles and practices for classifying such documents by Colon Classification; and the provision of rules and devices for classifying them by Dewey Decimal Classification and Universal Decimal Classification. We shall elucidate the difference between Basic, Compound and Complex subjects first, thereafter as suggested, study the way they are handled in the different systems of classification. In addition, in this Unit, the need, the development and the different types of common isolates and their use in CC, DDC and UDC will be highlighted.

BASIC COMPOUND AND COMPLEX SUBJECTS

It is useful to begin with the definitions of Basic Subject (BS),

Compound Subject (CdS), and Complex Subject (CxS) in order to get a clear notion of phase analysis.

* A Basic Subject is a subject which:
* Is enumerated in the schedule of BS;
* Cannot be expressed as the Compound Subject of any of the existing BS, *i.e.*, a subject without any isolate idea as a component;
* Is evolved through one full cycle of the spiral of scientific method as propounded by Dr. S. R. Ranganathan. They also exhibit different modes of formation of subjects;
* Calls for schedules of special personality, matter and energy isolates;
* Has some specialisation-academic and/or professional segmentation. The indicators for this are:
* Existence of professional societies
* Degree course
* Periodical publications
* Whole books on the subject

For example mathematics, economics, law

There are several varieties of BS. The correlation of modes of formation of BS to the kinds of BS is summarised as follows:

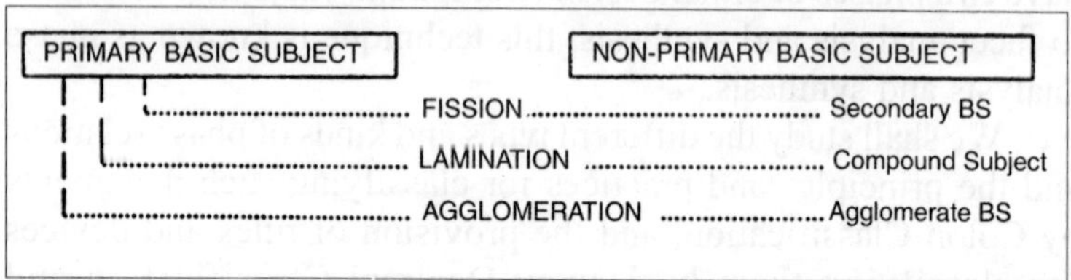

Primary Basic Subjects are the core frame for all other kinds of BS.

Compound Subject (CdS) is a subject with a BS and one or more isolate idea (Isl) as components. E.g.:

* Chemistry of alcohol-chemistry (BS),
* Alcohol (IsI) morphology of flowering plants-botany (BS),
* Flowering plants (IsI),
* Morphology (IsI).

Complex Subject (CxS) is a subject formed by a combination of two or more subjects-basic or compound. *E.g.*:

* General relation between economics and sociology
* Economics for statisticians
* Economics influenced by political factors

PHASE RELATION

A phase relation is the assembling together of two or more of

* Subjects (Basic or Compound)
* Isolate ideas (one and the same facet, or isolate ideas in one and the same array).

Assembling is done to express one or the other of possible relations between the components of the assembly. The result is a complex subject, complex isolate idea, or a complex array isolate idea, as the case may be.

Each component in the assembly, in its turn, is called a "phase". They are called "phase 1" and "phase 2" as determined by their sequence in the assemblage.

Types of Phase Relation

There are three types of phase relation.

The relation may be between

* Two or more subjects, known as Inter-Subject Phase Relation; or
* Two or more isolates within one and-die same schedule of facet isolates, known as Intra-Facet Phase Relation; or
* Two or more isolates within one and the same array of isolates, known as Intra-A" Phase Relation.

Inter-Subject Phase Relation

In inter-subject phase relation, we notice an interaction between two subjects.

Consider, for example, the following titles:

* Statistical analysis in library management
* Weather forecasting for the cultivation of the rice crop
  Sociology for economists

In the first example, two main classes are involved; ~ sociology and economics. The specific: subject of this title is sociology, expounded to suit the special needs of economists. In the second example, the statistical analysis is a tool subject used in managing libraries. Here, the two subjects involved are library science and statistics. ‘

The two compound subjects in the third example are weather forecasting from meteorology and rice cultivation from agriculture.

Intra-Facet Phase Relation

In intra-facet phase relation, we see two isolate ideas of the same facet interact to form, a complex subject, For example:

* Comparative study of Buddhism and Jainism
* Difference between democracy and oligarchy
* Influence of aristocracy on rural folks

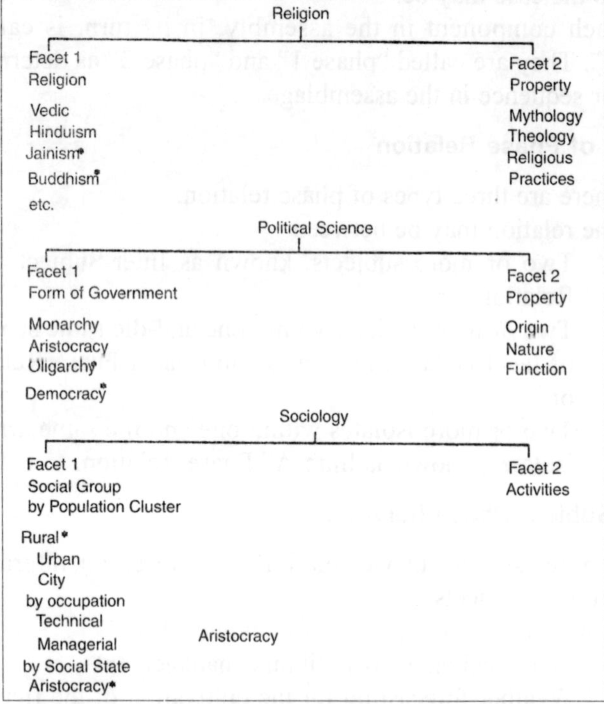

In the first example, the comparative study is between two religious faiths belonging to the facet religion. In the second, the study is between two isolates of the same facet type of state in political science.

In the third example, what is studied is the influence of aristocracy on rural people. Both these isolates belong to the same facet social groups in sociology. The following diagram displays the infra-facet phase relation. The asterisk marks indicate relation.

The component which is the primary focus of exposition in a two-phased subject is referred to as the primary phase and the second component that interacts to expound.the first phase is known as the secondary phase. In the examples given in this subsection, the first and second phases are -easily identifiable.

Intra-Array Phase Relation

In intra-array phase relation isolate ideas belonging to the same array of a facet are in a relation with each other.

Complex subjects of this type are illustrated below:

* Comparison of rural and, urban life
* Difference between laws relating to dacoity and theft
* The relationship between politically handicapped and socially handicapped persons in psychology

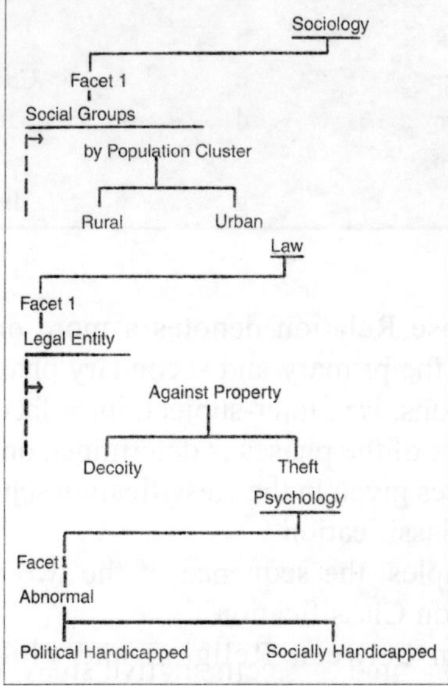

In We examples, be relation is between isolates of the same array of a facet. In the first example, isolate ideas rural and urban belong to the same array of the facet social groups in sociology. In the second example, isolate ideas dacoity and theft belong to the same array of the facet legal entity. In the third example, isolates politically handicapped and socially handicapped belong to the same array of the facet entity. These three concepts are presented diagrammatically here.

KINDS OF PHASE RELATION

In colon Classification six kinds of Phase relations have been recognised as given below with their indicator digits.

* General
* Bias
* Comparison
* Difference
* Tool
* Influence

Table of the indicator digits.

Intra-Array	Intra-Facet	Inter-Subject	Kind of Phase Relation
t	j	a	General
u	k	b	Bias
v	m	c	Comparison
w	n	d	Difference
x	p	e	Tool
y	r	g	Influence

General Phase

General Phase Relation denotes a more or less complete relation between the primary and secondary phases, inclusive of any type of relations, *viz.*, inter-subject, intra-facet or intra-array.

The sequence of the phases is determined on the basis of the sequence of classes given in the classification schedules of any of the schemes of classification.

In the examples, the sequence of the two phases is given according to Colon Classification.

* Relation between Religion and Philosophy (Inter-subject) Religion - Philosophy (Sequence in CC) Q&aR

* Relation between anatomy and physiology.,(Intra-facet) According to CC, Anatomy would precede Physiology; hence the sequence of the two phases is as follows: Medicine, Anatomy, Physiology L;2&j3
* Relation between Audio and Visual learning in Education. Here again, according to CC, Audio would precede Visual and hence, the sequence of the two phases is Education, Learning, Audio, Visual T;416&t7

Note in this case the two isolates belong to the same array and hence it is intra-array relation.

Bias Phase

The Bias Relation between two subjects indicates that the exposition of one subject (Phase 1) is biased towards another subject specialist (Phase 2). This means that the exposition of a subject is specially attuned by the selection, arrangement, choice of illustrations, etc., of the topics as per the needs of a specialist. Here, Phase 1 is known as Biased Phase and Phase 2

* Statistics for librarians BT&b2
* Statistics for Engineers BT&bD
* Statistics for Biologists BT&bG

The sequence of the three subjects of the Biasing Phase are in accord with the CC. There appears to be no literary warrant to give examples of intra-facet and intra-array relations.

Dewey Decimal Classification, for the first time in the 18th edition made provision for the use of phase relation. It is done through the Standard Subdivision -024. The numbers for the above subjects in DDC will be

* Statistics for librarians 310.24092
* Statistics for engineers310.2462
* Statistics for biologists 310.24574

In UDC the connecting symbol for phase relation is colon; however, UDC does not make any difference between levels of phase relation. For all types of relation there is only one connecting symbol. The numbers for the subject will be:

*	Statistics for librarians	31:02
*	Statistics for Engineers	31:62
*	Statistics for Biologists	31:573

The sequence of the three subjects of the Biasing phase are in accord with the CC. There appears to be no literary warrant to give examples of intra –facet and intra-array relations.

Comparison Phase

This Phase Relation denotes cases where two subjects are compared. Consider the following examples:

* Comparison between plants and animals (Inter-subject)
* Botany - Zoology (Sequence in CC) I&cK
* Comparison between morphology and physiology (Intra-facet)
* I;2&m3
* Comparative psychology of man and woman (Intra-array)
* Psychology, Man, Woman (Sequence in CC) S,55&v6

Difference Phase

This Phase Relation denotes cases of documents where the difference between two subjects is expounded.

For example:

* Difference between political science and history (Inter-subject)
* History - Political Science (As in CC) V&dW
* Psychological difference between sick and abnormal persons (Intra-facet)
* Psychology, Sick, Abnormal (As in CC) S, 4&m6
* Difference between meditation and worship (Intra-array)
* Religion, Worship, Meditation (As in CC) Q;413&w4

Tool Phase

This Phase Relation deals with cases of documents where one subject is used as a tool to expound the other.

For example:

* Literature Through.Art: A New Approach to French Literature (Inter-subject) O,122&eN
* Classification as a tool to study circulation service (Intra-facet) 2;8&p5

* Rural sociology as a tool to study urban sociology (Intra-array) Y,342&x1

This phase Relation has been recognised as one of the phase relations to classify documents which display such relations. This device, however calls for further investigation to assess its full implications. It is also referred to as 'Exposition Phase'.

* Influence of nourishment on education (Inter-subject)	T&gL;573
* Influence of intellectuals on ruling classes (Intra-facet)	Y,417&r53
* Influence of direct tax on indirect tax (Intra-array)	X 72,01 &y2

The sequence of the two phases in the two phases in the three examples are:

*	Education	Nourishment
*	Ruling Classes	Intellectuals
*	Indirect Tax	Direct tax

The subject that is influenced is in the First Phase by the subject that influences.

So far, six kinds of phase relations have been identified. It is quite possible that a few more may be encountered. The noteworthy point is that ' a method has already been provided, as in Colon Classification, which may be helpful for handling complex subjects of the future.

Such elaborate devices exist only in CC. UDC and DDC have not made provision to distinguish different types of relations. Through UDC has provided a single connecting symbol for all types of relation, however, few in DDC we can recognise intra-facet relation like:

* Foreign relations between India and UK = 327.54Q41

In this case India and UK are from the same facet and hence can be stated as intrafacet relation. As suggested, make a comparative study of the Phase Relation in all the three schemes, if classification later in this Unit.

PHASE RELATIONS IN CLASSIFICATION SCHEMES

As has been stated in the introduction to this Unit, phase

analysis and synthesis have been developed to accommodate interdisciplinary subjects which have been steadily increasing in the past several decades. Dewey Decimal Classification has provided a few rules and instructional guidelines to classify complex subjects. The Universal Decimal Classification has made limited provisions for handling complex subjects. But among the, three Classification Schemes with which we are concerned in this Course, it is the Colon Classification that has given a full treatment to this area of classification.

Colon Classification

In Colon Classification, phase relations have been explicitly identified and categorised into types and kinds. It has provided specific rules for classifying complex subjects. Just as facet analysis has given a logical and helpful framework for classifying multifaced subjects, phase analysis has provided a similar frame work to deal with interdisciplinary subjects. These devices have been based on theoretical foundations to obtain a helpful and practical arrangement of documents on library shelves and of entries in catalogues and bibliographies tuned to user requirements.

The following titles are examples of complex subjects, displaying different types and kinds of phase relations with their class number:

Inter-Subject	Kinds of Relation	ClassNumber
Relation between religion and philosophy	(General)	Q&aR
Statistics for engineers	(Bias)	BT&bD
Comparison between plants and animals	(Comparison)	I&cK
Difference between political science and history	(Difference)	V&dW
Literature through art, a new approach in French Literature	(Tool)	0,122&eN
Influence of nourishment on education	(Influence)	T&gL;573
Intra-Facet	(General)	L;2&j3
Relations between anatomy and		

Table Contd...

physiology		
Comparison between morphology and physiology,of plants	(Comparison)	I;2&m3
Psychological difference between sick and abnormal person's	(Difference)	S,4&n6
Indian music through painting	(Tool)	NR-(44)&pN6
Influence of intellectuals on ruling classes	(Influence)	Y,417&r53
Intra-Array	(General)	T,522&t5
Relation between education of blind and dumb		
Comparison between psychology of man and woman	(Comparison)	S,55&v6
Difference between meditation and worship	(Difference)	Q;4 I 3&w4
Rural sociology as a tool to study urban sociology.	(Tool)	Y,342&x I
Influence of direct tax on indirect tax	(Influence)	X72,01&y2

The seventh edition of Colon Classification has been used for constructing the class numbers. Ampersand (and) is the connecting symbol for phase relation in the 7th edition of Colon Classification.

Dewey Decimal Classification

Dewey Decimal Classification, being an enumerative system of classification, has very limited provision for the explicit use of phase analysis and synthesis. Its recognition of complex subjects, however, can be noted in the provision given for classifying such subjects.

These provisions are:

* Enumeration of complex subjects in its schedules: Example: Enumeration of Science and Religion at 261.55
* Use of Standard subdivision for Bias Relation

Examples: Standard subdivision - 024 Works for specific types of users makes this provision.

* Mathematics for Engineers 510.2462
* 510 Mathematics
* 024 Works for specific users
* 62 From Table 7 (persons occupied with engineering and allied operations and manufacturing)

Rules given at some places in the schedule for phase analysis and synthesis.

Example: Foreign relations between India and China.

* 327.54051
* 327 Foreign relations
* 54 India (from area table)
* 0 Connecting digit
* 51 China (from area table)

This is an example that can be regarded as a case of intra-facet relationship. It must be noted that these provisions in DDC are not adequate for classifying complex subjects.

Universal Decimal Classification

In Universal Decimal Classification, the relation sign colon (:) is used to indicate all types and kinds of phase relations. The same sign is also used for facet relations. The following examples illustrate these statements.

*	2:5	Religion and science (inter-subject–general phase relation)
*	51:62	Mathematics for Engineers (inter-subject–bias phase relation)
*	22/28:294.3	Comparison between Christianity and Buddhism (intra-facet–comparison phase relation)
*	595.141:591.142	Difference between simple marine worms and earth worms (inter-array–difference phase relation)
*	7:8	Influence of literature on art (inter-subject–influence phase relation)
*	8:7	Literate through art, a new approach (inter-subject - tool phase relation)

The sequence of Phases are reversible as in the case of facet relations. This is in accordance with the principle of flexibility in UDC.

Examples of colon (:) for facet relation		
*	635.91: 632.38	Virus diseases of indoor plants
*	669.14:621.791	Welding on steel
*	371.212:373.5	Admission to grammar schools
*	624.21:625.1	Railway bridges

Comparison between CC, DDC, and UDC

Below are given a few examples of phase relation and their class numbers by DDC, UDC and CC which will make you understand how complex subjects have been handled in CC.

Name of the Subject	DDC	UDC	CC
Examples of Inter-phase Relation			
Relations between philosophy and religion	100 or? 200	1:2	Q&aR
Psychology for teachers	150.088379	159.9:371.1	S&bT
Comparison between philosophy and religion	100 or? 200	1:2	Q&eR
Difference between philosophy and religion	100 or? 200	1:2	Q&dR
Influence of religion on Philosophy	100 or? 200	1:2	R&gQ
Examples of Intra-facet ralation			
Relation between Primary and Secondary education	372 or? 373	372:373	T,15&j16
Epistemology for metaphysics	121.08811	11:165	R2&k3
Comparative study of epistemology and metaphysics	110 or? 121	11:165	R2&m3
Difference between Epistemology	110		

Table Contd...

and metaphysics	or? 121	11:65	R2&n3
Influence of logic on ethics	170 or? 160	17:16	R4&r1
Examples of Intra-array ralation			
Relation between import and export duty	336.264 or? 336.265	339.543.3	X72,951&5
Import duty biased towards X72,951&u5 export duty	336.264 or? 336.265	339.543.3	
Comparative study of spring and autumn seasons	551.6 ?	551.583 ?	U2,761&v3
Difference between undergraduate and Postgraduate education	378.1552 or? 378.1553	378?	T,181&w2
Influence of wind on cyclones	551.552 or? 551.518	551.55?	U2,736&y3

The worked out numbers in the table gives a clear picture that only in CC every type of inter-disciplinary subject can be classified co-extensively. In UDC we cannot distinguish between the different types of relations because of the single connecting symbol for all relations. DDC has yet to make provision for these types of relations. At present we can give any one number as shown in the table.

Bibliographic Classification

According to Mills, the concept of Phase is recognised by Bibliographic Classification and "The hyphen (-) is now generally used as a phase link, comparable with the UDC Colon."

COMMON ISOLATES

Several families of isolates can be recognised within the universe of isolates as sub-universes. These include families of geographic isolates, featured time isolates, physiographical isolates, action isolates in general, property isolates in general, etc, Institution isolates can form components of several compound subjects going with each of all or almost all of the basic subjects. Each isolate in each such family is called a Common Isolate (CI). Schedules for each of the families of common isolates are given as a set by themselves in practically every scheme of classification, except LC and RIC, without any particular basic subject as the context.

Meaning of Common Isolates and their Need

Ranganathan defines common isolates as "an isolate idea denoted by the same isolate term and represented by the same isolate number, quite irrespective of the compound subject in which it occurs, or the basic subject with which the compound subject goes". In DDC, it has been explained as "a special kind of patterned repetition Any subject can be presented in several forms. It could be in the form of outline, history, theory or dictionary. It could also be in the form of a periodical or a handbook. It could as well be a presentation of how to study or teach that subject. These common forms and modes of presentation are called standard subdivisions.

It has been found that certain kinds of concepts keep recurring and may be found in many subjects, *e.g.*, proceedings, periodical, dictionary or encyclopaedia. These are all referred to as forms of presentation. Publications like Journal of Economics, Encyclopaedia of Philosophy and Proceedings of All India Library Conference have their own subjects. All these subjects, however, are presented in particular forms. The forms involved here such as journal, encyclopaedia and conference proceedings are commonly referred to as outer forms. There are inner forms also, *i.e.*, forms of approach to the subject. For example, theory, study and teaching, history and biography are various approaches to the subject and they are known as inner forms.

We also find that subjects are treated in the historical and geographical contexts, which are usually called by the terms time and space respectively. Thus, inner and outer forms of presentation and historical and geographical treatment are features common to all or most subjects. They, therefore, recur throughout the scheme of classification. In library classification, such recurring concepts are standardised. This standardisation results in economy of size, as it restricts the length of the schedules in a scheme by listing these common features only once. Incidentally, standardisation also lends mnemonic value to the recurring concepts, as they are consistently expressed by the same set of symbols. Hence, in a scheme of classification, separate tables are provided for common isolates and directions are given for their application.

History of Common Isolates

There are several things which go to the credit of Melvil Dewey. The concept of common isolates is one of them. In the beginning he called them form divisions. They were first introduced in the second edition of DDC brought out in 1885. Since then they have undergone several changes. The name form divisions continued up to the twelfth edition of DDC published in 1922. This name was changed to common subdivisions in the thirteenth edition appearing in 1932. These common subdivisions were listed under three different categories, *viz.*, miscellaneous common subdivisions, viewpoints and form divisions. This whole set reappeared as just form divisions in the fifteenth and sixteenth editions and was renamed as standard subdivisions in the seventeenth edition. The seventeenth edition also identified space and time isolates as common isolates and listed them as such. Until the publication of the seventeenth edition, the history schedule had been used for space isolates.

In UDC, common isolates are called auxiliary subdivisions. Broadly, there are two types of auxiliaries in use in UDC: common and special. Auxiliaries of form in UDC are like the standard subdivisions of DDC. Space and time isolates are treated as common auxiliaries and listed separately. The use of auxiliaries in UDC is an important aspect in number building.

In the first edition of CC, there were three different schedules for common subdivisions of which space and time were two. The number of common subdivisions was small initially. It was only in the fourth edition of CC that these were recognised as anteriorising and posteriorising common subdivisions. In the fifth edition, they were named as common isolates. After several changes through successive editions an exhaustive list of common isolates has emerged in the seventh edition of CC.

Kinds of Common Isolates

According to the definition of the term "Common Isolate Idea" , the different kinds of common isolates include language isolate ideas, time isolate ideas, space isolate ideas and anteriorising common isolate ideas. There can also be common personality isolate ideas, common matter isolate ideas, and common energy isolate ideas.

It may be noted that among the manifestations of the Fundamental Categories Energy, and Matter, some will be special isolate ideas and some others will be common isolate ideas. The matter common isolate ideas consist of properties and values and not of materials. However, these common property isolates and energy common isolate ideas too need enumeration. Further, it is found that energy common isolate term and matter common isolate terms are often found coalesced into a single term in the documents; one has to separate them. Also, one and the same common isolate idea is not always denoted by the same term at all times; their reduction to a single term is time-consuming.

Common Isolates in Colon Classification

The common isolates in CC are quite different from those studied in DDC. Though the purpose and need for common isolates are the same, the number of common isolates and their application differ in CC. It has clearly differentiated common isolates. Common isolates are defined in CC as those which denote the same isolate term and are represented by the same isolate number. The family of common isolates in CC is also very large. There are several types of common isolates which can be seen at a glance from the diagram given below.

Types of Common Isolates in CC

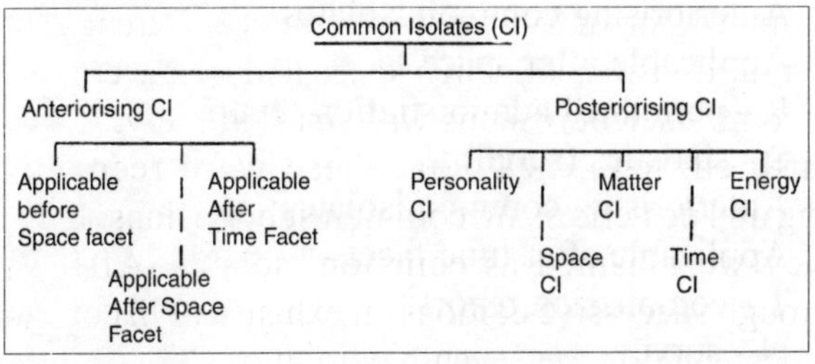

Up to the sixth edition of CC there had been a clear distinction between anteriorising and posteriorising common isolates. Anteriorising common isolates were attached to a host (core) number without any connecting symbol, whereas posteriorising common isolates were attached with a connecting symbol. In the seventh edition that distinction has been removed. However,› they have retained the same function assigned to them in the earlier editions.

Anteriorising Common Isolates in CC

Anteriorising common isolates mean that they have precedence in arrangement over the class numbers to which they have been attached. In short, the anteriorising common isolates have the anterior value. To explain this with an example, in the arrangement of class numbers V,54 and,54"a, V,54"a comes before NF,54 in the sequence of classes. Documents such as bibliographies, encyclopaedias, periodicals and histories of a subject are approach documents, and as such, they must precede other core documents on the subject in the arrangement on the shelves.

Some of the anterionsing common isolates are listed below:

* Anteriorising common isolates
* Applicable before space facet
* A - bibliography
* C - concordance
* D - table
* F - atlas
* K - cyclopaedia
* M - periodical
* P - conference proceedings
* V - history
* W - biography
* Anteriorising common isolates
* Applicable after space facet
* R - periodical administration report
* S - statistics (serial)
* Anteriorising common isolates
* Applicable after time facet
* T - commission report
* t4 - survey

* V - source material
* V46 - genealogy
* V6 chronology

Posteriorising Common Isolates in CC

Posteriorising common isolates are of three types, personality, matter and energy' common isolates. They are to be attached to the host (core) class with their respective connecting symbols, *viz.*, comma, semi colon and colon.

A personality common isolate stands mainly for institutions, some of which - are as follows:

* F- investigating- institution
* F2 - observational institution
* F3 - laboratory
* G - learned body
* H6 - museum
* Y - cultural organizations

Matter, Energy, Space and Time Isolates in CC

There is an exhaustive list of energy and matter common isolates on pages 93 to 104 of the seventh edition of CC. The number of energy common isolates in the sixth edition of CC was small. The matter common isolates appear for the first time in the seventh edition.

Space and time are regarded as common isolates and are listed separately. They can be attached to any host class number whenever warranted.

Application of Common Isolates in CC

We have seen that in CC there are different types of common isolates. The application of each of these types is illustrated below with suitable examples.

Anteriorising Common Isolates

The following examples illustrate the use of anteriorising common isolates:

* C"aN7 - 'Bibliography of physics books up to the 1979s
* C"k73;N3- - Encyplopaedia of physics, first published in the USA in the 1930s C"m56,N5 - Physics journal

first published in the UK in the 1950s '

* C"p44,N7 - Proceedings of physics, conference held first in the 1970s in India
* C"1v - History of physics
* C"wM88 - Biography of a physicist, born in the year 1888(C.V. Raman)

Note that the connecting symbol double inverted comma (") in the examples has no ordinal value. As stated earlier, all the numbers have precedence over the basic class C (physics). The anteriorising common isolates, in the example's, are applied before the space facet.

Now let us see a few examples of anteriorising common isolates which are applied after the space and time facets.

* T,4.44"r	Report on adult education in India.
* T,4.44"s	Statistics on adult education in India (Published regulariy, a serial).
* T,4.44'N75"t	Indian adult education commission report, published in 1975.
* T, 4.44'N75"t4	Statistics of adult education in India published in 1975 (a stray publication)

The first two are cases of a common isolate being applied after the space facet and the last two are cases where it is applied after she time facet. You will also notice that several common isolates in CC have their own facet formula which is shown along with the common isolate at appropriate places in the schedules.

Posteriorising Common Isolates

Under these, we have to study personality, matter, energy, space and time common isolates. As suggested,, therefore, take them up one by one in that order.

Personality Common Isolates

These represent institutions or organisations. A personality common isolate is ordinarily added after the space facet. The institutional element in the number can be worked out by what is known as the alphabetical or chronological device. The alphabetical device consists of the initial letter of the institution's name used to represent it in the number. The chronological device consists of the year of establishment of the institution. The alphabetical device is used when the year is not known. The chronological number is preceded by 9, if the institution is a national body. A few examples worked out below will help you to understand the use of the personality common isolate.

* Indian Mathematical Society founded in 1931	B.44,g,9N31
* Delhi University	T,18.44,t4,N21.
* Poona Observatory	B9.44,f2,P

Given below is the expansion of the numbers so as to enable you to know the rules:

* B Mathematics:
* 44 India (all space isolates are added with a dot() as the connecting symbol)
* G Learned body (all lower case Roman letters represent common isolates. An element added with a comma as the connecting symbol indicates personality facet)
* 9N3 1 A national body is represented by 9 and the date of foundation; N31 is 1931
* T Education
* T,18 University education. 18 from personality facet under the main class T
* 44. India
* T4 An institution of higher education. t4 is a personality common isolate.
* N21 Founded in 1921. Delhi University is a localised body and so 9 is not prefixed.
* B9 Astronomy
* 44 India
* F2 Observational institution (f2 is a personality common isolate)
* P Poona (alphabetical device)

Matter Property Common Isolates

An exhaustive list of matter property common isolates appears for the first time in the seventh edition of CC. A matter property common isolate is applied with a semi-colon as the connecting symbol.

Given below are a few examples:

* The outgoing Tamil Nadu ministry - V,4411,2;aP5
* Where, V History
* 4411 Tamil Nadu
* 2 Cabinet(Ministry)
* AP5 outgoing- Matter property common isolate
* The intrinsic value of paintings - N6;a72
* Where, N6 is painting
* A72 is intrinsic value

Energy Common Isolates

On page 93 of the seventh edition of CC a list of energy classification common isolates.is given. An energy common isolate, is attached with the connecting symbol colon. First a class number appropriate to "the subject on hand is worked out and then, if necessary, a common isolate to be attached is determined. Some of the energy common isolates are:

ab	- Establish, inaugurate	eb	- Mixing
af3	- Differentiate	eg	- Cleaning
ak	- Compensate	ev	- Washing
aD2	- Infiltrate	e3	- Boiling
aR	- Investigation, research	fZ6	- Preserving
aR2	- Observing	p2	- Describing
aT	- Evaluation	pR4	- Printing
dl	- Designing	u1	- Surveying

1	BX	- Astronomy	Worked out According to the Facet Formula for BX
	3	-Sun	
	57	- Eclipse	
	aR2	-Observation-energy Common Isolate	
2	L	- Medicine	Worked out According to the Facet Formula for L
	25	-Intestine	
	4	-Disease	
	74	-Ulcer	
	aR	- Research - Energy Common Isolate	
3	NA	- Architecture	Worked out According to the Facet Formula for NA
	9(2)	- Library Buildings	
	3	- Plans	
	dl	- Designing - Energy Common Isolate	

What is given above is only a sample of energy common isolates. A few examples are worked out below indicating the use of energy common isolates.

* Observing solar eclipse	BX,3;57:aR2
* Research on the ulcer of the intestine	L,25;474:aR
* Designing architectural plan of library buildings	NA,9(2);3:dl

The expansion of the above class numbers is as follows:

Space and time as common isolates: As space and time can be added whenever warranted, they have been treated as common isolates. They are also listed separately in the scheme. The application of space and time is much simpler and also easy to understand. However, a few examples are worked out here for your benefit.

University libraries in India - 2, 34.44

* Where,
* 2 - library science
* J4 - university libraries
* 44 - India

Mass communication in India in the 1980s - 4.44'N8

* Where,
* 4 - mass communication
* 44 - India
* NS - 1980s

In the second example, both space and time isolates are present.

COMMON ISOLATES IN DEWEY DECIMAL CLASSIFICATION

In DDC, common isolates have undergone several changes in both nomenclature and presentation. They were spelled out by different naives in different editions of DDC. The different names used so ıar are form divisions, common subdivisions, viewpoint numbers and standard' subdivisions. From the seventeenth edition onwards they have been called standard subdivisions.

Types of Common Isolates in DDC

The following are the different types of common isolates in DDC.

*	01	Philosophy and theory
*	016	Indexes
*	02	Miscellany
*	022	Illustrations and models
*	028	Techniques, procedures, apparatus, equipment, material
*	0285	Data processing
*	0288	Maintenance and repair
*	03	Dictionaries, encyclopaedias, concordances
*	05	Serial publications
*	06	Organisations and management
*	07	Study and teaching
*	072	Research
*	08	History and description of-the subject among groups of persons
*	09	Historical and geographical treatment

A note along with table states that "the notations are never be used alone but may be used as required with any number from the schedules". It is, thus, clear that the above numbers are not used independent of the core numbers from the subject schedules. Every number in the above table is preceded by a dash which merely shows that the number never stands alone. The dash is to be omitted when it is added to a core number taken from a subject schedule.

Space and Time Isolates In DDC

Up to the sixteenth edition of DDC there was no separate table for space isolates. Whenever required, they were taken from the history schedule. They were separately listed for the first time in the seventeenth edition. Some class numbers are in complete without the addition of area numbers especially where the subject treatment is on a geographical basis. Take, for example, subjects like Foreign policy of India, Economic conditions of China, and Political parties of the United Kingdom. In all these cases, the element of geographical area (space) is so important that wit out it the class number is incomplete and incomprehensible. Hence, all schemes of classification have made provision for space isolates.

In DDC, the,eater part of Volume I is devoted to area numbers.

Broadly, the division of geographical space is represented as under:

* Area, regions, places in
* Persons regardless of area, region and place
* The ancient world
* Europe
* Asia
* Africa
* North America
* South America
* Other parts of the world.

Having seen the space isolates in DDC, let us now examine the time isolates in it. Provision of time isolates is not as extensive in DDC as it is in UDC and CC. The time isolates in DDC are in the form. of historical periods and given in table as part of the standard subdivisions. Their use is limited. The treatment of time in subject schedules is on the basis. of a few very broad historical periods as under:

*	0901 -	to 499 A.D.
*	0902 -	500 - 1499
*	0903 -	Modern period, 1500
*	0904 -	20th Century, 1900-1999
*	0905 -	21st, Century; 2000-2099

Application of Common Isolates in DDC

A given document is first analysed to find the subject and then assigned an appropriate subject number. It is further examined if an additional number from the standard subdivisions table is called for. If the book you are classifying is, say, The teaching of geography, it is to be first given the number for geography. To this number is added the standard subdivision notation for teaching from table. You already know that a standard subdivision is added to a core number by first applying zero (0) to the latter. In our example, the number will be 910.7 where 91 is geography and 07 is study and teaching from table. Some other examples are:

*	Medical dictionary	- 610.3	610 plus 03
*	Encyclopaedia of religion	- 203	200 plus 03
*	Journal of agriculture	- 630.5	630 plus 05
*	Research in crystallography	- 548.072	548 plus, 072

All the underlined elements of notations in the examples are standard subdivisions. They are applied with a zero. However, there are instances where initially a zero has been used for the divisions are given in the schedules whether one has to use two or more zeros. Note a few examples worked out below:

*	Encyclopaedia of oriental philosophy	-	181.003
*	Dictionary of political science	-	320.03
*	Journal of social welfare	-	361.005
*	Journal of engineering	-	620.005
*	Journal of public administration	-	350.0005

Mark the contrast between the numbers in these examples and those in the earlier examples. The underlined elements of the notations are standard subdivisions. They are connected with the core numbers with the addition of two, three or even four zeros. Such use is stated in the schedules and hence there is no difficulty encountered while classifying. The only precaution you have to take before applying the standard subdivision numbers from table is to check in the subject schedule whether one or more zeros are required to be added.

A common isolate for space also can be added to a class number taken from the relevant schedule. Here again, before applying a space isolate it is to be checked in the relevant schedule if provision for applying the space element already exists there. If yes, the number is built as stated in the scheme.

It is only when there is no provision in the schedule and without the application of a space isolate, the class number would be incomplete, you can apply the space isolate frorn the standard subdivisions. Take, for the example of income tax in India. Here, no provision chas been made in the schedule for area numbers. In all such cases we can construct the full number, taking the space isolate for India from the standard subdivisions. Thus:

*	336.24	Income tax
*	09	Historical and geographical treatment as given under standard subdivisions
*	54	India, Under 09, them is a direction to add country number from table
*	336.240954	Income tax in India.

COMMON ISOLATES IN UNIVERSAL DECIMAL CLASSIFICATION

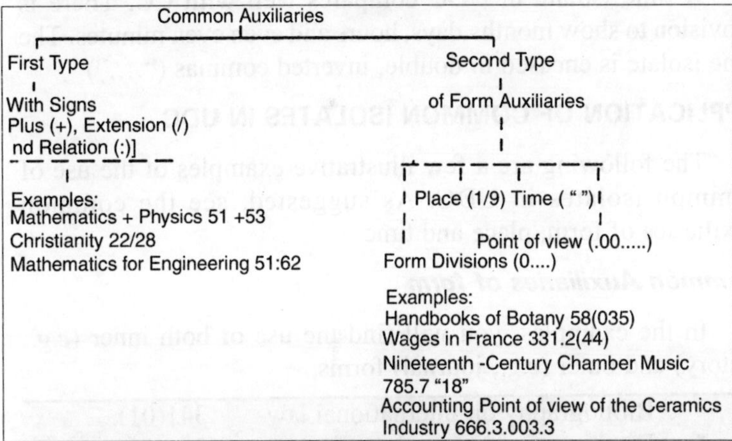

In UDC, common isolates are known as auxiliaries. Broadly, they fall into.two categories:general and special. The general category pervades the whole scheme, whereas the special category is relevant to only specific parts of the scheme.

Again, the general category can be divided into two groups:

* Those that are signs to join other notational elements, and
* Those that introduce explicit tables of subdivision.

The following diagram will explain the concept further:

The common auxiliary of forms in UDC are like the standard subdivisions in DDC and the anteriorising common isolates of CC.

Connecting Symbols for Common Isolates in UDC

The connecting symbols or indicator digits in UDC play a major role in the building of class umbers. As in CC, the indicator digits in.UDC reveal the type of facet used. That is the reason, by in depth classification, UDC has become very popular throughout the world. The common auxiliaries of form are put in parentheses with a connecting symbol nought (0..). They are used more for outer forms of presentation like dictionary, journal, etc. They are also used for a few inner forms.

Space isolate in UDC is like an area number in DDC. In UDC, it is put in parentheses (1 /9). As in CC, it contains a part from the political division and there is also provision for ones, orientation, physical features, etc.

A time isolate in UDC compares well with CC. There is provision to show months,days, hours and even even minutes. The time isolate is encased in double, inverted commas ("....")

APPLICATION OF COMMON ISOLATES IN UDC

The following are a few illustrative examples of the use of common isolates in UDC. As suggested, see the common auxiliaries of form, place and time.

Common Auxiliaries of form

In the examples, you will find the use of both inner (*e.g.*, history) and outer (*e.g.*, journal) forms.

*	Bibliography on international law	341(01)
*	Dictionary of international law	341(03)
*	Journal of international law	341(05)
*	Teaching of international law	341(07)
*	History of international law	341(09)

The common auxiliaries of form in the examples are put in parentheses with a zero as the connecting symbol.

Common Auxiliaries of Place

Like DDC and CC, UDC also provides a fairly exhaustive schedule of geographical isolates. This schedule covers political as well as physiographical divisions. All these are called common auxiliaries of place. Their application is simple and easily understandable. A few examples are given below for your benefit.

You will notice that the place number is always put in parentheses without any prefix.

* 327(540) - Foreign policy of India, where 327 is foreign policy and (540) is India.
* Bilateral relations between two countries can also be shown with ease. Thus,
* 327(540:41) Bilateral relations between India and the U.K.
* The number for the second country (41 U.K.) in the above case is joined with a colon.
* 33(540-22) - Economic conditions of rural India where 33 is Economics, (540) is India and (-22) is rural zone (zones or defined areas can be joined by a hyphen to another place).

Common Auxiliaries of Time

The time isolates in UDC are applied wherever needed. These are almost similar to those in CC. The connecting symbol for the time element in UDC is two double inverted commas ("). Even months, weeks, days, hours or minutes, as slated earlier, can be represented. The minus sign (–) in the time isolate indicates periods before Christ. A few examples illustrating the use of time isolates are given below:

* 1988	"1988"
* 15thAugust 1947	"1947.48.15"
* 6th November 1987	"1987.11.06
* 32 B.C.	"-0032"
* 6th Century,	"05"
* 19thCentury	"18"
* 1950s (1950-1959)	"195"
* 18thto 2Centuries	"17/19"

Applying a time number is also very simple.

For example,

* Economic conditions in India in the 19th Century: 33(540)"18" (33 - Economics, (540) - India and "18" - 19th Century)

SUMMARY

In this Unit, we have discussed the following points:

* Interdisciplinary subjects which display relations between two subjects are known as complex subjects. They are to be distinguished in classificatory work for the purpose of helpful arrangement.
* These complex subjects display phase relations, the first subject is the primary phase and the second one is secondary.
* They display phase relations between two subjects (inter-subject), two isolates of the same facet (intra-facet) or two isolates of the same array (intra-array of a facet).
* Besides these three types, there are six kinds of them *viz.*, General, Bias, Comparison,,difference, Tool and Influence.
* The types and. kinds of phase relations have been explained with illustrations.
* The treatment of phase relations in Colon Classification, Dewey Decimal Classification and Universal Decimal Classification is explained with examples.
* The types and kinds of common isolates have been explained.
* The application of common isolates in Colon Classification and Dewey Decimal Classification and Universal Decimal Classification have been given with illustrative examples.

11

Current Trends in Library Classification

INTRODUCTION

The history, trends and developments in library classification can be traced from the epoch making year of 1876 when Melvil Dewey published Decimal Classification. During the past twelve decades (1876-1996) developments have taken place in the field of library classification. During the period many general as well as special schecmes have been published. Some of the major general schemes, *viz.*, Dewey Decimal Classification, Universal Decimal Classification and Colon Classification have witnessed major developments.

Many national and international organisations and eminent classificationists took the cause of library classification. Several international, regional and national conferences were held to discuss various aspects of classification. The output of literature covering various facets of library classification in terms of both macro and micro-documents is very impressive. The following parts briefly deal with trends and developments especially during the last five decades.

THREE DISTINCT PERIODS

While tracing the trends and developments during the hundred years of classification, Ranganathan recognised three distinct periods, namely,

* Pre-facet Period (1876-1896);

* Transition to Facet Period (1897-1932); and
* Facet Period (1933-1972).

In Pre-facet Period Melvil, Dewey's Decimal Classification (1876) and C.A. Cutter's Expansive Classification (1879) were published. In the Transition to Facet Period Universal Decimal Classification (1897-1905) and Library of Congress Classification (1902) were published.

The Facet Period witnessed the publication of Ranganathan's:

* Colon Classification (1933),
* ILE. Bliss's Bibliographic Classification (1935),
* Library Bibliographic Classification (1960) and
* Fernmont Rider's Rider's International Classification (1961).

Some of theses classifications have an organisation or an institution to take up the responsibility for their revision, development, maintenance and application.

DEVELOPMENTS IN DDC

Until the publication of the 16th edition of Dewey Decimal Classification (DDC) in 1958, different editions were published at infrequent intervals. The 16th edition was edited by Benjamin Custer who set the pattern of a seven-year cycle. In this edition, an attempt was made to reconcile the conflicting aims of integrity of notation and provision of new topics. The 17th edition was published in 1965 in two volumes, *viz.*, V.1. Tables; V.2. Area Table and the Relative Index.

This edition showed a trend towards more synthesis than earlier editions. The main thrust of the 17th edition was to remove certain anomalies that have crept in between the use of form divisions with zero and division of subjects with the help of zero.

18TH AND 19TH EDITIONS

The 18th edition published in 1976 was in 3 volumes, *viz.*, V.1. Tables; V.2. Schedules and V.3. Index. For the first time five more auxiliary tables, *viz.*, T3. Subdivisions of Individual Literatures, T4. Subdivision of Individual Languages, T5. Racial, Ethnic and National Groups, T6. Languages, and T7. Persons were added. These were in addition to the existing T1. Standard

Subdivisions and T2. Aims. The 19th edition was published in 1979 in 3 volumes. The policy that was initiated in the 17th edition was also carried out in this edition.

The important features we can notice in this edition are:

* A diagram showing how hierarchical classification proceeds from the general to the specific in DDC;
* A practical guide to the use of classification; and
* A very detailed step-by-step instructions for building numbers in the main class.800 Literature.

20TH AND 21ST EDITIONS

The main objectives of this edition are: user convenience, clear instructions, more explanations, greater accessibility through expanded summaries and elimination of duplicate provisions for classifying single subjects.

The 21st edition was published in 1996 in four volumes and edited by Joan S. Mitchell *et al.* The thrust of this volume is users' convenience, which includes:

* More information located strategically to guide the classifier;
* Numerous captions have been rewritten to eliminate vague headings;
* 'Example' and Contain notes' were replaced with 'including notes';
* The relative index has more entries than the index to the 20th edition;
* Expanded manual; and
* Special attention has been given to reduction of U.S. and Christian bias.

COMPUTERISATION OF DDC

In July 1988 Forest Press, hitherto the publishers of DDC, became a division of Online Computer Library Center (OCLC). With this change DDC joined the computer generation.. Forest Press has been the publisher of DDC since 1911, when Melvil Dewey first used the name as imprint. Until 1988, Forest Press was a part of Lake Placid Educational Foundation, also founded by Dewey. Edition 19 of DDC had been printed from the computer tape in 1979.

The following years witnessed the emergence of a sophisticated computer-based editorial support system and database used to produce DDC 20 and 21 editions. DDC 21 appeared in two formats:

* In print; and
* Dewey for Windows, a Microsoft Windows TM-based version (released in August 1996) (CD version). Dewey home page contains current information on the Dewey Decimal Classification.

DEVELOPMENTS IN UDC

As we have discussed in earlier units, Universal Decimal Classification (UDC) was developed on the basis of Decimal Classification.and was first published in 1905 entitled Classification Decimale Universalle. The scheme is revised and updated from time to time by the-Intenational Federation for Information and Documentation (FID).

In response to a demand from several quarters for comprehensive short editions in English, abridged editions are being brought out by the British Standards Institution (BSI), the official agency. The abridged edition BS1000A was first published in 1948. The second abridged edition with radical revision was brought out in 1957. The third abridged edition was brought out in 1961.

IME 1985 AND 1993

The International Medium Edition (IME) was published with more extensive divisions to replace abridged English editions. The IME, English Text comprises of two parts, Part I - Systematic Tables published in 1985 and Part II - Alphabetical Subject Index published in 1988. This edition contains about a third of the material in the full editions brought out in English, French and German. In addition to various signs and symbols already provided in Abridged English Editions (ABE), two more new symbols: →4(the arrow) meaning, *e.g.*, 159.9 Psychology →4 (301.151; 591.51; 621.821; 616.89, and = (parallel divisions) meaning "subdivi-sion as" have been introduced.

* *E.g.* 611.3 Digestive system. Alimentary canal

* 611.3 a (616.3, *e.g.*, 611.31 Oral cavity)

Another IME in English was published in 1993 in two parts. The digit 4 used for Linguistics has been frozen and the Linguistics divisions have been shifted to class 8.

UDC IN COMPUTER-BASED INFORMATION RETRIEVAL SYSTEMS

It was suggested as far as back as 1934 that UDC was suitable for 'mechanical sorting'. The Royal Society's Scientific Information Conference held in 1948 noted the need to explore the potentialities of UDC in mechanised retrieval. The research programmes carried out in the USA, Britain, Germany, Denmark and Switzerland in the sixties helped UDC to be usable as an indexing language for computerised control and processing of information in the fields of knowledge. The most significant research work in this respect was the American Institute of Physics UDC Project under Freeman and Atherton. Other experiments carried out during the late sixties in using UDC for special mechanical applications include, the indexing of Geo-Science Abstracts and the maintenance of user profiles in the metallurgic fields.

UDC AND UNISIST

FID thought of making UDC a 'Roof Scheme' under which it could be hung the relevant special classifications, thesauri or descriptor lists as well as the more detailed UDC divisions themselves for those who prefer a homogeneous UDC-based system. The concept received encouragement in the efforts to make UDC adopted as the switching language for UNISIST (United Nations World Science Information System), a joint project of ICSUJUNESCO. An ASLIB study for UNISIST stated that UDC was found 'least unsatisfactory' of the major existing schemes.

COMPUTERISATION OF UDC

For more than three decades UDC has been used advantageously in computerised bibliographical and abstracting services not only for the production of subject indexes but also for information retrieval and SDI. In the forefront of UDC mechanisation has been Rigby who, as early as 1964, showed in the Conference at Elsinore the printouts of Meteorological and Geoastrophysical Titles that had started the use of the computer for author and subject indexing. A more comprehensive survey on the use of computers with the UDC was compiled by Rigby with the description of more than sixty experimental or operational systems in fifteen countries and four international projects.

DEVELOPMENTS-IN CC

You are aware that the first edition of Colon Classification (CC) designed by S.R. Ranganathan was published in 1933. It remained a Rigidly Faceted Scheme until 1952. The first attempt at breaking the rigidity of a pre-determined facet formula was made in 1950. Thereafter, CC appeared as an Almost-Freely Faceted Scheme for Classification in Edition 4 (1952). Developments in CC since 1950s were more and more towards a scientific method. The feature of analytico-synthecity increased in each edition especially after the 4th edition. The major structure of CC is its Basic Subject Schedules and the Schedules of Isolates. The schedule more special to a basic subject is the schedule of Personality Facet.

PUBLICATION OF 7TH EDITION

The 7th edition of CC was published in 1987. It was proposed to be brought out in 3 volumes, *viz.*, V.1 Schedules for Classification; and 3 Index and Worked-out Examples. But only MI Schedules for Classification was brought out in 1987. The other two volumes have not seen the light of day. In this edition, in addition to existing indicator digits in the 6th edition (1960), a few more indicator digits, *viz.*, & (ampersand), + (plus), = (equals), * (asterisk) and " (double inverted comma) have been added. The fundamental category Matter [M] has been transformed into Matter Method (MM), Matter Property (MP) and Matter Material (MMO. This edition also provided for environmental divisions. The schedules of Basic Subjects have been greatly expanded. It also provides for Common Matter Property Isolates. The schedules for Language, Time and Space have been greatly expanded.

COMPUTERISATION OF CC

Developments in Case Western Reserve University, Ohio, indicate the influence of facet analysis. Dr Fugman (ISKO, Germany) used facet analysis in his chemical analysis system. Facet analysis is also used for shelving purposes in online information search, Syracuse University, New York, was using PMEST in their computer-generated indexes.

In India, DRTC in 1967 wrote some computer programmes based on facet analysis and tried to experiment with the use of CC in computers to construct class numbers. CC was also used in computer programming for SDI services and for chain indexing and cyclic indexing. The Western Ontario (Canada) School of Library and Information Science used CC schedules for developing a thesaurus. In 1968, DRTC initiated experiments to determine the feasibility of using general purpose computers in a document finding system based on a classified catalogues system using a freely-faceted version of CC.

INTERNATIONAL CONFERENCES

In the past twelve decades major developments and trends have taken place in library classification giving it an international perspective when compared to other traditional branches of library science such as cataloguing, indexing and abstracting. During the past four decades, to be more specific since 1957, a number of international conferences have been held on library classification/knowledge organisation organised by FID/CR and the International Society for Knowledge Organisation (ISKO).

FIDICR—INTERNATIONAL STUDY CONFERENCES ON CLASSIFICATION RESEARCH (ISCCR)

Since 1957, FID/CR has organised six International Study Conferences on Classification Research (ISCCR). The first ISCCR was held at Dorking, England, during May 13-17, 1957. Ranganathan, in his opening address, dwelt upon "Library Classification as a Discipline". The recommendations of this conference dealt with:

* Scope of classification;
* Schemes of classification;

* Need for research;
* Use of classification schemes;
* Differences between systems;
* Construction and application of schemes;
* Notation for such visually scanned systems as the card catalogue;
* Machine systems;
* Research projects;
* A general scheme for classification;
* Development of classification schemes; and
* Furtherance of. Research.

The second ISCCR was held at Elsinore, Denmark, during September 14-18, 1964. Ranganathan delivered the presidential address entitled "Library Classification Through a Century".

The papers presented to this conference were grouped into five areas:

* General theory of classification;
* Research in mechanised classification;
* Selected and special schemes;
* Evaluation techniques; and
* Directions for future works.

The third ISCCR was held at Bombay during January 6-11; 1975. The recommendations of this conference centered on:

* General aspects of designing ordering systems for global information networks;
* Use of empirical methods and theoretical models ford signing ordering systems for global information networks;
* Systems evaluation;
* Interdisciplinary contents;
* Education;
* Needs and problems of developing countries.

The fourth ISCCR was held at Augsburg, Germany, during June 28 - July 2, 1982. The theme of the conference was "Universal Classification, Subject Analysis and Ordering Systems".

The fifth ISCCR was held at Toronto, Canada during June 24-28, 1991. The theme of the conference was "Classification Research for Knowledge Representation and Organization".

The papers presented to this; conference fall into three broad categories:

* General Principles and Policies;
* Structure and Logic Classification; and
* Empirical Investigation.

The sixth ISCCR was held at University College, London, on June 16-19, 1997 on the topic "Knowledge Organisation for Information Retrieval". The University College, London, ASLIB, Classification Research Group (CRG) and Internatio-nal Society for Knowledge Organisation (ISKO) sponsored this conference.

The themes discussed in this conference were:

* Role of classification in information management;
* Classification research for retrieval of information published electronically;
* Automatic methods of classification;
* Researcher and the real world;
* Tools for classification and classification as a tool; and 6. Data modelling.

LIBRARY RESEARCH CIRCLE (LRC)

This was founded in Delhi by S.R. Ranganathan in 1951. This circle used to meet on Sundays at Ranganathan's residence to pursue research on various aspects of classification, especially relating to Colon Classification. Its members concentrated on fundamental categories, indicator digits, rounds and levels of manifestation, zone analysis and on requirements for depth classification. The work entitled Depth Classification, published by the Indian Library Association, 1953, provides ample testimony to the contributions made by members of LRC. Its activities withered away from 1954.

FL/DCR

On the initiative of Ranganathan, FID formed a Committee on Classification Theory (FID/CA) in 1950. Later in 1961, FID/CA was renamed as the Committee on Classification Research (Fill/CR). This Committee has been stimulating classification research. The activities of FID/ CR are communicated through a serial publication entitled FID/CR Newsletter, published four times a year listing classification research projects in progress. FID/CR has so far organised six international conferences. The present chairman of FID/CR is Dr. I. C. Mcilwaine.

CLASSIFICATION RESEARCH GROUP (CRG)

This Group was forned in London in 1952. The early work of members of CRG is reflected in Sayer's Memorial Volume (London, Library Association, 1961). CRG as a whole published a brief outline of its views on faceted classification in 1953 and later issued a memorandum entitled 'The need for faceted classification as the basis of all methods of information retrieval' in 1955.

From 1952 to 1960 members of CRG turned their attention to the design of special schemes of library classification. CRG was of the opinion that no general classification existed which was suitable for computer retrieval. Therefore it was decided to develop a general classification scheme in association with the MARC Project for an automated retrieval system.

Since the 1970s, CRG has been actively engaged in the following areas:

* Revision of Bibliographic Classification of I LE. Bliss, by Mills;
* Formulation of Broad System of Ordering (BSO);
* Classification Scheme on LIS; and
* Precis.

DOCUMENTATION RESEARCH AND TRAINING CENTRE (DRTC)

DRTC was established in Bangalore in 1962 by S.R. Ranganathan. It actively promoted different levels of research in library classification. These are:

* Development research to develop depth schedules;
* Fundamental research to develop postulates and principles; and
* Systematic testing of depth schedules developed by faculty and alumni of DRTC.

It has been organising annual seminars on thrust areas of Library Classification and Information Science, conducting short term courses and workshops. It is bringing out, in collaboration with Sarada Ranganathan Endowment for Library Science a quarterly journal "Library Science With Slant 'to Documentation and Information Studies" (1964-).

INTERNATIONAL SOCIETY FOR KNOWLEDGE ORGANIZATION (ISKO)

This society was founded at Frankfurt, Germany, in 1989. Its founder-president is Dr Ingetraut Dahlberg. The principal aim of this society is "to promote research, development and application of all methods for organisation of knowledge in general and in particular fields, by integrating especially the conceptual approaches of classification research and artificial intelligence. The' society stresses philosophical, psychological and systematic approaches for conceptual objects". The society provides for personal contact and opportunities to the worldwide community of colleagues who devote themselves to the creation, expansion, revision and application of tools for the organisation of knowledge according to the conceptual point of view. The society has already organised four international ISKO conferences. The society is also bringing out a quarterly journal entitled "Knowledge Organisation", formerly known as International Classification. This is devoted to concept theory, classification, indexing and knowledge representation.

ESTING OF CLASSIFICATION SYSTEMS

A number of studies have been undertaken to determine the best and most effective classifying and indexing methods. Most of the studies have not tested classification schemes as such but rather their application in information systems. The best known studies were carried out at Cranfield, England, under the direction of C. Cleverdon in the early sixties.

UNISIST AND BROAD SYSTEM OF ORDERING.. (BSO)

The UNISIST (United Nations World Science Information System) programme was started in 1971 by UNESCO as an intergovernmental programme. The programme was launched on the basis of the recommendations made by the first intergovernmental conference held in 1971. The said report consists of a chapter on technical developments where it suggested that a standard list of broad subject headings might be useful to locate and transfer large blocks of information rather than specific document data.

ASLIB was requested to examine whether existing classification schemes would serve the purpose. An ASLIB committee felt that none of the schemes were suitable. Therefore, UNISIST has come to the conclusion that a completely new scheme should be developed as a Standard Reference Code (SRC). Later it came to be known as BSO.

FID PROPOSAL FOR STANDARD REFERENCE CODE (SRC) AND BSO

FID/CCC (International Federation for Information and Documentation/Central Classification Committee) had been working on the feasibility of transferring UDC as a 'roof scheme' for other classification systems before it entered into a contract with UNESCO on the development of BSO in 1971-72. But at the FID conference held in 1972 at Budapest, Hungary, it was decided to enlarge the size of the FID/CCC panel formed in 1971 to serve as a working group called FID/SRC for the purpose of preparing a Standard Reference Code (SRC) which could serve as the BSO as desired by UNESCO.

A small committee known as FID/BSO was constituted to develop the proposed new scheme. After two and a half years of study, the Committee presented a draft scheme called BSO, which consisted nearly two thousand subject fields in a brief hierarchical order but without a notation. FID published the "BSO - Broad System of Ordering: Schedule and Index" in 1978.

SPECIAL SCHEMES OF LIBRARY CLASSIFICATION

The past five decades have witnessed the emergence and publication of a number of special schemes of library classification to meet the requirements of special libraries and information centres. The problem of making special schemes, has been subjected to intensive investigation especially by the members of CRG and DRTC. Major problem in constructing special schemes have been largely resolved with the development of faceted schedules.

The norms and procedure for formulating depth schedules have been formulated by classificationists especially by S.R Ranganathan's Design of Depth Classification Methodology (1964). The members of CRG have brought out a number of faceted special schemes. DRTC between 1963 and 1975 brought out fifty depth schedules to classify a variety of subject fields. From 1967 to 1973, another 71 depth schedules were designed.

Some of the prominent special schemes are listed below:

* Soil Earth Science, by B.C. Vickery.
* Classification of Social Sciences, 1961, by B.F. Kyle.
* British Catalogue of Music Classification, by E.J. Coates.
* Diamond Technology, by J.E.L. Farradane.
* Organising the Arts, 1968, by Peter F. Broxis.
* Classification of the Performing Arts, 1968, by Anthony Croghan.
* A Classification for the Literature of Jazz, 1970, by D.W. Langridge.

LIBRARY CLASSIFICATION AND COMPUTER

World War II ushered in the electronic age. The computer is a versatile tool to relieve us of much of repetitive routine work with some creative element. Can we depend upon computers for classifying documents?

Ranganathan opined that "classification involves judgement of the subject of the document in all its facets and arrays manifested in it. This cannot be done by statistical analysis of the words in the document, which alone the machine can do. At present the computer can do a good deal of work not requiring judgement. But, classification will have to be done by humans until the computer can have the faculty of judgement built into it".

But, right from the 1970s, research work is being carried on an automatic classification by K.P. Jones, Rigby, R. Freeman and others. According to Jones "Computers have encouraged statistical rather than conceptual approaches to classification. There is a real difference between automatic and manual classification in that the computer can be more exhaustive than the human classifier." Jones further observed that the prospects of automatic classification for library purposes are not very bright. Appropriate methods and applications of classification have not yet been established.

INTERNET: LIBRARY CLASSIFICATION SCHEMES

Internet, the largest storehouse of information, has around 100 million pages of information. To find the required information contained on the Internet is a complex task. Attempts have been made to apply library classification schemes for retrieval of information contained on networks.

The advantages of adopting library classification schemes are:

* Enhanced subject search facilities;
* Possibility of offering multilingual access;
* Interoperability with other services; and
* Facility for partitioning of large databases.

Moreover,- if the Internet service provider uses an existing and popular classification scheme, it has better chances of being up-to-date as it is revised at regular intervals and is popular with users.

CONCLUSION

The preceding parts have already indicated to us that library classification/knowledge organisation will have greater relevance and importance and a distinctive role to play in the 21st century in the context of the emerging Information, Society. Library classification/knowledge organisation shall remain as the main focus of attention and discussion at international for as, thanks to FIDICR and ISKO. Needless to say, no other branch of the Library and Information Science has reached such heights as library classification/knowledge organisation. We have to thank the vision and contributions of Ranganathan and other eminent classificationists, to few like Sayers, Vickery, Fosket, Langridge and Mills, who laid strong foundations for the growth and development of the subjects, for this. Of late eminent personalities like Dahlberg, Nancy Williamson and I.C. McIlwaine have given a new direction to library classification, transforming it into Knowledge Organisation and making it a topic of discussion at international foras.

Bibliography

Ahmad, Lone: *Cataloging and Classification,* Jammu Kashmir: South Kashmir Press, 2006.

Anand, K.: *Library and Information Services for the Public*, Haryana: Haryana University, 2001.

Bajapi, K. P.: *The Secrets of Short Catalogue and Classification Entries*, New Delhi: Penguin Books, 2002.

Britto, G.: *Position Classifications and Salaries for Library Workers in the Public Service*, New Delhi: Rawat Publications, 1999.

Gaidhane, M.: *Library Classification,* Mumbai: Oxford University Press, 2000.

Gowri, R.A.: *Cataloging and Classification for Library Technicians*, New Delhi: Rawat Publications, 1999.

Gupta, R.: *Library Classification Facts and Analysis*, Rajesthan: Journal of the Association of Physicians of India, 2006.

Gururaj, G.: *Library Classification: Evolution of a Dynamic Theory,* Dharwar: Karnataka University Press, 2007.

Kapil: *Library Classification and Browsing*, New Delhi: Sege Publications India, 2001.

Kapoor, S. L.: *Library Classification: Fundamentals & Procedure*, New Delhi: Sterling Publishers, 2003.

Kaur and Gulati: *Classification, the Ubiquitous Challenge:*, Delhi: International Marketing Conference on Marketing and Society, 2007.

Krishnamurthy, S.: *Classification: Options and Opportunities*, Haryana: Haryana University, 1997.

Mahantra, J.: *Library Cataloguing and Classification System*, Mumbai: Oxford University Press, 2000.

Majir, J.P. and Basnet, J.: Decimal Classification, Delhi: *Indian J Community Med*, 2008.

Malhotra, C.: *Library Classification and Numbering System,* Mumbai: *Indian Jouranl of Pediatrics*, 2007.

Manjusha, C. H.: *Elements of Library Classification*, New Delhi: Sege Publications India, 2001.

Nanda, S.: A Modern Outline of Library Classification, India: *Indian Journal of Preventive and Social Medicine*, 2006.

Pagare, D.: Library Journal, Mumbai: *Indian Pediatrics*, 2005.

Panicker, R.: *An Introduction to Library Classification*, Delhi: International Marketing Conference on Marketing and Society, 1998.

Ranganathan, S.: *Practical Handbook of Dewey Decimal Classification*, Chennai: T.T.Ranganathan Clinical research Foundation, 2008.

Rey, D.M.: *Theory of Library Classification*, New Delhi: Vikas Pubishing House, 2001.

Saluja: A Practical System of Classification for Medical Libraries:, Tripura: *Indian Journal of Pediatrics*, 2007.

Sarangi: The Cheltenham Classification: A Library Classification for Schools, Orissa: *Indian Journal of Community Medicine*, 2008.

Sharan, P.: Yale Law Library Classification, Delhi: *Journal of Indian Association of Child Adolescence Mental Health*, 2006.

Singh, G.: *Stanford Law Library Classification*, Punjab: Social Defence, 2001.

Sinha, D.N.: Problems in Library Classification:, Patna: *Indian Pediatrics*, 2005.

Tarapot, P.: *Philosophy of Library Classification*, New Delhi: Vikas Pubishing House, 2001.

Toumbourou, J.W.: Library Classification and the Field of Knowledge, Mumbai: *Indian Jouranl of Pediatrics*, 2007.

Tripathi, B.: A Classification Scheme for Law Books, *Indian Journal of Pediatrics,* 1999.

Index